Scripture, Canon, &
Faith in Pursuit of Conversation

Book 1 of the Series:
40 Things Everybody Should Know about the Bible

What Readers Are Saying . . .

William "Chip" Kooi, Ph.D., Associate Professor of Theology, Oklahoma Christian University, Edmond, OK.
"No topics are more vital to the future of the church in America than those addressed by Gary Collier in this book. Positions on issues of canon and inspiration are frequently formulated *a priori* and then imposed onto the Biblical text—Collier's treatments clarify the issues and help the reader see and consider evidence typically ignored or glossed over, either for lack of knowledge or out of fear of the implications. If all truth is God's truth, then Christians should have no fear of honest inquiry. *Scripture, Canon and Inspiration* opens the inquiry and offers us an entry into conversations that we absolutely must have if Christian faith is to continue to be a significant voice in our culture."

Carson E. Reed, D.Min., Senior Minister, Northlake Church of Christ, Tucker, GA.
"Fans of the *Coffee With Paul Classroom* website will not be disappointed with Gary Collier's new work, *Scripture, Canon, & Inspiration.* Collier does what he does best; he provokes active thought and conversation through his engaging, conversational style. Relying on his own extensive textual work in biblical materials as well as more broadly with other ancient sources such as Philo, the author draws the reader into important, current conversations about the Bible by looking at the texts themselves."

Brian Casey, D.Arts., Houghton College, Houghton, NY.
"All Bible reading plans aside, all devotional methods aside, all creeds and all ecstatic worship experiences aside ... that's right, put them ALL aside. No matter how popular the method or the speaker or the author, don't follow charisma or some 12 easy, magic steps 'for your life' supposedly based on the Bible. Do, on the other hand, listen to both the details and the overarching messages from Gary Collier in this book. You will emerge from this read with a newly fleshed-out respect for scripture, although you might have sustained a wound or two along the way. We are baseless if we do not sit in rapt attention before ancient scripture, engaging with it honestly, and I am persuaded that renewal based in what scriptural texts actually say can make all the difference in and for Christians."

Michael Wilkinson, M.D., F.A.C.P. Palestine, TX.
"*Scripture, Canon, & Inspiration* is not written for scholars. Gary Collier is a scholar and is capable of discourse on that level, but this book is written for the rest of us. If you are a student of scripture, a church leader, a Bible teacher, or simply a committed but curious follower of Jesus, then this book is for you. I highly recommend it. Your faith will be strengthened and you will never read the Bible the same way again."

Patrick Spicer, IT professional, Bible student and teacher, Houston, TX. (Quoted as the headline on the back cover.)
"Hailing from a tradition that boasts a high view of scripture, it was hard to imagine the possibility of an even higher view—but Gary Collier proposes exactly that. And if Gary is correct about the canon of the earliest Christians, we are recovering something not of mere tradition but of sheer beauty. Whether slightly or radically, all careful and objective readers of *Scripture, Canon, & Inspiration* will be compelled to adjust their thinking about this crucial topic."

Huey Edwards, Mended Hearts Ministry (A Clown Ministry), Bronson, KS.
"In my own home, Gary Collier's book has sparked lively discussion—it is a breath of fresh air! He gives the Scriptures a significance that has been lost by teaching the reader how to converse with its authors and each other. Collier opens the doorway to real-time interaction with those people of faith that have gone before us. The author challenges the reader to come into relationship and engage with the authors of the Bible. The end result is a greater and fuller relationship with our God."

Dawn Gentry, Director of a children's ministry (11 years), now an M.Div. Student, Emmanuel Christian Seminary (focusing on Christian Ministry), Johnson City, TN.
"As Christ followers, whether or not we acknowledge the fact, how we view the Bible impacts every other theological decision we make. Collier's conversational approach engages the reader while his academic depth provides plenty of challenge for scholars. I thoroughly enjoyed the conversational style all through the book, and Collier's joy of God's word comes through loud and clear. I was not surprised or disappointed by anything I found. I also especially resonated with the 'what if' section at the end of chapter 9, and I agree with constantly asking 'what can we do to make things better?' Those who are willing to read without assumptions will find a conversation partner worthy of our time and respect. If you can imagine a faith community that values dialogue as we pursue Christ above all, begin here."

Robert C. Belville, Retired businessman & Hickory Church of Christ elder, Morganton, NC.
"*Scripture, Canon, & Inspiration* provides the Bible teacher and serious student with a treasure of invaluable material on the nature and purpose of holy scripture. Collier's style is friendly, his readers need not be scholars; but his thesis is sharply set out. Much of what is assumed by many people about canon and the proper use of scripture is naive and even false. It is a great disservice to Christians, particularly young people confronted by glib non-believers, for church authorities to stifle the open discussion about and with scripture. This discussion will be helpful in pointing to Jesus as Lord in a book (the Bible) that has become, as Collier aptly characterizes, an honored but ignored relic."

Beverly L. Watkins, Pastor of New Members Ministry, Promise Land Christian Community Church, Indianapolis, IN.
"*Scripture, Canon, & Inspiration* is a powerful book. It is so awesome that I had to read some and digest it before I could continue. I strongly recommend that every serious Christian, student of the Bible or any other interested person read the book. The more I read, the more I wanted to read. I found myself being challenged in my belief system quite a bit more than was comfortable, however, it was extremely profitable to me Spiritually. It is a powerful tool for any study group or individual who wants to understand what the Bible is and is not, and much more. This book will cause you to engage in conversations with it and raise questions that you probably would not have thought of before reading it. It is a must read for everyone, whether you are serious about the Bible, curious about the Bible, or just want to know. I challenge you to pick it up and begin to read, you won't be able to stop until you have finished."

A. C. and Ruth Oliver, Retired evangelist/wife, Missionaries, Students of the Word - Lubbock, TX.
"Gary Collier's *Scripture, Canon, & Inspiration* is a book that needed to be written. It will challenge the mind of the person who has come into an inherited, honest, but wrong assumption that the Bible was somehow delivered to men whole, complete, and free from human error—and that no further questions concerning its veracity or its God-breathed authority are acceptable or allowed. Collier asks (even insists in a very humble and non-pugilistic way) that believers at least take part in a *conversation* which is part of their faith—a *conversation* that has been ongoing from the earliest of the old covenant scriptures to the century in which we live. If our core belief is that Jesus is the Christ, and that the Good News concerning Him is contained in these documents (Collier seems to be saying) let us look deeply and sincerely into their origin (enter into the *conversation*) without fear. We wish the book every success with God's blessing."

Sherrod Lee, M.D., Portland, OR.
"'Don't believe all you think, or think you know.' At least, not without being willing to constantly re-examine your thinking, add to your knowledge, and let new light shine on your thoughts. Gary helps us do that by introducing materials most of us have never considered, and leading us in careful critical rethinking of some of our accepted teachings. This book is challenging, but not overwhelming or bent on wholesale change. It is a provocative conversation-starter."

John Eoff, Believer, Kerrville, TX.
"This book is about canon (a closed list of acceptable documents for inclusion in The Book) and will be held in disagreement by those who are more interested in upholding the traditions which they have been taught than they are of seeking true understanding of those holy scriptures. 'This cannot be a closed subject—and especially not an assumed subject' (pg 175). 'Do you have an opinion that the Bible should be

used as a science textbook? You are welcome to that opinion, but I don't want you teaching my kids!' (pg. 136). This is good reading for everyone who is interested in examining truth about the Bible."

Jack Gibbert, Retired preacher, Texarkana, TX.
"This book will bring a whole new look and hermeneutic into the life of any serious Christian Bible student. The system is as simple as you will ever find. You may still seek 'what's in it for me' and 'what should I do' but your focus will shift from those views to seeking this single truth: 'Jesus Christ, his name is **Lord**.' Collier is not about making you into a 'Collierite,' but rather a Bible student in search of a conversation with God."

Doug Lemon, HSSBC (Humble Servant Saved By Christ), Minister, Whippany, NJ.
"Nineteen Eighty-Nine was the best worst year of my thirty-six year career in industry. I literally sat as nursemaid to a comatose business. I opened an office every morning and sat by myself where there had been six or seven other employees. I had many long hours available for Bible study, reflection, meditation and prayer. Not being a 'scholar' or having earned a number of degrees or possessing many academic resources I just read and prayed and reflected. It was a 'lay' study, not that of a theologian. During that year I raised questions that I had not thought of before. How long was oral tradition passed on before it was put to stylus and clay? If Paul's lost letter to the Corinthians was ever found and documented to be authentic, would we re-edit the Bible to include it? How many other epistles by accepted NT or OT authors lie buried in some yet undiscovered cave or under and unexcavated tell? If Jude could quote Enoch, of what authority was Enoch? Would all of his prophecy be inspired or only that part quoted by Jude? These and similar questions piqued my interest. *Scripture, Canon, & Inspiration* addresses my questions and takes my inquiry to a much higher level. Collier's style speaks to me, the untrained lay person while his thorough research and documentation would seem to address those with more academic training. I highly recommend this author and this book to any who have questioning minds."

Zoe Hagan, President, Little Mermaid Club House and Castle.
"I'm only four and can't read, but Gary is a good monster and chases me when I come over."

Scripture, Canon, & Inspiration

Faith in Pursuit of Conversation

by

Gary D. Collier

Foreword by Edward William Fudge

CWP Press
Cloverdale, Indiana
May 10, 2012

www.CoffeeWithPaul.com

Citation Information
Collier, Gary D. *Scripture, Canon, & Inspiration: Faith in Pursuit of Conversa-
tion.* 40 Things Everybody Should Know about the Bible, Book 1. Cloverdale,
IN: CWP Press, May 10, 2012.

Editor's note: This book was formatted in MS Word 2010, which does not
always properly hyphenate words. The indexing feature is also inadequate
for producing the desired outcomes for references to ancient texts.

Concept, Translation, Commentary, Format, & Design by Gary D. Collier

Unless otherwise indicated, all translations of Old or New Testament texts
are by the author based on the following standard biblical texts:

New Testament
Nestle, Eberhard and Aland, Kurt (Eds.). *Novum Testamentum Graece.* 27th
ed. Stuttgart: Deutsche Bibelgesellschaft, 1993.

Aland, Kurt; Black, Matthew; Martini, Carlo M.; Metzger, Bruce M; Wikgren,
Allen (Eds.). *The Greek New Testament*, 4th ed. New York: United Bible Soci-
eties, 1993.

Old Testament
Elliger, K. and Rudolph, W., (Eds.). *Biblia Hebraica Stuttgartensia* Stuttgart:
Deutsche Bibelgesellschaft, 1977.

Rahlfs, Alfred (Ed.). *Septuaginta*, Stuttgart: Deutsche Bibelgesellschaft, 1979.

Contact Information
CWP Press
452 W. Water Street, Cloverdale, IN 46120
Email: cwppress@coffeewithpaul.com   Website: coffeewithpaul.com

Book Cover
Bridwell Papyrus 1, verso. For discussion and acknowledgements,
see chapter 6.

Table of Contents

Appreciation 12

Read This First (A Personal "Heads Up") 14

Foreword 16

The Day the Church Stood Still 19

PART 1: The Bible as Conversation 41

1 Bible Reading Today 43
    A. Community and Faith 43
    B. Mirror, Mirror... 53

2 Seeing the Bible Alike 63

3 Scripture and Canon 73

4 Whose Idea Was "Canon"? 93

5 Should the Canon Be Open? 109

6 "Jars of Clay" and Inspiration 121

7 "The God Who Kills Babies!" 135

8 The Bible as "Collections"...................................145

9 The Earliest Christian Canon...............................159

10 Conclusion 171

PART 2: Engaging in the Conversation 177

Introduction 179

11 What's Wrong with Da Vinci 181

12 Canon 183

13 Scripture..189

14 Law & Prophets 251

15 The Word of God...261

16 The Name Above Every Name 279

PART 3: Partners in the Conversation 289

Conversation Partners.. 291

Abbreviations... 301

Index... 307

Meet the Author.. 326

*To
Lanette*

Appreciation

This book has been in the making for about 30 years in innumerable ways. It was in actual writing for 15 months and went through approximately 43 continually emerging drafts. This has allowed me to have enduring conversations about this topic with numerous people from all kinds of backgrounds and to make ongoing revisions, adjustments, and updates as a result of those simply wonderful interchanges. One might think that after such a process the book should be perfect—or that perhaps somewhere along the line I would have listened more to my detractors and correctors. But then where would the adventure be? So, there are numerous people I wish to hold up to you by name.

At the very top of the list are Terry Armstrong and Jeff Kochvar for their personal encouragement.

I also wish to express my heartfelt appreciation, albeit inadequately, to Brian Casey, a doctor of music, whom I have never met in person, but whom I have grown to love and respect over the years as a brother. He thoroughly read this manuscript in several forms and both encouraged me and argued with me the entire way.

To Michael Wilkinson, Patrick Spicer, and Carson Reed for reading the nearly finished manuscript in detail and for providing me with point-blank challenges that led not only to some minor corrections, but also to some substantial revisions.

To Portia Regan, my (actual) little sister, who has for years relished every opportunity to point out my faults, and who now, as a lead trainer for the State of Indiana, brought her considerable expertise to bear.

To the Bridwell Library of Southern Methodist University (Dallas, TX) for their gracious consent to use the 6th century Bridwell Papyrus 1 (P[26]) on the front cover of the book.

And to Don Haymes, Research Librarian and Archivist at Christian Theological Seminary (Indianapolis, IN), for his invaluable assistance in all questions "books," above and beyond the call of duty.

I also wish to express my appreciation to some others who have played a role in this work whether they know it or not:

- To Jeff Faull, the quintessence of Christian grace, who maintains the ability of open conversation in the midst of deep concern.

- To the numerous participants who left questions, comments, and challenges on the original video discussion pages of www.biblestudytips.org including especially these frequent commenters: Keith McDonald, Jack Gibbert, Beverly Watkins, Granville Russell, and Larry Diersing.

- To many others on that website including Brenda Causey, Rob Lilienthal, Darcy Heavin, Heather Weeda, Judy Black, Shannon Hayward, Karen Fry, Lynnette Linkenhoker, Oscar Miles, and numerous others as the list continues to grow. My gratitude extends to all.

- To Doug Lemon, A. C. and Ruth Oliver, Sherrod Lee, John Eoff, and Neika Stephens for their encouragement and support.

- To my son Craig, a gifted writer, whose insights and willingness to converse have benefited me greatly during this writing.

- To my wife Lanette, without whose incredible support and faith and encouragement, I might have long since abandoned writing this book. It is to her that this book is affectionately dedicated.

Finally, I am grateful to God for the time and opportunity of wanderings in the desert and for being allowed to explore and then share the contents of my heart; never wishing to blame God (or anyone else) for the hallucinations of a parched mind, yet ever conscious that I could never *find* the rock, much less speak to it, were it not for divine presence and grace.

Read This First
(A Personal "Heads Up")

To my readers,

The Christian world is on the brink of a major shift in its view of the Bible. Many will not welcome this shift, and many are not aware that there is, right now, a raging conversation about it. This is no trivial conversation.

Recently I was asked whether this topic is not merely faithless haggling over minutia. It was a clear demonstration of the urgency of the problem: How could any Christian not understand the relevance of the concern about the makeup and nature of the Bible?

*So, let us be clear from the start: the "origins and nature of the Bible" is not just a sensitive topic, it is potentially **explosive!** It is often more a deeply rooted emotional issue than a carefully studied concern. And that emotion often lies just (barely) beneath the surface.*

For the benefit of all of my readers, I want to be as open as possible about where I'm coming from. I am a Christian, and I write as an invested member of the Christian family. I believe there are few things in life that are more precious than the ancient scriptures. Everything I write in this book is from that perspective. This is my very best effort to be true to those scriptures and to offer something worthy of the ongoing conversation.

But I have been around long enough to know that my commitment to the ancient scriptures—which I have just stated—will be doubted or second-guessed by some readers because of the following reality: **This book, although written from great concern, will not hold back in directly and pointedly challenging all of us to think seriously about—and even to reconsider—some widely held opinions about the Bible.**

As I have pursued this project, a few readers have become personally offended, feeling that I'm calling them "dummies" or that I'm attacking the Bible. It is never my desire to hurt anyone. So I have worked hard to word my concerns to distinguish clearly between challenging opinions (which I certainly do) and attacking people or the Bible (which I don't at all intend to do). Through it all, I am attempting to make a positive contribution to my larger Christian family for how we think together about the Bible.

There are many Christians who love the Bible who are also seeing traditional understandings of the origins and nature of that Bible as old wineskins about to burst. **I'm one of those people.** I'm not only not ashamed of that, I'm evangelistic about it! And yet, my main concern is not that you agree with me; rather, I want to be part of a Christian family that seeks open and viable conversation with each other as we, together, pursue conversation with God.

This book is about allowing **the scriptures** to be the scriptures; about understanding the nature, strengths, and limitations of **canon**; and about being open to the **word of God**—and knowing that these three are not the same things.

Blessings,
Gary D. Collier
May 10, 2012 (Happy Birthday Lanette!)

Foreword

In case anyone has not noticed, faith is under fire. Even subjects once considered safe—"Scripture," "canon," "the Bible," and "inspiration"—enjoy no privileged safe haven. Some who write books on these topics do so with evil intent. Sensing that, it is an instinctive reaction to circle the wagons, pass the ammunition, and shoot at anything out there that moves. However, merely tightening the definitions and increasing the volume accomplish nothing. Far more fruitful to examine our own position to ensure that what we believe and say and argue is dependable for us and defensible against attackers.

Gary Collier is persuaded that much of our present discourse is neither dependable nor defensible. When we talk about "scripture," "canon," or "the Bible," or when we discuss concepts like "inspiration" and "inerrancy," says Collier, we very often fail to choose the best words to communicate what needs to be said. At the very least, Collier insists, we should accurately repeat the Bible's own language on these subjects—and acknowledge that, concerning some of them, it says nothing at all. These shortcomings and omissions make easy targets of us and those we love.

Surrounded as we are by purveyors of doubt and disbelief, Collier's counsel feels strangely counter-intuitive. In this situation, he urges, less is really more—and in this book he explains what he means. And be forewarned: Collier challenges several deeply-held convictions—

which admittedly causes discomfort. But remember, too, that all growth requires change, and change often feels unsettling, disorienting, frightening, even threatening. Little wonder that Paul instructed Timothy to correct with gentleness those who were confused by error. Correction is traumatic enough even when kindly administered—but the Bible specifically identifies "correction" as one intended function of scripture.

In this book, Gary Collier speaks clearly and logically, building on evidence, not on assumptions. He challenges our present thinking, directly but gently, kindly but with persistence. He speaks with integrity and with transparency. He does not talk down to his readers but dialogues humbly as a conversation partner. He sounds like a man who is concerned but not angry.

In the end, Collier's purpose is not to attack but to equip, not to undermine faith in God but to strengthen it. Our reward, he believes, will be to encounter in the Bible not merely abstract truth—however inspired, infallible, or inerrant—but also the living God, with whom we can walk and have conversation all the days of our lives.

Edward William Fudge
GracEmail
edward@edwardfudge.com

Author of
The Fire That Consumes: A Biblical and Historical Study of the Doctrine of Final Punishment (3rd edition, 2011)

Hebrews: Ancient Encouragement for Believers Today (2009)

The Day the Church Stood Still

Throwing Down the Gauntlet

Still, now, in the first quarter of the 21st century, one of the most assumed topics among many well-meaning Christians is the viability and vitality of the Bible.

Unfortunately, it is often taken as a given—already proven (by someone) beyond reasonable doubt or beyond the need to rehearse the details yet one more time—

- that the Bible is synonymous with the Word of God, planned and brought into being by God, and that such a claim is made clearly within the Bible itself;

- that either the Protestant or Catholic Bible (only one) is the only real and true Bible, planned by God from the foundation of the world;

- that the Bible is complete and "closed," with exactly the books that God had planned, and could not have more or fewer books;

- and that only skeptics or non-believers would think of challenging any of this.

It is also widely envisioned that a review of "how we got the Bible" is more a rehearsal of detail and useless technicalities than an urgent matter for current faith.

When all of this is added to an unfortunate reputation (at least among some) of being unwilling to listen to one another about much of anything at all, the chances that there might actually be any real conversation in the wider Christian communities about the nature of the Bible are admittedly low.

The Same Table

This sad state of affairs is reminiscent of a line from the original 1951 movie, *The Day the Earth Stood Still*, when Mr. Harley, the secretary to the President, is speaking to Klatu (a spaceman who traveled 250,000,000 miles to earth to throw down the gauntlet against nuclear aggression). When Klatu asked for a meeting with all the heads-of-state of the earth, Mr. Harley was not at all hopeful: "They wouldn't sit down at the same table with each other."

Unfortunately, it isn't science fiction to say that, today, Christians of all stripes talk a lot about things like "unity" and the "table of the Lord" and about "the Bible as the final authority in faith and practice," and other such high-sounding things. Yet, when it comes to the willingness or ability to have open conversation on truly significant topics—like the nature of the Bible itself—many Christians often will not sit down at the same table with each other. At least, not for very long.

Now I do not wish to appear harsh or condescending to anyone when I make such statements. I speak more as a family member concerned for my family, which in this case I define as all Christian communities around the globe. In fact, it is my deepest wish to appeal to the similar frustrations that countless others may feel and to the experiences they may have had as devoted members of Christian communities. So, maybe you can identify with my frustrations and longings in what I'm about to say in this book.

For when it comes to understanding what the Bible actually is, large segments of the church in the earliest part of the 21st century are simply standing still. This can be blamed on any number of things like apathy, ignorance, a lack of theological nerve, stubbornness, religious fossilization, a lack of Christian spirit, a sense of spiritual arrogance or sectarian separatism, being sidetracked with the cruelties (or pleasures) of daily life, and even a widespread and growing biblical illiteracy among the Christian masses.

On the surface, at least, this *does* sound horribly harsh, and who among us wants to look in the mirror and see such things; or even worse, who wants to sit quietly by while some guy comes flying in on a spaceship to tell us everything that is wrong with us? I don't, and I doubt that you do either.

So here is what I'm asking from you. Let us all assume that we each have a deep love for our Christian heritage, and that we all recognize that many things in our mirror need attention. And instead of me throwing down the gauntlet to you, I'm asking that we together take up this gauntlet and throw it down together for the sake of us all.

Now some may wonder what in the world I'm talking about! Why do we need to throw down anything at all? And so it becomes part of the burden of this first volume of this new series to address some of what is at stake right now in the whole question of the nature of the Bible. So, let me assure you that this will be no rehash of anything else, and this will not be an attempt to rebuild the same old walls. It is, in fact, an attempt to address a growing problem that many people already see when it comes to the Bible and the church in the 21st century.

In order to set the stage for this series, then, I will now set forth four immediate needs in the 21st century church relating to the Bible. They are an attention to fundamentals, an aim of biblical literacy, a need for an atmosphere of conversation, and a willingness to address anew the foundational question of the nature of scripture, canon, inspiration, and the role of the Bible in our lives.

1. Basics

There is a continual need for church leaders and Bible teachers not only to address but to model "the basics" of good Bible study.

Although there are many devoted Bible readers, there is always a need to reiterate and demonstrate the fundamentals of good Bible reading. Whole sections of libraries are written on this topic, but here is a rapid-fire overview of a few extremely important Bible study tips that every reader should, by now, not only know but faithfully practice. Unfortunately, it is more than too often that even church leaders (including pastors and teachers) are derelict in their responsibility to adhere to these principles or to teach them to others.

Read humbly and with prayer. As much as possible, read contextually and responsibly, taking whole documents at a time. Avoid hopping, skipping and jumping all over the place. Actually ask the questions Who,

What, When, Where, and Why—and then pay attention to the answers. Learn the differences between the types of literature in the Bible and respect those differences. (Don't read poetry like prose, or apocalyptic literature like law, or a letter like a Gospel, or theology like science.) Learn the value of using scholars as conversation partners. And finally, use the PUABARI method: Pick Up A Bible And Read It! There's so much more, but these are basic. Let us encourage each other to make a practice of such things.

2. Literacy

There is a crying need for church leaders and teachers to address the problem among Christians of biblical illiteracy.

This is not simply my opinion; it is, instead, official: Christians are biblically illiterate! You might know this by merely paying attention. But the Barna Group (http://barnagroup.com) published its ten year findings in December of 2009. Sobering. The details should be read, posted on thy wall, and worn as frontlets between thine eyes.

We live in the "deep-sea-fishing" time of more Bible translations and Bible helps than at any other time in the history of the world. And Bible software! Push a button and you can now do more Bible research in the blink of an eye than the Bible faculty of your alma mater could do in a whole semester! Christians today generally have a high view of the Bible, calling it the most important book in the history of the world.

And yet all of this rings hollow against a demonstrated ignorance by the Christian masses of how to maneuver within that book. This is not about the ability to re-cite biblical facts and trivia. This is rather about grasp-ing biblical concepts and principles and how to properly read and apply the ancient scriptures in a 21st century context. When it comes to the Bible, a frighteningly high number of people want to eat the fish without knowing or caring how to fish.

3. Conversation

There is a desperate need for church leaders and Bi-ble teachers to help create an atmosphere of genuine conversation (thoughtful interchange) about the Bible, especially on tough subjects where people are going to end up disagreeing with one another.

The question is:

How do we create and maintain a healthy Christian community in which open conversation is not only allowed but encouraged?

Is it possible for us to pursue a thinking atmosphere of *"supportive engagement"* in which we can learn to in-teract with each other and yet still support one another as a loving Christian family despite disagreement?

I'm not talking, here, about the so-called "agreeing to disagree" thing, where we all tend to believe whatever we want for no particular reason. I'm talking about a think-ing environment in which we study together and chal-lenge each other and end up supporting each other de-spite disagreeing in good conscience.

For this to happen, we need to be focused not on *what* to think, but on *how* to think; not indoctrination, but clear Christian goals with effective thinking skills and conversation skills.

Unfortunately on the whole (and there are certainly exceptional people and places), popular Christian culture today is not a "thinking" place where intelligent and challenging conversation about the Bible is encouraged and where people are trained in the art of Christian discourse. Instead, today's churches tend to avoid genuine Christian discourse; and it is all done for the illusion of unity.

This does not mean, of course, that there are no stirring sermons or lively Bible class conversations in such a place. It means that the topics and directions of conversations are generally carefully guided and controlled so that, in the end (whether stated or not), emphasis is placed on official indoctrination. In other words, a clear pronouncement of what the Bible "actually teaches" on the topic is stated as the grand finale.

I have so many examples of this it would fill-up this book, but I'll give you just one. I was attending a large suburban church in which one of the elders approached me to teach a class on the role of women in the church for all adult classes combined. When I explained that my view on this topic was different from the practice of this church, he said he knew it and wanted me to proceed anyway.

Because this was a fairly conservative church, I decided to put together a four person panel: two men and two women. One man-woman team would advocate a more traditional role, the other would advocate a more inclusive role. Both teams were heartfelt in the positions they represented. This was not a debate; it was clearly

25

laid out as an open and friendly discussion of ideas. Each class was video-taped. During each session, both members of each team made a presentation and fielded questions. The purpose of the approach was clearly and often stated:

> *To demonstrate that Christians of good conscience can openly discuss and even disagree on important biblical topics and yet still support each other.*

My team had the task of presenting a view that was different from the official position of the leadership. Even so, we continually stated that although we arrived at different conclusions than the official position of the church leaders, we could submit to and support that position, since it was a studied position of good conscience. As members of a large family, we respectfully disagreed on this topic, but we supported the judgment of our leaders for our church.

This was all going well until the elder who invited me to teach this six-month class up-and-moved a thousand miles away right in the middle of the class. At this point, a new elder was appointed and the dynamic of the leadership completely shifted. When the class ended, the new elder (who had never attended even one of the classes) stood before the whole church and denounced my positions as heretical (that was the term). It was not enough that I *supported* the elders, I had to *agree* with their assessments of biblical texts.

Now, the issue here is not about the role of women in the church. The subject could just as easily be any other topic: abortion, genetic engineering, social justice, inerrancy, you name it. And whether you agree with the first elder (who encouraged discussion) or the second (who was concerned about heresy), consider these two questions:

1. Is it possible for intelligent people of good conscience to diligently study the Bible and then honestly arrive at different conclusions?

2. Is it a requirement that everybody has to agree with each other to support each other?

Forced indoctrination maintains the illusion of unity. But approaching the Bible and Christian community in this way creates two huge problems:

First, a climate is created in which many Christians not only *don't know* how to have an open and thoughtful conversation about the Bible, they are encouraged *not to care* about open discussion. The main concern is about everybody coming to agreement on right positions. Or at least keeping quiet if you don't.

This not only keeps people fat, dumb, and happy (an illusion of peace and tranquility), it sets them up to get eaten alive by outsiders who are right now reading voraciously about the origins, history, and nature of religious texts. This is especially happening with people who are fed-up with the traditional church and who are tired of being, what they consider, "spoon-fed the party line."

By comparison, Christians within the churches are tending to be woefully ignorant about the nature of the book they say is at the center of their lives, and they tend to be less and less conversant with the real issues current today. Not only so, they tend to show little or no alarm about this.

Second, a climate is created in which many Christians adopt the style, attitude, methods, and approaches of current-day political systems. I'm not choosing between Republicans and Democrats here, I'm talking about political styles and systems being co-opted as preferred modes of Christian interaction.

Far too often, Christians (regardless of their political leanings) are influenced in their "conversational style" more by political talk-radio and party-bashing rancor than by anything Jesus had to say. Whether it is in a Bible class or the church lobby on Sunday morning, or by email, instead of being salt and light in the world, Christians too often more like hot sauce, mimicking the barbs, acrimony, and slanderous "us-versus-them" attitudes of the political realm, and then they overtly parade and defend an obnoxious spirit of meanness or arrogance—all in the name of "taking a stand for truth."

This is not only not Christian behavior, it militates against intelligent Christian engagement over biblical issues. Certainly, Christian behavior is about the pursuit of truth and good works; but biblically speaking, Christian truth and good works should be based on something other than political styles or social mandates (2Tim 3:17).

This very book is an exercise in conversation about the nature of the Bible. I'm writing exactly what I think should be written. But I have no delusions that all readers will accept my thesis. Why? Because this book will directly challenge the status quo about the nature of the Bible, and it will offer a different path.

Even so, my main concern throughout this book is not that you *agree* with me; it is rather that you *think* with me. The book is an effort at Christian conversation.

One of the most needed skills for today's church is the ability to have open conversation with each other about important questions. But whenever we disallow that, all that can happen is indoctrination and the delusion of unity, or of Christian spirit, or of the pursuit of God.

4. Scripture, Canon, and Inspiration

There is an urgent need for Christian leaders and teachers to give renewed, focused, and serious attention to the nature of scripture and canon, and to the related topic of inspiration.

Not that we dust off some old notes from school, but that we set ourselves to a renewed evaluation of the issues involved and a real conversation of the topic.

Just say the word "canon" in a group of Christians and watch how many don't have a clue what you are talking about. What's worse, say the word to a group of church leaders and watch how many think you are talking about principles for proving how the earliest Bible among Christians was equivalent to the Protestant Bible until the Catholics added a bunch of books to it—and that this is obvious to anyone who has true faith.

This is a vitally important topic.

The Da Vinci Code is but one example of public relevancy of this topic. Certainly, this story is filled with inaccuracies, including an overly clever suggestion that computer graphics can be used on da Vinci's "The Last Supper" to cut out and move the depiction of John (who, in the painting, is said to be Mary Magdalene) revealing her secret love affair with Jesus. But Christians get outraged at this statement from the book:

The Bible is the product of man, my dear. Not God. The Bible did not fall magically from the clouds. Man created it as a historical record of tumultuous times, and it has evolved through countless translations, additions, and revisions. History has never had a definitive version of the book.[1]

Of course, *The Da Vinci Code* did not *create* this issue; it's a piece of well-done fiction that merely helped bring it into popular view. Further, this approach is not an aberration. Take a quick look, for example, at just two titles published as recently as 2011 by a well-known and controversial agnostic NT professor:

2011—Ehrman, Bart D. *Forged: Writing in the Name of God— Why the Bible's Authors Are Not Who We Think They Are.* HarperOne, 2011.

2011—Ehrman, Bart D. *The Orthodox Corruption of Scripture: The Effect of Early Christological Controversies on the Text of the New Testament.* Oxford University Press, 2011.

A tremendous amount of work has been done on "canonical studies" in the last half century—and to say that these studies do not necessarily support the popular view among Christians or the status quo on Christian college campuses is an understatement. If nothing else, this small volume you hold in your hands should be considered a wake-up call to many Christians who don't have any idea what is taking place in this field of inquiry (or how it will impact them); or to many religious leaders in churches and teachers on college campuses who might

---

[1] Dan Brown, *The Da Vinci Code* (Doubleday, 2003) p. 231.

even be well acquainted with these things but are being very quiet about them.

To be very clear, this book is not a call to take up arms or to march against heretical views of the Bible; this is a call to a vitally important conversation that is already taking place, but that many Christians don't even know about.

For example, two of the leading works that ought to be studied carefully and discussed in depth among college teachers, church leaders, and all thinking Christians include the following two books:

2011—Lee Martin McDonald, *The Biblical Canon: Its Origin, Transmission, and Authority* (3rd corrected ed. Baker Academic, 2011); and

2011—Lee Martin McDonald and James A. Sanders (eds), *The Canon Debate* (Baker Academic, 2011 [a collection of essays by over 30 authors]).

I single out these two books because of their immense importance in this field of research on the biblical canon, representing a wide variety of scholars, and also speaking adeptly about the "canonical process." The point is not that Christian leaders will all agree with everything in these books or with each other in the process of discussion, but rather that the conversation is vital. And to the books above should be added other important works by Abraham, Barton, Beckwith, Bruce, Childs, Ehrman, Gamble, Metzger, Sanders, Sundberg, Tov, Ulrich, and more,[2] representing a variety of viewpoints and asking a variety of extremely important and engaging questions:

---

[2] See "Discussion Partners" in Part 3 of this book.

- What were the scriptures of the earliest Christians?

- Does scripture imply the notion of canon, and how do we decide?

- Was canon an earlier or later consideration of Jews and Christians?

- Can we know for sure when, how, and why biblical canons began to take shape and when they were finalized?

- Is it more proper to speak today of a single biblical canon or of a variety of biblical canons?

- What does the phrase "canonical process" mean and what role (if any) does "adaptability" to new situations play in the rise of scripture and canon?

Looking at such things, we will most assuredly open Pandora's box, something that we generally avoid like the plague. But this is no less an important issue to Christians in the 21st century church than the question of banks dealing in sub-prime markets was to our nation's financial wellbeing. An open conversation about such books and concepts could usher us into an appreciation for the complexity of the problems involved.

Whatever our current beliefs about these and related questions, and however unsettled it makes us to consider such things, thinking Christians are faced with the incredibly important question of how to appropriately raise this topic to a level of careful and responsible discussion. The topic is as potentially explosive as it is "titanesque." And yet, it is often assumed to be beyond question. This assumption, left alone, will prove to be a colossal and fatal mistake.

Faith by Inertia

In the "Gospel according to Klatu" (the spaceman mentioned earlier), "inertia" is the property of matter by which it remains at rest or in uniform motion unless acted upon by external force. In many Christian circles, when it comes to open and useful conversation about the Bible, it almost always takes external forces to change things. Long-held theological positions (especially when groundless) do not usually die gracefully.

One well-known and oft-quoted example of this is that there was a time not so very many years ago (a century or so) that a good number of biblical scholars, along with many exuberant churchmen, regarded the Greek of the NT to be a special language of God, a "Holy Spirit" Greek given just for the revelation of Jesus Christ into the world. This, of course, was evidence of its inspiration.

However, that all broke down under the weight of discoveries of Greek literary papyri showing the NT documents to be a part of the larger world of *Koine* Greek prevalent at the time. And even though the NT brand of *Koine* cannot be called the common everyday "street language" spoken by people in the market places (an overstatement often made today), it is still a form of *Koine.* It is rather more a "Biblical *Koine*," a literary speech steeped in the idioms and phrases of the Hebrew Bible, but especially as those had been rendered into Greek through the Septuagint (the many Greek translations of the Hebrew scriptures). It is also a form of *Koi-*

ne that is not at all homogeneous, which means it has a variety of styles and applications among the various NT documents. This can be easily seen, for example, by contrasting the rudimentary Greek of John with the more highly stylized of Luke-Acts or Hebrews.

The claims that the Greek of the NT was a special Holy Spirit language created just for the revelatory purposes of God was a good idea. But it flew in the face of growing evidence, and it did not have a leg to stand on.

I suggest that the church is right now at no less a momentous juncture for its description of the canon and inspiration of the Bible. For right now, regardless of what church you can name, there is no reason or call or excuse for Christian individuals or churches or church leaders (or academicians for that matter) to be standing still in their attitude towards the Bible. Not today. Not only is it not necessary, it should be wholly repellent to us. There are too many things at stake to live in the past or to be satisfied with overly simplified views of the Bible that do not stack up with what we now know about the origins of Christianity, the nature of canonicity, the history of biblical manuscripts, and so much more about the Bible.

While many are content to live in ignorance about such things, or with woefully inadequate formulations from the past on the topic, there are also many thinking people today who are tired of "faith by inertia."

New Series

Keeping all of this in mind, then, this new series, *40 Things Everybody Should Know about the Bible,* will attend to the basics, encourage biblical literacy, pursue a culture of interchange and conversation, and engage in the cultural "war on the Bible" in what will hopefully be renewed, informed, and relevant terms. And in the course of this war, there will be no delusions about agreeing on everything, or merely confirming what we've always believed, or making either the Catholic or Protestant or independent hierarchies happy, or proving others wrong, or playing it safe. For honest Bible study is about seeking and finding, not about impressing, pleasing, or placating the powers that be.

And so, in this pursuit of seeking and finding, this series will explore 40 things that everybody should know about the Bible. And as you read, you should at least be aware that these 40 things were originally 40 video lessons made for the internet. The script for those lessons is serving as the basis for the body of this series, although here that script has been augmented and expanded, often significantly.

For that reason, the style of writing will be more conversational than formal, more popular than technical. And yet, the goal has been to make this material responsible and well-founded.

As the upcoming volumes are developing (an expected total of four), the concept and direction may evolve as well. If you wish to participate in the weekly video series, please go to

www.coffeewithpaul.com

This series of books will focus primarily on the NT, and the emphasis will be on reading scripture contextually, responsibly, and conversationally, all of these being explained as we proceed.

Seven Important Things

There are seven important things about this series to keep in mind.

First, I'm not going to please everybody. That would be nice, but it is not likely. If you ask 40 Bible teachers what the top 40 things are that everybody should know about the Bible, you'll get 40 lists. This is my list. I'm talking about what I consider to be one of the most important topics in the world: what the Bible is and how it relates to us now.

Second, this won't be fancy. I'm not here to wow you with erudite words or flowery, poetic language. This is coming from my own experiences and struggles and from my love for what I for 25 years have called "Bringing the Word to Life." I will attempt to speak in plain, everyday language.

Third, these won't be long or technical chapters. This is by design *not* a scholarly book, and I'm certainly not writing for scholars. However, it is not a devotional book, either. This book covers some very rugged territory in a very non-technical way. I certainly intend to be responsible in my approaches, suggestions, and content. I might get a little excited now and then, because for me, this is an exciting topic.

Fourth, this won't be business as usual—and that's a promise. What I have to say in this volume (at least for some), will be potentially disturbing or controversial. It is not because I want to be; it is because, to be honest about this topic, I have to be. One has to be mad (bonkers) to challenge the long-entrenched view of the Bible that is so widespread. It goes something like this:

We believe the Bible to be the inspired, verbal, ple-nary, infallible, and inerrant Word of God, without error in the original autographs, the complete reve-lation of His will and the divine and final authority for all Christian faith and life.

Naturally, this is intended as a good thing; it is seen as a high view of the scriptures. It lets everyone know that we value the Bible. So then, doctrinal "statements of faith" like this one are put everywhere: in our bulle-tins, charters, websites, sermons, Bible classes—everywhere. Such sentiments are so widely prevalent that **they themselves begin to function like scrip-ture.** In fact, sometimes we don't know the difference between what the Bible *says*, and what we think it *means* on this topic.[3] (We'll talk more about this as we go.)

I *do* understand the history of the discussion that has led to such statements, and I know that they are of the highest intention. Still, when such things lock us away from needed reassessment, there is a problem. When something is "required" and yet is beyond discussion, that is when discussion simply must begin again. If there is anything that should disinterest us, it is ossifica-tion—when it becomes wrong to ask questions.

Personally, I am all in favor of pursuing a high view of the scriptures. But, I would guess that you will agree that no view of the scriptures can be said to be a "high view" which puts words in the mouth of the scriptures, to make them say things they do not say, so as to protect long-held theological tradition. So, as we pursue a high

---

[3] This comment is offered in all seriousness and is not intended as glib or dismissive. It will appear as a theme throughout this book, and will be dis-cussed at length in chapter 3.

view of the scriptures together, we should understand up front that this won't be business as usual.

Fifth, that being the case, I am asking you to join me in elevating this crucial topic to a high level of fearless, unhindered, and responsible discussion in the larger Christian community. To that end, I have made these chapters fit for private study or small group discussion. As you will see, what I present will be so different from the norm on some things (not on everything, of course) that it will be natural for there to be hesitation or even fear in reaction to what I have to say. However, the subject ought to be at least honestly and openly discussable.

So, whether you agree with what I have to say or not, consider the importance of the topic and the necessity of raising it to a higher level of Christian consciousness. You can even use this book along with the 12 to 15 minute videos (corresponding to each chapter) on the website to start a small group *(BibleStudyTips.ORG)*.

And now to the final two points, both of them extremely important:

Number six. I not only will challenge many things, I will offer something very positive in response—an alternative to the norm. In every chapter, we'll consider one new thing that everybody everywhere ought to know about the Bible. And yet, we will not be jumping around topic to topic. Instead, we'll be pursuing a very specific and deliberate path, unpacking and evaluating the following statement as the central thesis of this book:

> ***The Bible is an act of faith,***
> ***by people of faith,***
> ***in pursuit of a conversation with God.***

This is a small and seemingly simple statement. It almost looks like a ho-hum throw-away line, and I have noticed that readers sometimes don't quite know what to do with it—so they just pause for a few seconds, and not knowing what else to do, they treat it as a kind of cute little side-statement that they will just ignore. Astute readers, however, will see that **this is, in fact, the central thesis of the book!**

For some readers, the statement appears to be very awkward, since how can the Bible (a *thing)* be an act? We'll get to that. Over time we'll see just how *important* and *packed*, and in some ways how *revolutionary,* this small statement actually is (or perhaps *threatening,* depending on one's point of view).

And finally, number seven. Talk to me! Although I certainly cannot control this in my readers, I am asking you to stay with me and think with me in these chapters. Argue with me! Not in a nasty way of course, but in the higher calling of engagement of the mind, heart, and soul. Talk to me in the margins and on the note pages at the back of the book. And then talk to me on the website *CoffeeWithPaul.com/respond,* where you can ask questions, disagree, offer suggestions, or leave comments.

Now, in this next statement, I am not trying to be offensive. All I can say is that this is my personal experience in many different locations: *Christians have the unsavory habit of not being able or willing to listen to anything they don't already believe.* In other words, we do not generally prize a "culture of conversation." Exceptions to this are a beautiful thing. But far too often, Christians tend to *argue* about the Bible, they do not *dis-*

cuss it. I would guess that you have experienced this yourself.

Let's not be part of that. Rather, let's talk.

So here is how I understand my task in this book: It is not my job merely to tell you what you already know or believe, or what makes you feel good, or to agree with what your preacher says, or even with what mine says. My job is to think and to try to challenge you to think—and to challenge both your preacher and mine to think.

In the hopes of encouraging intelligent conversation, I am going to intentionally try to take you into areas that may not always be comfortable. So I'm asking you up front to stay with me, think with me, and talk with me.

And so, like my sci-fi hero, Klatu, who traversed 250,000,000 miles of space to throw down the gauntlet, and like Paul, who utilized the 250,000 miles of Roman roads for the same thing, let us together consider how we might throw down the gauntlet for our larger Christian family. Not, of course, to start a fight with them, but that we may offer a challenge worthy of the faith and message we espouse.

When it comes to the Bible, can we be a people who pursues genuine discussion and the open exchange of ideas? I know that this is quite possible with many people; I also know (unfortunately) that it is not possible with some others. (Some people have no intention, desire, or willingness to pursue conversation—for them, it is all about lecture. This is a dead-end road and not worth our energy.)

I'm asking you to join me in bringing this about.

PART 1:
The Bible as
Conversation

ʹΙΕΡΑ ΓΡΑΜΜΑΤΑ

(hiera grammata)
Sacred Writings
2Tim 3:15

Coming to know the sacred writings.

1. Bible Reading Today
2. Seeing the Bible Alike
3. Scripture and Canon
4. Whose Idea Was "Canon"?
5. Should the Canon Be Open?
6. "Jars of Clay" and Inspiration
7. "The God Who Kills Babies"
8. The Bible as "Collections"
9. The Earliest Christian Canons
10. Conclusion

1
Bible Reading Today

A.
Community and Faith

Just what is the Bible?

Of course, there are about a billion ways to answer this question depending on who you are and what your prejudices are. We Christians tend to think we own the Bible (like it's ours), but we also tend to be schizophrenic about it. For example, we will say it is the most important book in the world; and then we don't read it.

A good friend of mine says the Bible is a Rorschach test, you know, an "ink blot" test, where "what you see" says more about you than what you are looking at. In other words, the Bible is whatever we want to make it. We've all seen that happen.

And naturally, that can be said of everything, so calling something a Rorschach test is more about how that thing is used than anything else.

50 First Dates

Instead of getting mired in the muck of all the ways the Bible has been, is, or can be used, I'm going to suggest a way of understanding the Bible that I'll bet you have never thought of before. And it will probably sound a bit odd.

The Bible is 50 First Dates.

Have you seen that movie, "*50 First Dates*"? As a result of a car wreck, a young woman has brain damage and has no short term memory. Every night when she sleeps, she forgets everything from the day before.

Her family and friends support her. But to help her gain a memory of her life from one day to the next, she keeps a daily journal. Every day when she wakes up, she reads the journal to see who she is. The movie is mostly about her courtship with her boyfriend.

Essentially, this describes Christians with the Bible.

Faith Communities

It's not that the Bible is a bunch of love letters. That's not it at all. It is rather that the Bible is a collection of documents relating to a courtship: a courtship between communities of faith and God. And a key word in this is the word "pursuit."

I'm not trying to be cute with this imagery. I'm trying to find a way to illustrate a very serious point. So, let's get more specific. The Bible is an ancient collection of widely varied documents which span hundreds of years; and these documents are stories, accounts, and other records of God pursuing us, and of us pursuing God. And it all happens in community.

From start to finish, this is a *community* pursuit. And if you will allow me to reach out of this page right now and shake you, I want you to get this much: *The Bible was not written by God to you. It was written by people of faith in pursuit of God and for the benefit of other people of faith in pursuit of God.* It is not about you. It is not about me. It is about us as we exist in community and as we together pursue God.

No, this does *not* discount *revelation.* Nor does it devalue *scripture.* It certainly *does* challenge some existing theories on the topic. We will get to all of that soon enough; but for now, the focus is the origin and nature of scripture in community.

When I was born, I was born into a faith-family. A community of faith. And the Bible was already there. I didn't own it. They didn't own it. (Although some of us always thought we did). It turns out that we have all just been allowed to hold it for a while. When they all die, and when I die, the Bible will still be here, only then in the hands of somebody else.

My mother read the Bible all of her life. My grandfather was an elder for 40 years in a church dating back to the 1800's. Before that, my great-grandfather was an elder in the same church, also for 40 years. That's three generations of Bible reading in my family that I know about, all in one church—a single faith community! That's a long time.

However, the Bible does not predate me by three generations. It predates me by about 50 generations (using biblical generations), some parts even more; and all of it within a context of faith communities of one kind or another.

Within these many and varied faith communities, every generation "wakes up," not knowing who they are, with a short amount of time to figure it all out before they fall asleep. And the Bible is a journal to remind them. The Bible is 50 First Dates: a continuing courtship with God, and all within the context of faith-communities.

Act of Faith

Actually, this is an ancient concept. So let me say it another way:

> *The Bible is an act of faith,*
> *by communities of faith,*
> *in pursuit of a conversation with God.*

Please look closely at this statement. I've mentioned it before. But because it is an unfamiliar concept, it appears for some "not to work." As one example among several, a close friend of mine states his discomfort:

> *I'm having a problem with the fact that the Bible, as an object or set of objects, **is not itself an act.** Could your intent be clearer by saying that it **represents** an act? I can see how this may sound like it's weakening your incisive thesis, but **a thing cannot be an act,** strictly speaking.* [4]

I appreciate the willingness of my friend to boldly go where many friends are hesitant to go. And as I said to him (with tongue in cheek), it reminds me of the movie Star Trek (V) when Kirk, McCoy, and Spock are sitting around a campfire singing "Row, Row, Row Your Boat." They stop their quasi-musical rhyme with "Spock, you're not singing!" To which Spock objects incredulously: "*Life* is *not* a dream!"

---

[4] Private emails during the fall of 2011. Emphasis mine, gdc.

I intend no personal slight of my friend (or of anyone who might agree with him) when I state the following: **In fact, it is this one-dimensional view of the Bible as "a thing" (even a "holy thing")—a view unbelievably entrenched in our "Christian culture"—that is so much in need of being dismantled and replaced.** So, quite intentionally walking in the opposite direction of common assumption, and with neither tongue in cheek nor blushing cheeks, I assert that "Bible" is quite literally *act*.

But that was not the end of this discussion, for during this same period of time, I had sent a proof copy of this book to my son, formerly a teacher in Japan and now a grad student in creative writing. I was intrigued when, without any prompting, he sent me a long email in support of this very point of *act* vs. *thing:*

> *Can one think of a pirouette as both a thing and an act? What about a dance? A ballet? A series of performances? All performance? Culture?[5]*

---

[5]Craig A. Collier, private email, November 04, 2011, in response to the objection raised as stated in the book (he had no access to the private emails of my friend, and we had not discussed the matter). He noted in a somewhat academic manner: "'Bible' is both a *thing*—i.e. a 'system' (system being our object) that generates in conjunction with history, culture, thought, time, etc., and it is an *act* ('generate' being one of our active verbs, 'converse' possibly better in some ways and not in others). That generation of/conversation with that system is a fully integrated and self-acting system—a collective, systematic act, **with which individuals and communities interact as both reader *(thing)* and architect *(act)*"**(emphasis mine, gdc).

Then, mentioning the views of philosopher and political theorist Joseph Oakshott, he personally reflected: "When I later encountered the ideas of Oakshott's view of the 'Human Conversation' (quoted by Kenneth Bruffee in 'Collaborative Learning and the 'Human Conversation' in part as stating that, 'Education... is an initiation into the skill and partnership of this conversation in which we learn to recognize the voices, to distinguish the proper occasions of utterance, and in which we acquire the intellectual and moral habits appropriate to conversation' p. 397) an attention to the conversation, not just in terms of literature, but in the **formation and participation in discourse com-**

These questions are both perceptive and on point.

In the same way, the words "Bible" and "canon," when *traditionally* understood, refer to a *thing* that God produced: an end product. External to us. Standing over us.

But when *properly* understood, these terms belong squarely *within* the contexts of the vibrancy of preaching, teaching, faith, and *ekklesia* (community)—acts of faith, all. *The Bible is not merely a* **result** *of these things; it* **is** *these things.* The Bible as scripture and canon was a gradually unfolding *process*—an ongoing act by struggling, believing, writing, searching, adapting, conversing communities of faith. Indeed, it is those unstoppable acts by various communities of faith that are what make anything at all to be thought of as "canon."

Later still I was reading Wilfred Cantwell Smith's *What is Scripture?* I do not equate scripture and canon, or scripture and Bible, but he correctly and directly challenges the static view of scripture as "thing" or "object" apart from human interaction, noting that:

> *There was a time when Western scholarship on the world's scriptures approached each as an object—a text. [This approach] ignored human involvement in them, and therefore their scriptural quality.*[6]

---

munities, began to take hold. Oakshott's conversation is also my conversation, and it is unavoidable if you accept that **history is somehow engaging us in conversation.** Every other discourse, by analogy, must also be doing so" (emphasis mine, gdc). Kenneth Bruffee above is in *Cross-Talk in Comp Theory: A Reader.* Ed. Victor Villanueva, Jr. Urbana: National Council of Teachers of English, 1997.

[6] Wilfred Cantwell Smith, *What is Scripture?* (Fortress Press, 1993) 222. Although I am not following Smith's agenda here, his emphasis on human interaction with text as essential in the definition of scripture is on target.

He continues from this point to insist that "Scriptures are not texts" but the trilateral *engagement* "among humans, the transcendent, and a text."[7] This sounds like a *conversation* to me.

To say "the Bible is an act of faith" is both an apt description and a corrective *desperately* needed. For whatever else we think it is, when we open the Bible (any Bible), we hold—right there in our hands—thousands of years of community effort, love, fear, dispute, life, and death—acts of unrelenting faith, all. But it is not simply past act; it is ongoing.

Early in my marriage, my wife surprised me with a hand-crocheted winter scarf. Others might see it as a piece of clothing; but when I wear the scarf on cold winter days, I see her working in secret to produce something special. This scarf is not just a piece of cloth; it is an act of love offering warm embrace.

In the movie *Gladiator*, Marcus Aurelius longs for Rome—but not for what Rome had become:

> *When a man sees his end... he wants to know there was some purpose to his life. How will the world speak my name in years to come? Will I be known as the philosopher? The warrior? The tyrant...? Or will I be the emperor who gave Rome back her true self?* **There was once a dream that was Rome.** *You could only whisper it. Anything more than a whisper and it would vanish... it was so fragile. And I fear that it will not survive the winter.*[8]

---

[7] Ibid. pp. 223, 239.

[8] Richard Harris in *Gladiator*, 2000.

Rome a dream. To call the Bible a book is like calling Rome a bunch of buildings.

Finally, when this book was well into the final stages of publication, I happened upon the following quote. In 1952, Robert Hutchins, then president of the University of Chicago, gave a speech announcing the publication of the *Great Books of the Western World*—a collection designed to represent what is called the "Western Canon," the best and most influential writings of western civilization. He said this:

> *This is more than a set of books, and more than a liberal education. Great Books of the Western World is an **act of piety**. Here are the sources of our being. Here is our heritage. This is the West. This is its meaning for mankind.*[9]

I call upon this same sense now. The Bible is not merely or even primarily an end result: a thing in a pew rack or with gold edges. As "canon" it is a concept conceived in community, produced by community, and kept alive in community: an idea, a dream; personified, it is an **act of faith**, *alive, still in process*. The Bible is not a neuter noun: static, dead, motionless. It was not dropped out of heaven and found on a stump. Nor was it carved in stone. Nor was it even bound!

And to anyone who might be concerned whether God is being somehow left out of my description, I point again to the word "conversation": that God is able to speak within community. We do not deny God when we refuse to put words in his mouth!

---

[9] http://en.wikipedia.org/wiki/Great_Books_of_the_Western_World, my emphasis, gdc.

From its very inception as "a collection of documents," the Bible has always been a part of community. Whatever else the Bible has become, it is intimately related to the communities that began writing, repeating, and collecting it, as well as those that keep reading it (whether "faith communities" or "academic communities")—the communities that say in some sense: "This book is special for us."

But I fear that what the Bible has become in the hands of many who hold it is a thing it should have never become. For when it ceases to be *act* and only becomes *thing*, the death of the scriptures has already set in. This is too important not to explore.

A Relic

A Bible sitting on a shelf is no different from any other closed book. It is simply closed. Like or not, if the Bible is simply a closed book in the community that says, "We follow it," then despite all the high-sounding talk in the world, the Bible is then nothing more than a relic: an object; an artifact; a *thing* worshipped *for what it represents* to those who revere it and not *for what it has to say* from its own words. Like old nails or pictures. [10]

What Christians Say

So is that what the Bible is? A relic?

---

[10] And if you don't "get" the significance of what I'm saying here; if you think I'm merely being dramatic or overstating my case you had better ***start*** getting it. Not because of me and all of my erudition, but because the Bible as a relic is exactly what Christians are presenting to people all around—and those people all around ***are*** getting it.

If you ask most Christians what the Bible is, they'll tell you a very high-sounding set of things:

The Bible is God's inspired Word.
The Bible is our guide to life.
The Bible is our blueprint for living.

Christians of different stripes will vary over exactly how they say it, but the Bible (they will tell you) stands behind all of their controversial positions on hot topics and debates: like politics, science, creation, evolution, abortion, social justice, slavery, homosexuality, holy war, pacifism, whether Satan is real or metaphorical, whether heaven and hell are real or metaphorical, whether God exists, the ultimate meaning of life, ethics, morals, church structure and polity, women in ministry, miracles, tongue-speaking, divorce and remarriage, whether the U.S. is a Christian nation—and every other topic you can possibly think of.

At least in theory, Christians generally end up calling the Bible *"the most important book in the history of the world."*

But I have a question right here: Do Christians even believe this? Not just in theory but in fact? Do they really think the Bible is the most important book in the world?

B.
Mirror, Mirror

Christians say, "The Bible is the most important book in the history of the world." But do they mean it?

Well, let's see. There have been numerous polls taken since 2000 to gauge the depth of Bible readers. To take only a few examples:

In 2010, The Pew Survey found that those who score highest on religious knowledge tests are not at all mainline or evangelical Christians, but atheists and agnostics.[11]

In 2007, Stephen Prothero (a Boston University professor) wrote that "Americans are both deeply religious and profoundly ignorant about religion," proving his case through published studies, opinion polls, and other means.[12]

In 2005, Newsweek Magazine[13] noted that whereas 45% respondents to the survey say they read once a week or more, only 2% associate reading the Bible with their closest connection to God, falling behind personal prayer, nature, a house of worship, and praying with others. This statistic is striking in that many Christians, at least,

---

[11] http://pewforum.org/Other-Beliefs-and-Practices/U-S-Religious-Knowledge-Survey.aspx

[12] http://pewforum.org/U-S-Religious-Knowledge-Survey-Preface.aspx

[13] Newsweek Magazine, August 2005, and on the Newsweek website for the same month.

will insist that the Bible comprises "the very words of God," or some such.

But these polls pale in comparison to the next.

Polls by George Barna: 2000-2009

1. Biblically Illiterate

George Barna of the Barna Group, as a result of extensive review of the top trends in 2005, made the following comment:

> *American Christians are biblically illiterate. Although most of them contend that the Bible contains truth and is worth knowing, and most of them argue that they know all of the relevant truths and principles, our research shows otherwise. And the trend line is frightening: the younger a person is, the less they understand about the Christian faith.*[14]

Among many other specifics, Barna says, that according to research, the belief system of young people is more the product of the mass media than the result of Bible reading, teaching from their churches, or their parents.

Again in late 2009, Barna identified four major themes to summarize that year. The third was headlined as follows:

> *Biblical literacy is neither a current reality nor a goal in the U.S.*

---

[14] The Barna Group is not associated with Coffee With Paul© in any fashion and there is no effort here to suggest that it would sanction any of our efforts. However, the results of that group's polls do give indications that we feel are pertinent to our interests. All articles mentioned below are found on their website: http://www.barna.org/.

Among other things in this section, he noted:

Bible reading has become the religious equivalent of sound-bite journalism. When people read from the Bible they typically open it, read a brief passage without much regard for the context, and consider the primary thought or feeling that the passage provided. If they are comfortable with it, they accept it; otherwise, they deem it interesting but irrelevant to their life, and move on. There is shockingly little growth evident in people's understanding of the fundamental themes of the Scriptures and amazingly little interest in deepening their knowledge and application of biblical principles.[15]

Noting that many preachers and Bible teachers misconstrue the belief-systems of those they attempt to address, Barna suggests that most Christians confuse what they already believe with what the Bible says, neither knowing the difference, nor caring.

All of this is another way of saying (in my own words, not Barna's) that most Christians don't know the difference between what the Bible says and what they think it means. And they don't seem to be bothered by that much at all.

2. Reasons for Bible Study Oblivion

In the same study, Barna says the research shows that "people are oblivious to committed study of the Bible" for a variety of reasons:

---

[15] Ibid.

People think they already know what they should know;

Teaching Bible text has been de-emphasized in many churches;

Families no longer emphasize Bible teaching as a family endeavor or priority;

Most parents leave Bible training to the churches, but churches use volunteers who are not properly trained or prepared to properly train others in the Bible;

There is often a lack of understanding of the role of culture when teaching biblical themes.

These reasons are serious enough in their own right, but it is helpful when they are viewed against earlier poll results that point in the same direction. As a result of earlier polls, Barna had noted at least two other reasons that are especially worth consideration as to why American Christians are oblivious to Bible study.

3. Shot Gun Approaches

On November 28, 2000, Barna had pointed to what can be called "shot gun approaches" (not his terminology) in many churches that try to become all things to all people but end up becoming more confusing than helpful when it comes to an emphasis on Bible study.

The result is that churches feel they have fulfilled their obligation if they provide a broad menu of courses, events, and other experiences, but such a well-intentioned but disjointed approach leaves people confused and unbalanced.[16]

4. Sound-Bite Theology

Two years later, on December 17, 2002, Barna noted that we live in a "sound bite" world where people expect quick and simple answers.

In a sound bite society you get sound bite theology. Americans are more likely to buy simple sayings than a system of truth that takes time and concentration to grasp. People are more prone to embrace diversity, tolerance and feeling good than judgment, discernment, righteousness and limitations. People are more focused on temporal security than eternal security and its temporal implications.[17]

The polls of the Barna Group, especially because they span many years, are extremely helpful in seeing trends. There are many other conclusions drawn that are not reflected here, and are worthy of study in their own right. Among them is the tracking of fluctuations in Bible reading habits among American Christians.[18]

Of course, one does not need official polls to know that among the majority of Christians, Bible reading is in deep trouble. Although there are many avid Bible readers, there are many more, even long-time Christians, who have only a vague familiarity with the Bible on its own terms. Add to this a rising number of preachers, teachers, and other Christian leaders who, in the name

---

[16] Ibid.

[17] Ibid.

[18] Ibid.

of relevancy, insist upon a so-called "high view of scripture," and yet focus less on biblical text than other "hot topics" or daily concerns, and we have the makings of something that is far less than biblical Christianity.

Put Up Or . . .

All right, then. I have a simple question here:

If Christians really believe that the Bible is "the most important book in the history of the world," then why aren't they reading it? Why don't they know more about it? Why aren't they just burning up with desire for it?

Oh, what we don't know about the Bible!

A good way to illustrate this is to look at how Christians react to current-day books or movies.

Like *The Da Vinci Code.*

This book, and the movie that followed, left many Christians shaking in their boots about some terrible secret kept from us by the supposed power-hungry, woman-hating Vatican. In essence, it says Christianity is one big lie, a carefully constructed concoction of the Catholic Church. Here's a quote:

> *Many have made a trade of delusions and false*
> *miracles, deceiving the stupid multitude. . . .*
> *O! Wretched mortals, open your eyes!*

So said Leonardo da Vinci against the Bible, according to the bestselling book, *The Da Vinci Code*, by Dan Brown. And the book goes on to make this very clear:

> *The Bible is the product of man, my dear. Not God.*
> *The Bible did not fall magically from the*
> *clouds. Man created it as a historical record of tu-*

multuous times, and it has evolved through count-
less translations, additions, and revisions. History
has never had a definitive version of the book.[19]

In the movie, the main character (played by Tom Hanks) makes it very clear that Jesus was a good man. Nothing else can be known or proved. Faith must take one beyond that point.

In fact, as we soon discover, the legacy of Jesus is actually a surviving oblivious female descendant of Jesus from his wife, Mary Magdalene—proved by quoting the *Gospel of Mary* and then the *Gospel of Philip* that "Jesus loved her more than the other disciples and that he used to kiss her on the mouth." All of this is viciously attacked by the Roman Catholic church in order to protect its own power. And so there arose a whole secret order of people dedicated to protecting the "truth" of the existence of the lineage of Jesus and Mary. The holy grail was not a cup, but the life of our unsuspecting heroine.

In the movie we have the bonus of seeing this unlocked through computer graphics by transposing a picture in da Vinci's painting of the last supper.

Now, despite what you might think, I'm not trashing the book, here, or the movie. I actually liked them both and think that all Christians everywhere should at least watch the movie. No, I'm making the point that most Christians know so little about the history of their own Bibles, or of the whole realm of apocryphal literature, that they are unable to fairly evaluate a whole gamut of current movies and books about Christianity:

---

[19] Dan Brown, *The Da Vinci Code* (Doubleday, 2003) p. 231.

59

1. Some books and movies try to be supportive of Christianity but are rejected anyway: *The Last Temptation of Christ* was an OK novel and B-movie that aroused the ire of Christians all across the country for all the wrong reasons.

2. Some books and movies are very revisionistic of Christianity with so-called new discoveries: *The Passover Plot, The Da Vinci Code, The Jesus Family Tomb, The Jesus Papers*, and more. These are really not new, but are often sensationalized versions of longstanding theories or traditions. Books like these receive mild interest from scholars, but they don't take the books seriously.

3. Some books and movies bring a new slant or challenge to Christianity: *The Gospel of Judas* raises questions outside the box about canon, characterization, and early Christian history; and *The Jesus Dynasty* is a highly speculative look at the family of Jesus by a controversial, prolific American NT scholar. Books like these are highly debated among scholars, which means scholars take them seriously even though some or many disagree with them in the strongest terms.

All of these books or movies are (intentionally) a direct challenge to what might be called "traditional Christianity," even if they are not all of the same class or genre of writing.

Now, what is disturbing about all of this is that many Christians do not know how to respond to such things except through complete apathy (if we ignore it, it will go away), or irrational arguments or even panic (making Christians look desperate and ignorant, not even understanding the basics of the book to which they claim devotion).

Responsibility

Now my point is not that all Christians are ignorant or that all should become scholars, or even that all "informed" Christians will agree with each other. Hardly! It is, rather, about a need for truly becoming responsibly conversant with the texts we say we hold so dear—with our hearts, our souls, and our minds. Whether mindless Christianity or heartless Christianity, it is still not Christian.

Christians need to understand this: the attacks on Christianity and the Bible are hardly at an end. As a matter of fact, "you ain't seen nuthin yet!" Much more is on the horizon relating to the identity of Jesus, what it means to refer to the Bible in any way as "canon" or as "scripture," and the viability of faith, especially Christian faith, in an increasingly secularized and diversified world such as ours. But the fact is, most Christians don't even know what these things mean, let alone are they "conversant" with them.

The 1st Thing

Based on all of this from parts 1 and 2, the first thing that everybody ought to know about the Bible is how it is actually being regarded by the faith community that calls it "The Word of God."

So, how is it regarded by that community?

Well, in theory, the Bible is held very high. Many high-sounding things are said about it, and a lot of "chest-beating" goes on.

But in fact, Christians are increasingly, just plain and simple, biblically illiterate.

The first thing that everybody ought to know about the Bible is, that to most Christians (not all, of course, but most):

The Bible is, in practice, nothing more than a relic—something that is honored for what it represents in their own minds, but not really for what it says from its own pages. And the truly sad part is, they have no idea that this is what they think. And they don't care!

And if you think it makes me happy to say this, or to end this chapter this way, you are mistaken.

This generalized complacency about "sacred writings," this detachment from sacred text, in fact, is not what gave rise to the Christian faith or even to the Bible itself in the first place.

Instead, the Bible itself, on nearly every page, is an ongoing love-affair with previously written scripture, in search of a conversation with God; something that cannot be said about current-day Christianity.

2
Seeing the Bible Alike

In chapter 1 we saw that, although in *theory* the Bible is often praised as the most important book in the history of the world, in *fact* it is often nothing more than a relic among Christians. For this to change, Christians will need to give it more than high-sounding talk.

In this chapter, we have a 2-part question:

Can we all see the Bible alike? And, what is the role of conversation when reading the Bible?

The Perfect Bible

When I was a kid growing up in church, I often heard a sermon called "Can we all see the Bible alike?" It generally went something like this:

1. Yes, we can all see the Bible alike! Because if not, then God did not know how to write the Bible, and he would be the author of confusion, which 1Corinthians 14 says he is not.

2. 1Corinthians chapter 1 says we should all "speak the same thing," "there should be no divisions" among us," and we must "be perfectly joined together in the same mind and in the same judgment."

3. 1Corinthians 13 says, "But when that which is perfect is come," meaning, the Bible, God's perfect and complete revelation.

4. And finally, Revelation 21, which in wonderful apocalyptic fury brings a curse on anyone who "adds to or takes away from this book." And anybody with half a brain knows that "this book" means the Bible.

Ok, so let's summarize:

1Cor 14:33	God not author of confusion
1Cor 1:10	All must agree completely
1Cor 13:10	The "Perfect" = the Bible
Rev 21:18-19	"This book" = the Bible

By the time we get done with the sermon, we have a perfect Bible and the ability for all of us to see it the same way. Anybody who disagrees with this is denying the plain Word of God.

Now, although I understand the effort here (to say that we can all have confidence and that we can all agree about the Bible), the manner of argument is simply bad. This message strings proof-texts together all out of context, forcing a pre-conceived assumption that they all refer to the same thing—which they do not. Unfortunately, the case is manufactured.

1Cor 14:33 is not talking about the author of the Bible but is addressing the problem of discord. In 1Cor 1:10, the context is conflict, not biblical interpretation. In 1Cor 13:10, there is nothing at all contextually that points to "that which is perfect" as being the Bible. And in Rev 21:18-19, "this book" is not the Bible, but the book of Revelation.

64

When it is all said and done, such an argument for a perfect Bible or for a unified understanding of it is from flawed, imperfect human beings.

Imperfect People

Now, I don't have time to do a detailed analysis of this, so let's just cut to the chase. The question is whether we as human being can all see the Bible alike.

Well, think about this. Can you name *any* topic that we all can see alike? Is there even one? Even those of us who agree together that God exists do not have the same perceptions or understandings of the person of God.

Even specialists don't agree with each other. Why do we get "2nd or 3rd opinions" from medical doctors? Why don't our political leaders all agree about how to understand the constitution? The truth is, if you put two scholars in a room—on any topic—you get nine opinions. But you don't have to be a scholar for that to be true. Try having kids so that you can raise them up to be little versions of you. At least you and your little clones will see everything alike, right?

Especially on the Bible, you can bet your boots that people are always going to disagree over what this or that thing means. If you are looking for perfect harmony on what the Bible means, forget it. It will never happen. And it is never promised.

But why would we even expect this? Not even Jesus' closest followers got it. Yes, Jesus prayed for them. And then Judas betrayed him. Peter denied him. Paul at first wanted to lock them all up or kill them, and he later called Peter a hypocrite to his face and in front of the whole world. Only God knows what Peter privately thought of Paul. Can we all see the Bible alike? Forget it!

Conversation

Well then, what's the point? Why even read the Bible if we can't all understand it the same way? Well, let me ask you this: why get a 2nd opinion from another doctor before having major surgery? Why not just give up and give in?

This is where part 2 of our question comes in: "conversation." Just what is the role of "conversation" in all of this?

"Conversation" is what allows us to participate in the decisions being made for our lives. "Conversation" is where we start to evaluate and process the information we receive. Without conversation, opinions tend to become rigid, etched in stone, and even overbearing or, in extreme cases, life-threatening.

For example, take the opinion (we call it a doctrine) that "the Bible can never be wrong on any topic." That sounds good. It sounds biblical. It sounds right!

Until it is read as supporting the view that Jews, who murdered Jesus, have an inherently evil nature, like Hitler did in World War 2; or in support of slavery, like many southern churches did prior to and during the civil war; or in support of the mistreatment of women, as some still do. And on the list can go.

By starting with a simple, holy-sounding premise, a premise that has been debated fiercely for nearly 1500 years—that the Bible is perfect and cannot be wrong—well-intentioned people can then use the Bible for anything they like, even pushing aside, explaining away, or ignoring other statements of justice and brotherly love.

Without conversation, the Bible can become any wicked or destructive tool that any individual or any particular group wants it to be. And all in the name of God. And as such, it becomes just another agent of soul-battering. Without conversation, it will stay that way.

Conversation allows us to challenge abuses carried out in the name of God; to evaluate how we read and apply scripture to the continually changing and evolving issues of our daily lives; to engage in a quest for truth, as well as to engage each other along the way. It is one of the most important tools we have when reading the Bible.

But conversation is not something that we as whole Christian groups have been very good at, traditionally. In some cases, we may even see a call to conversation as a call to weakness or a lack of Christian nerve.

In many circles, this is a very fragile subject. But I want to bring out something that many Christians are conditioned not to see. Many Christians are so conditioned and cajoled and instructed to look at the "unity and perfection" of the Bible, that it becomes forced.

Intertextual Conversation

So please consider this:

The Bible itself, as it has been handed down to us, is an ancient collection of widely diverse documents; documents that are in unending conversation with one another about seeking and experiencing God in the world. As such, they sometimes

67

stand in tension with each other, and they some-times present alternate points of view about those experiences.

I have time only to illustrate this, so don't consider this an attempt to offer a detailed argument. Also, this is the point where some may be tempted to simply "shut me off" because what I'm about to say will *not* be the standard fare. So consider this an exercise in conversation on a very politically energized topic.

My first illustration is Genesis chapters 1 and 2, because they present two different creation stories side-by-side. Most of us aren't trained to see this, and are in fact trained not to see it. We normally read these chapters through the lens of current questions about science and evolution, something the Genesis stories were not talking about on any level. But when the stories are allowed to stand on their own, and within their own contexts, they offer alternative understandings of then-current creation stories from Egypt and Babylonia which honor gods of all different kinds. In other words, our Bible *begins* in conversation with its own world. Yes, there's more to this, but this is a start.

But it isn't simply a rebuttal, an "us against them" sort of thing. For the two Genesis accounts stand also in conversation with each other, offering alternative views of creation from each other, not so much as though they are competing with each other, or debating one another; but rather as different ways of approaching the topic, including some details that don't exactly match each other (such as the name of God, the number of days, or the precise order of creation). The two stories make very different points: Genesis 1 focuses on who did the creating (certainly not Bel, or Baal, or Marduk, or the sun-god, or some crocodile god); Genesis 2 shows the divine origins and purposes of marriage. They stand side-by-side in conversation with each other about the activity of God in the world.

Even though these are not generally the things stressed in Christian Bible classes or sermons, perhaps we should consider that this practice of putting alternative depictions side-by-side without having to decide "which one is right" is typical of Jewish teaching.

For example, another clear illustration of this can be found in the accounts of Kings and Chronicles. These are not bald histories that tell "just the facts, ma'am"; these are national histories or annals written from particular—and competing—points of view. It would be like the Democrats and Republicans (all loyal Americans despite what they often say about each other), each writing their own version of the history of the U.S. and expecting them to match!

This Jewish habit of including varying viewpoints side-by-side, in conversation with each other, continues well into the traditions of the Jews known as the Mishnah and the Talmud, some 600 years after the birth of Jesus, in which various interpretations would be put side by side without any felt-need to reconcile "which one was right."

A third illustration is the collection of the Gospels themselves. We Christians have sometimes been trained to read these as four witnesses on the stand in court after watching a car-wreck from four different street corners. (I've often wondered why anyone would want to compare witnessing to Jesus with a car wreck! But that was the illustration!) And it seems to be part of Christian culture everywhere (from preachers to Bible class teachers to the church janitor) to throw all of the Gospels into a blender (maybe I should have said the church cook), or they read them as pieces of a large puzzle, reconstructing the "real" history of the life of Jesus, which *none* of the Gospels is felt to tell.

I'm not trying to be sarcastic or glib. I'm actually trying to smile a bit at a perfectly horrible approach to the Gospels that we have all seen hundreds and thousands of times. The Gospels should not be read this way. Although Christians become very nervous about even the slightest suggestion that there might be a difference between one Gospel or another, the real miracle is that they were allowed to stand next to each other in the first place! The fact that there are four Gospels presents an ancient, yet living conversation about the significance of Jesus Christ in the world from different points of view.

These are only a few of the places in the Bible that demonstrate intertextual conversations taking place. The ancient prophets are in continual conversation not only with people of their times but with sacred texts that came before them: such as the "water from the rock" texts found in Exodus and Numbers, adapted and reinterpreted in later texts like the Psalms, and Isaiah, and Nehemiah, and still later in 1Corinthians (and in many other ancient texts which are not in our Bibles). Early Christian authors routinely are carrying on a conversation with other scripture texts just under the surface, like the Gospels with the *Wisdom of Solomon*, or Paul with other religious writings, or Jude, who directly quotes what we call a "pseudepigraphical" book (*1Enoch*), and alludes authoritatively to several others. Even an early

Christian book like, *The Acts of Paul and Thecla* (a book of the NT Apocrypha), was directly carrying on a conversation that was friendly towards 2Timothy but not towards 1Timothy. In fact, it is an early letter which tends to generally dispute 1Timothy as genuinely from Paul.

All of this conversation going on within these texts cries out for further attention—a subject to which we will return. But for now it is enough to say that "Conversation" is a part of the very makeup of the Bible we read. To say that

> *the Bible is an act of faith,*
> *by people of faith,*
> *in pursuit of a conversation with God*

is a way of acknowledging what is right in front of our faces in the book we say we hold so dear. The scriptures were written in conversation with each other.

Taking the scriptures seriously on their own terms, the way they appear right in front of us—regardless of how that might challenge some longstanding views about them—is the responsibility of all Christian communities everywhere.

The 2ⁿᵈ Thing

The second thing everybody should know about the Bible is that *no matter how much we want to pretend that it can be so, we will never all see the Bible alike.* Because we are so many people from so many backgrounds and with so many prejudices, concerns, preconceptions, and experiences, it is not even possible.

But here is what *is* possible. If we so desired, as Christian brothers and sisters, we could simply decide to put an end to our hostility, enmity, strife, bickering, and selfishness over our arrogant presumption that how we ourselves see the scripture is the same as scripture itself.

We might not all agree on every detail any more than our earliest Christian teachers agreed with each other; but we can decide to engage each other in open and genuine conversation about such abiding differences and thus demonstrate to all the world that in Jesus Christ it is indeed possible to live in peace and harmony.

3
Scripture and Canon

So far we have been laying the groundwork to help us unpack this statement:

The Bible is an act of faith,
by people of faith,
in pursuit of a conversation with God.

First we pointed out that although we Christians say the Bible is the most important book in the world, we increasingly see it as a relic, and we are increasingly (as a whole) biblically illiterate.

Next we noticed the importance of being in "conversation" *with and about* the Bible, something that we are often neither willing nor able to do. We then noticed that the Bible itself is an ongoing conversation from beginning to end, a conversation in pursuit of a relationship with God.

In this chapter, we start talking about the third thing that everybody ought to know: the difference between scripture and canon.

Where Angels Fear to Tread

There is a difference between scripture and canon. They are not the same thing. However, to press this point among some Christians and to pursue its natural ends is like setting off a bomb in the middle of a city.

Why is this so dangerous a topic?

1. First and foremost, the topic is often considered as *closed*. God closed it. To raise questions about it is regarded quite nearly a heresy in itself and is taken as an attack on the Bible and a denial of the Christian faith.

2. Second, the topic is considered as *divisive*, not worth the effort compared to the amount of disharmony that can result.

3. Third, the topic is frankly *massive*, making mastery of the details elusive and discussion all the more difficult.

Whatever the reasons, to date, there has been virtually NO open conversation about the "nature of scripture" within the Christian community at large—except in very traditional, longstanding, and orthodox terms. And so we find ourselves in a time of increasing attacks from books and movies like the *Da Vinci Code* in which the "conversation" is being controlled by critics of the Bible, forced upon a Christian population that is, by and large, ill equipped and unprepared.

The Starting Point

You've heard of the tipping point, where a point of critical mass is reached and momentum or direction changes. Well, in our attempt to positively affect the momentum of our Christian population, we can never reach a tipping point if we can't find the starting point. And as a starting point, the question of the "nature of scripture" deserves—no, it *demands*—a renewed, focused, and detailed conversation within the Christian community.

So then, such a conversation must consider a bare minimum of three things:

1. What the scriptures *claim* for themselves (a contextual re-examination, including definitions).

2. What the scriptures *show* about themselves (a careful attention to the "inner workings" of biblical texts).

3. What *role* faith communities and academic communities have had with the scriptures through the ages (the give and take of canon and community.)

For "conversation" to take place, devoted Bible students must be willing to re-examine biblical texts and opinions about them—always; but always in a context of respect. This is not a game. Whether we as a people are willing and able to address the issues in a context of lively faith should be a matter of great concern.

With that on the table, then, I return to the starting point for this very important topic:

Scripture and Canon are NOT the same thing.

If we don't know the difference between these two, we are in trouble from the start.

What's What

Now I can't just say this and move on, because many Christians, including Christian leaders, are extremely muddled about this. And there are plenty of people who not only assume, but *insist*, that these words imply each other. They don't. So let's define them very basically right now according to ancient usage:

"Scripture" is an English translation of the Greek word *graphē* (pronounced as *"grah-fay"*), which means "a writing." In ancient Jewish and Christian texts relating to our concern, *graphē* took on the meaning of "sacred writing" or "sacred text." Through the Latin *scriptura* (which means merely "writing"), the word came into English as "scripture." Originally, there was a difference in the singular and plural:[20] (1) **"The scripture"** was a single document or scroll considered holy or sacred; or it was a particular excerpt, text, or passage. (2) "**The scriptures**" referred to an undefined group of sacred texts.

All of these were believed to be inspired of God and therefore to carry the authority of God. The word "scripture" was *not* exclusive, which means it did not imply that only this scripture (among other texts and documents) was inspired. So by definition, all books believed to be inspired would have been considered as "sacred texts" and could have had the term that we translate as "scripture" applied to them.

Because the current-day usage of the word "scripture" carries with it so much baggage (should it be capitalized? Does it imply "canon" or not? etc.), I will often use the phrases "sacred writings," "sacred texts," "holy writings," or the like instead of and in place of the word scripture. This topic is covered in detail in chapter 13 of this book.

"Canon" is itself a Greek word (*kanon*) and specifically means "rule" or "measure." In a very general sense, the term can refer to any group of documents widely

---

[20] It is often assumed and stated that the singular could stand for "Scripture as a whole," but in chapter 13 below, I will show this to be an inaccurate assumption.

read by any group of people. For example, the "Western Canon" often refers to books considered essential or rec-ommended for reading as the most influential for West-ern culture. They include such books as Homer's *Iliad* and *Odyssey*, Plato, Shakespeare, and many others.[21]

But quite honestly, when talking about the Bible, this general sense is not the sense that is normally intended. Canon, with respect to the Bible, is primarily viewed by Christians as God's express intention from before the foundation of the world and which God gradually re-vealed through Christian history of just which books are the books he intended. For most Christians, canon is as-sumed to be a matter of divine intention.

I'll discuss this more later, but for now we need to note this: The word "canon" is not used in any biblical text in reference to a list of books. Only later (after the 3rd century) is this term applied to books (in a list) that fit a given formal profile so that they might be accepted (recognized) as *authoritative and normative* in a given faith community.

So, unlike the word "scripture," and unlike the "gen-eral" approach to canon mentioned above, when it comes to talking about the Bible, the word "canon" *is* exclusive, seeking to recognize not only inspiration in a book, but other characteristics considered of equal or more importance (e.g., apostolicity, orthodoxy, availabil-ity, etc.) So, all books accepted in a canon would have been considered inspired, but not all inspired books

---

[21] An attempt to fully represent the Western canon is *The Great Books of the Western World,* published by Encyclopaedia Britannica.

would have been accepted into a canon. Following is a simple illustration.

In the history of canon development, a book's "inspiration" alone was not held to be sufficient enough to be definitive, since inspiration was applied to many books that were not apostolic, etc., and inspiration was also thought by many to be required if one wished to read and understand ancient sacred writings.

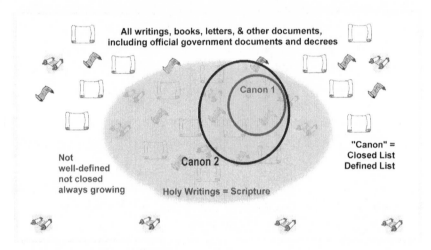

A **"closed canon"** refers to books (in a list) that fit a given profile and that are accepted as authoritative and normative; *and* that list is considered closed to further addition or subtraction. So, the Catholic Bible has more books in it than the Protestant Bible. That's a difference in closed canons.

So now let's summarize these basic definitions, *according to ancient usage:* Even by the standards of the 4th century A.D., all documents in a canon are considered inspired; but not all inspired documents are in a canon. In ancient terms, any document considered to be *scripture* uses inspiration as authority; but *canon* determines authority and normativity more formally and broadly, where inspiration is only one criterion among many. So, not all of the ancient scriptures ("sacred texts") are canonical; but all documents in a canon are considered scripture. A closed canon is a particular list of scriptures which may vary from another canon.

Now if this is sounding confusing, I want you to understand something: I did not create this mess, I'm just trying to explain it. And we should understand that it **is** a mess, and that so many people mean so many different things by all of these terms. But we're just now getting to the "fun" stuff. So hold on.

Eight is Enough

It is right here that the whole thing gets muddy. Today, it is common practice to ignore the ancient distinctions (mentioned above) and to use eight terms (or so) quite nearly interchangeably and even to force these redefined or later-defined terms onto ancient texts and time periods that did not use them in such a way or at all. It is all done quite innocently, as a matter of course:

1.	Scripture	5.	Word of God
2.	Canon	6.	Original Autographs
3.	Bible	7.	Inerrancy
4.	Inspiration	8.	Infallibility

By "interchangeably" I mean that these terms are often used to define each other, so that each word is said to give another aspect of a larger reality, and that they are all *implying* each other. When one of these words is used, the others are implied.

So, for example, it is very common for Bible readers, including preachers, teachers, and authors, to see the word **"scripture"** in the Bible—say, a common translation of 2Tim 3:16: "All scripture is inspired by God"— and to claim that this is a statement which implies canon. After all, the phrase "all scripture" is used, so that must necessarily imply *all* the scripture there is. For us this is the same thing as our canon, because for many today, our Bible (or canon) is complete and perfect and cannot be without any inspired document. So ...

Bible = Canon = Scripture = Inspiration

We take all of these as referring to the closed canon of the scriptures that God intended and gave through the apostles.

In this way, by summoning our *Hermeneutic of Interchangeability* (which is a kind of trash-compactor hermeneutic, since it specializes in smashing things together into one big lump), each of the terms is infused with new and broader meaning, each taking on the connotations of the other (an absolutely dreadful way of treating words in ancient texts, by the way).

I do not intend to be unkind, here. Rather, I want to be helpful, to aid us in seeing what we are doing (which I don't think is intentional). We are abusing biblical terms by reading them in light of our own theologies. In the process, we are then left with inane arguments that can best be called "*citational inspiration.*" That's where we propose (with a straight face) that a NT author can take a source that we consider "not inspired" (because it is not in our canon), but find a tiny part of it that *is* inspired, and then quote it for all the world to see as "inspired." Examples would include the factual mention of Jannes and Jambres in 2Tim 3:8 (who appear nowhere else in our OT or NT canons, but only in apocryphal or pseudepigraphical or other Jewish traditional sources); or the direct quotation of the pseudepigraphical book, 1Enoch 1:9 in Jude 14 as *prophecy*—but only that verse, because that is all that was quoted.

Ok, now let's add to this the phrase **"Word of God."** When this phrase occurs in the Bible, it is often simply assumed that this is another way of referring to Scripture (capitalized), meaning of course the closed canon, or the Bible. So, in this way of thinking, the line in Heb 4:12: "For the Word of God is living and active, sharper than any two-edged sword ..." or even Eph 6:17: "the sword of the Spirit, which is the Word of God," are not talking about the message of God, preached, but are both plain and simple commentaries on the previous text—and vice versa—and all are making reference to the Bible, a closed canon, Scripture, especially in its original autographs. In each case, by using our *Hermeneutic of Interchangeability*, the one implies the other and together they form an unbreakable "scripture on scripture" chain!

This all makes sense from inside of this grand scheme. And it is all attributed to the fore-planning of God. I suggest, however, that God might actually say, "Don't blame any of this on me, I had nothing to do with it." Sort of like world hunger and injustice.

So then, Christian authors and teachers might differ on specifics, but here's an often-repeated formula-statement of how these concepts all are said to fit together:

The original autographs of God's intended canon were inspired by God as holy Scripture, namely the Bible, the Word of God, inerrant in all its parts and infallible in its applications for life.

81

Statements like this are routinely offered as a "summary of faith" and are often considered to be an unassailable and inviolable biblical doctrine, almost as though the above statement itself were found in the scriptures. (So in function, it becomes a part of the canon. It is like getting paid "under the table," so we don't have to report it to the IRS.)

Another way of saying this is that by having this "doctrine of scripture" in place, we can then place it over the top of every occurrence of the words "scripture," "Word of God," etc. and insure that they all end up meaning what our doctrine tells us in advance that they must mean. Whether intended this way or not, it is a way of manipulating ancient words to support the doctrine we have created.

Now all of this hides under the term "theology." Thinking theologically is a necessary and good thing, if done carefully and appropriately, handling texts contextually and responsibly. But there is such a thing as bad theology and that is what we are dealing with here.

A good example of this is *The Chicago Statement on Biblical Inerrancy*[22] made in 1978 by a coalition of more than 200 evangelical scholars from a wide variety of backgrounds. Adopted by the Evangelical Theological Society and by many churches and schools, it is often considered to be the standard account of the doctrine of inerrancy.[23] The statement sets forth a "Summary," fol-

---

[22] Available from numerous places on the web. See for example: http://65.175.91.69/Reformation_net/COR_Docs/01_Inerrancy_Christian_Worldview.pdf

[23] However, there has been considerable disagreement over how to interpret this statement, and there is an ongoing power-struggle to control it.

lowed by 19 articles in a "We affirm . . . We deny . . ." format, and finally an "Exposition" of the doctrine in light of other perceived teachings of the Bible.

Although this statement is often compared to the Roman Catholic *Dei Verbum* (issued in 1965 as an authoritative statement on the relation of Tradition and Scripture), they are not identical statements, especially on the matter of inerrancy.

Text and Meaning

In all such approaches, various texts are brought together from all over the Bible, from which a biblical doctrine is derived. Once this is done, the *summary-statement* on the right in the chart below (a kind of *inerrancy code*) functions within faith communities as if it were the same thing as the *scripture texts* on the left.

Scripture Texts	The Inerrancy Code
2Tim 3:14-17 1Cor 2:10-16 2Pet 1:20-21 2Pet 3:14-16 John 16:13-15 Rev 22:18-19 Lk 24:44 etc.	*The original autographs of God's intended canon were inspired by God as holy Scripture, namely the Bible, the Word of God, inerrant in all its parts and infallible in its applications for life.*
What Bible says	**What we think it means**

This is all very well-intended. But it is important that we understand that things often get blurry right here so that, in this process, *we sometimes don't know the difference between what the Bible actually **says**, and what we think it **means**.* This is a crucial point. For when we don't know the difference between what the Bible says and what we think it means, just about anything can happen (and often does). To be clear, "what the Bible *says*" refers to the actual Greek or Hebrew words of a given text.

Let's take an example. According to the Nestle-Aland 27th edition of the Greek NT text,[24] 2Tim 3:16 specifically *says* this:

πᾶσα γραφὴ θεόπνευστος **καὶ** ὠφέλιμος...πρὸς **ἐλεγμὸν**...
*pasa graphē theopneustos **kai** ōphelimos...pros **elegmon**...*

That, in fact, is what the majority of ancient textual witnesses have. However, the bold print, here, indicates that the word *kai* ("and") is missing from some Latin witnesses dating as early as the late 4th century; and that *elegmon* ("refutation of error") is replaced by what is essentially a synonym, *elegxon,* in some important witnesses from the early 3rd century.

What difference does this make? Well, if you are wanting to know what a text *says*, it is important to know that not all ancient manuscripts are identical on this verse, even if the differences are eventually judged to be minor (as these appear to be). Biblical scholars called "textual critics" focus on determining what a text *says*. The main issue is what words were most likely in the text to begin with.[25]

---

[24] Referred to as NA27, the standard Greek text used by scholars today and documented on the copyright page of this book.

[25] The meanings of textual variants is certainly a concern for textual critics. However, their focus is to establish what the text was.

The next question is, what do these words *mean* in this context? Translators generally bring this into English as something like:

"All Scripture is inspired by God and is profitable"
"Every Scripture is God-breathed and is profitable"
"Every God-inspired writing is profitable"
etc.

The trouble is, not all of these translations have the same connotations. (Make no mistake about it: all translation is interpretation.) So, commentators, preachers, and other interpreters debate and discuss and arrive at some conclusions. They might then put forward a "position" on what a given text means. They might or might not proclaim that there is only one possible meaning of a text.

My point right now is a simple one: there is a difference between what a text *says*, and what we think it *means*. It is not only acceptable that we engage in debate and discussion about meaning, it is essential! However, at the end of the day, whatever we come up with as "this is what this text means," we must acknowledge that even though such a conclusion is the result of our best efforts, it is not the same thing as the text, and it should not be treated as the same thing. Who knows—later we might change our minds about what that text means! (Have you ever done that?)

There is a difference between what a text says and what we think it means. Unfortunately, it is very common for these two things to be confused. On all kinds of subjects! History is filled with this unfortunate practice.

85

Interpretation and Requirement

For example, the people who say, "We do not *interpret* the Bible, we just do what the Bible says," are especially good at this maneuver. It is not that they are devious, it is rather that they honestly don't see what they are doing. They have decided that if they look at a text and draw conclusions from it, that those conclusions carry the same weight as the text itself.

This is quite an easy thing to do, actually. We equate the two columns above. And at that point, the "doctrine," as stated, *functions* like scripture. And so, in practice, it is elevated to the status of "mandatory" for all Christians everywhere.

It is here that we must sharpen our focus. The short, concisely stated "biblical doctrine" (in the right column of the previous chart) is not found anywhere in the Bible! However well-intended, however much sweat and tears were spent on setting it forth, at the end of the day, it is still "a construct"—a statement pieced together from a variety of interpretations of a variety of texts and philosophical concepts. Or, put another way: no Bible on earth (whether Catholic, Protestant, or Jewish), includes this statement. Those who make this argument have to *theologically assemble it.*

Now, I'm not arguing here, that it must be abandoned, or that I alone do not speak from a construct of some kind. (This book is actually arguing **for** a particular construct—and it is not the one under discussion.) We all do, and the question is how aware are we of our particular constructs, and how well examined are they?

I am arguing that the "Inerrancy Code" above must be kept in perspective for what it actually is. *It is an interpretation, a theory, a tradition about scripture. Maybe a good one, maybe not. But it is not scripture.* Unless, of course, we decide to **regard it as such, and add it to our canon.** And in that case, we ought to be upfront about it.[26]

Battle of the Codes

A couple of chapters ago, we looked at the statement from the *Da Vinci Code*, which we now must see again. By comparing the two "codes" in the chart below, it is clear that these are diametrically opposite representations (constructs) of the Bible. On the left, critics of the

The Da Vinci Code	The Inerrancy Code
"The Bible is the product of man, my dear. Not God. The Bible did not fall magically from the clouds. Man created it as a historical record of tumultuous times, and it has evolved through countless translations, additions, and revisions. History has never had a definitive version of the book." (As noted earlier)	*The original autographs of God's intended canon were inspired by God as holy Scripture, namely the Bible, the Word of God, inerrant in all its parts and infallible in its applications for life.*

Bible are saying, "Use your **brain**! Look at the facts and don't be duped by Christian mumbo-jumbo." On the right, the popular Christian response is all-or-nothing:

---

[26] The Chicago Statement of Biblical Inerrancy is ironically becoming that functionally, especially as presented in Geisler and Roach, *Defending Inerrancy* (2012), in which, essentially, a Christian Mishnah and Talmud are emerging.

"This is biblical **doctrine**. If you reject this, you reject God."

Holding to the "biblical doctrine" on the right, many believers nonetheless understand the logic of the appeal on the left, and so are either afraid of it or drawn to it. Increasingly for many, a point of crisis comes when believers, who have staked their faith on the traditional Christian view on the right, come to realize that there are numerous areas that the "doctrine" about the Bible does not address or stack-up with the evidence! They then feel like they've been lied to, almost as if it's another Santa Claus story. At that point, the *Da Vinci Code* version (or one like it) looks like a logical alternative.

Getting In the Conversation

My suggestion is that the traditional Christian response does not understand what is at stake. Instead of *leading* the conversation, it is not even *in* the conversation. So, instead of continuing to fight old battles, I suggest that we should start fresh on this topic.

This does not, of course, mean a wholesale rejection of previous work on the topic. It means, instead, an open and vibrant conversation about it. Respecting the motivations, contexts, and efforts of those who forged earlier statements of faith, it is clear in our present context that renewed or even wholly alternative efforts are needed.

Specifically, we must energetically address the question of the relationship of canon and scripture, unhindered by the constraints of any previous doctrinal summaries or conclusions.

So, what does the Bible say about canon, scripture, the Word of God, and the like? What follows is a mere summary. For a detailed look at these topics, see Part 2 of this book.

1. Canon

First, this may come as a shock to some people, but the Bible has nothing at all to say about "a canon of scripture." Paul (and only Paul) uses the word four times in two texts[27] but not about scripture. And despite the fact that the concept of "canon" is often read *into* certain texts,[28] such a concern over a "canon" cannot be shown to exist within biblical texts or outside of them prior to the mid-2nd century A.D. (by the most conservative estimates)[29] or more likely until the 3rd or 4th century A.D. This is now extremely well documented by textual scholars and historians.

The biblical documents we have in our canon make no self-claims that "a closed-canon" is being assembled or planned by God or by the Holy Spirit or anything of the kind. Let's put it this way: if God had a "closed-canon Bible" in mind all along, he never told anybody.

This is not to say that no processes were underway already by the 1st century A.D. which contributed to a later

---

[27] 2Cor 10:13, 15, 16 and Gal 6:16 for the Gospel.

[28] Lk 24:44 and 2Pet 3:15-16 mention collections but are in no way specific; Rev 22:18-19 says not to add to or subtract from "the words of this book," in the tradition of Dt 4:2; 12:32; and Prov 30:6. Mt 23:34-35 and Lk 11:48-51 are used to infer a canon, but this depends on a preconception by interpreters; 1Cor 13:10 contains no contextual hints respecting a canon of Scripture and is best explained in other ways.

[29] Despite what I consider the circular reasoning of Andreas J. Köstenberger and Michael J. Kruger, *The Heresy of Orthodoxy* (Crossway, 2010. I will address some concerns about this book next chapter.

rise of a "canon consciousness." I will say more about the "canonical process" later. But regardless of this, the concept of "canon" is not mentioned, assumed, or implied, and it is certainly not required, in any biblical document.

2. Scripture

The word "scripture" does not imply "canon," but means literally "writing." It is a translation of the Greek word *graphē*

The word translated as "scripture" is an extremely important word in the Bible,[30] implying both divine influence and divine authority. But it is applied to a diverse array of writings and collections, including non-biblical writings. There is nothing about the word that implies a concern for garnering a list of books, whether open or closed.

3. Word of God

Although the phrase "the Word of God" might be used for sacred writings, it never implies "the Bible" as a closed list of books. The phrase "Word of God" is used numerous times in the Bible, most of the time to mean "God's message of Christ, preached." Early Christian writers emphasize the importance of the sacred writings as they bring readers to faith in Christ and as led by a life in the Holy Spirit as opposed to the letter itself. But they do not make the same distinction between the authority of the *written* word and of the *preached* word as con-

---

[30] The word γραφή (*graphē*) occurs over 90 times in the OT, Apocrypha, and NT, and over 50 in the NT itself. It has a variety of applications, including written Scripture, a holy, inspired writing.

temporary Christian doctrine does; if anything, they place the authority of the preached Word of Christ ahead of the written sacred text (never in opposition to it).

4. Original Autographs

There is never a concern, or even a hint, in any biblical text about original autographs, or about their status as inerrant. As a matter of fact, there is not even a preference given to "the original language" of a document being quoted, even when that language was available. The majority of the time when Christian authors (like Paul, Matthew, John, or the book of Hebrews) are quoting from the scriptures, they quote not from the Hebrew text, but the Greek translations. If they are ever concerned with an "original" anything, they never say so or act like it.

Of the several failures of the inerrancy approaches to the text of the Bible, one of the most significant is the failure to deal with the Greek Septuagint as the real source of sacred writings of the early church.

Another comment is in order about the concept of the original autographs. It is a nice idea. Imagine Paul writing his letter to the Corinthians (through Sosthenes—no matter). When he's done, there it is. According to the theory of inerrancy, it is perfect in all respects.

Do you think there was ever more than one draft of a letter? Did the authors (scribes) ever need to write a clean draft, or maybe a second or third draft? If so, were they all inspired? Or only the draft that got sent?

2Corinthians or Matthew, for example, both appear to have numerous structural elements that don't exactly match with other parts of the documents. In fact, they resemble documents that have gone through numerous stages of editing and revision. I don't know how much writing you've done, but documents like this aren't done only once. Does this mean that no draft of the document was inerrant until the last? Or were they written once?

I've heard the following statement numerous times: "If God could create the world from nothing, then I have no problem accepting the doctrine of the inerrancy of the original autographs." Seems logical.

How about the doctrine of a flat earth? The legitimacy of slavery? Polygamy? A theological case can be built for all of these from the Bible. I suppose that if God could create the world from nothing, we should have no problem with these either.

But the question is not what can we suppose. The question is what is claimed in the scriptures we accept. In fact, not one thing is claimed about an original autograph of any document. No matter how well intended, it is a theological fiction. We don't need it.

The 3rd Thing

The third thing that everybody should know about the Bible is that *scripture and canon are not the same thing. In fact, the difference between scripture and canon is the beginning of the conversation about the nature of the Bible, not the end of it.*

All of this adds up to the following three realities:

1. Scripture and canon are not the same.
2. Canon is not mentioned in the sacred writings.
3. A "closed canon" is a later development (not necessarily bad, but later nonetheless).

4
Whose Idea Was "Canon"?

In the first three chapters we saw that we Christians normally talk as if we have a "high view" of the Bible, and that many of us tend to focus on "formal doctrinal statements" about the Bible's divine origins, its perfect nature, and its continuing authority.

In sharp contrast, critics of the Bible are intensifying their attacks and becoming more mainstream in their approaches, pointing both to outright deception by the church and to glaring discrepancies in the history and transmission of the Bible. They also charge Christians with a-just-plain-gullible "lack of intelligence."

Unfortunately, we Christians—despite our high-sounding talk—tend to play right into the hands of our critics. Studies from Christian organizations report that many of us are in fact more and more treating the Bible as if it were "just another relic from the past," and that increasing multitudes of us are becoming ever more apathetic and "biblically illiterate." This is not me being mean to Christians; this is me looking in the mirror and relaying the facts of independent studies to my family. Like you, I care about this!

The effort of this series is to show that if we Christians are to reconnect with the book that theoretically resides at the heart of our relationship with God, we will—in all of our variety—need to catch a renewed vision of "Bible" as an ancient process of faith and canonical conversation:

- not in terms of past theoretical debates about the Bible, or artificial statements of "high-sounding" ecclesiastical doctrine;

- and not in terms that isolate the Bible from the plain evidence of its own inner-workings and rugged history;

- but rather in terms that the *origins* of sacred texts spring from "faith in the throes of conversation."

And so we have been considering the following statement:

The Bible is an act of faith,
by people of faith,
in pursuit of a conversation with God.

Beyond Innocence

As I've said before, this statement seems innocent enough, almost like a throw-away line, until it is understood that it offers a new path (new for Christians today, at least) for reconnecting with the Bible at its most fundamental level. Instead of focusing on the divinity and perfection of the Bible, untouched by human hands (which, of course, satisfies some ecclesiastical requirements, but removes the Bible from the mess of the faith-struggles in which it was born), this statement is actually an attempt to reconnect with the essential function of sacred writings in the life of the earliest believers. For "holy writings" emerge as expressions of an intensely interactive faith in the midst of life and struggle.

So in this chapter, we pick up with the question that we ended with last chapter:

"Whose idea was 'canon' in the first place? Was it God's idea or was it people's idea? And how do you know?"

For most Christians, this is a jarring question. Jarring and unsettling. It has that effect because Christians are not accustomed to talking about the Bible in such terms. They are so accustomed to hearing the Bible described as "God's perfect book" or as "God speaking," that it borders on heresy to suggest that the Bible as we have it might not be God's idea.

But is it heresy? Or, instead, is the statement "Of course canon was God's idea!" merely an unexamined assumption? Like putting words in God's mouth?

Take for example this statement from a website about the canon of the Bible:

> *Ultimately, it was God who decided what books belonged in the biblical canon. A book of Scripture belonged in the canon from the moment God inspired its writing. It was simply a matter of God's convincing His human followers which books should be included in the Bible.* [31]

My honest response to this is, "Wow! I want to jump on board of *this* bandwagon! So, how do you know this? Where is this claim made in the scriptures? I want to be the first on my block to share this with others!"

---

[31] http://www.gotquestions.org/canon-Bible.html I do not know the people of this website and am not attempting to belittle or attack them. I am, instead, dealing with a "concept statement" that this website repeats but which it does not originate. It is a widely held view.

Of course, it turns out that there *is* no claim in the scriptures like this; instead, this view is a so-called "logical" conclusion from the current doctrinal theories about inspiration. (It is another one of those instances where "we don't know the difference between what the Bible *says*, and what we think it *means*.") So, unfortunately, this is pure speculation stemming from unbridled assumption. But I'm supposed to trust it just the same.

Get Serious

But lest I be accused of avoiding a proper source for this concept, a recent attempt to support this widely proclaimed supposition is the book *The Heresy of Orthodoxy* by Köstenberger and Kruger. Here is a sustained argument (among the best to be found for this approach and position) that:

> the canon was "closed" by the beginning of the second century. At this time (and long before Athanasius), the church was not "open" to more books, but instead was engaged in discussions about which books God had already given.[32]

The book has many fine qualities, is well-written, and is promoted by some well-known biblical scholars.

However . . . the book labors to come up with a rationale for "canon" being God's idea, basically boiling down to this: The OT established the covenantal boundaries of both the OT and NT canons; God made apostles; the apostles job was to protect the message of God; and

---

[32] Andreas J. Köstenberger and Michael J. Kruger, *The Heresy of Orthodoxy* (Crossway, 2010), p. 170. This book came to my attention only after my book was finished. My comments here were added at a very late stage. In no way was my book written in response to their book.

that would include presiding over the writing of books. All of which means that God intended a specific canon, as we should have expected.

> *Inasmuch as early Christians were immersed in the Old Testament . . .* **we would expect that** *this same function of canon would* **naturally** *hold true in the new covenant time period.... So, just as covenant documents were delivered to Israel after the deliverance from Egypt by Moses,* **so it would seem natural** *to early Christians that new covenant documents would be delivered to the church . . . If Israel received written covenant documents to attest to their deliverance from Egypt,* **how much more would the church expect to receive written covenant documents** *to attest their deliverance through Christ?* (p. 114 my emphasis, gdc)

In fact, we can take this a step further:

> *the apostles . . . would have* **presided over** *the general production of such [NT] material even by non-apostolic authors.* (p. 117 my emphasis, gdc)

Well then, once again, with all of this "natural expectation," I'm wondering where any real evidence for this is to be found, especially if God had long intended a new set of books. Accepting the language above, *why didn't they tell anybody what they were doing?* Why don't we see something like that effort in Acts 15 which tells of a sort of conference presided over by James (apparently) and which sent a small letter *by the Holy Spirit and by the group* to various churches? They obviously knew how to do this on a small scale, why not on a large scale with the "Holy Apostolate Stamp of Approval" affixed to each document they were overseeing: "God has commissioned us to write a new set of Scripture in 27 volumes. Here's volume 3."

Yes, I've carried this too far, but to make a point. The whole concept is *fiction!* And it is just as much fiction as the *Da Vinci Code!* No matter how well intended, it is manufactured from a theological assessment about covenant based on an already assumed biblical canon to describe the making of that canon—and then used to describe what we might "expect" based on those conclusions. We're chasing our tales (pun intended).

One of the biggest problems of this book is that it continually throws everybody who is not on board with it under the bus of Bauer-Ehrman—the evil twins of the twisting of historical evidence. So, as just one example, McDonald's 550 page book published in 2007 (which I highly recommended above on page 31) is mentioned only once (in a minor note), and he is dismissed (along with others) as thinking of canon only in terms of "a later, after-the-fact concept imposed upon the New Testament books."[33] This actually reflects that the *substantial* assessments and arguments of McDonald's book are either not understood or are just plain ignored.

The Heresy of Orthodoxy is well-written and a valiant effort (I wanted to like this book). Unfortunately, as to canon, it would be better named *The **Fantasy** of Orthodoxy* in that one more time, we assume our case, construct our case, and then *require* our case by vilifying all others as under the spell of liberal bias.

---

[33] Ibid., p. 107.

We can do much better than this.

The Rise of Canons

Let's take this one step at a time.

Last chapter we saw that the terms "canon" and "scripture" are not the same thing.

From all documents of that time, we learn that "the scriptures" are writings deemed "holy" and as having their origins with God. But the term "scripture" is not in itself exclusive. It does not imply that "*this* is scripture, and nothing else is." There can even be collections of accepted scriptures—like the five books of Moses, or non-specific references to the Prophets or even Paul's letters (whatever these collections might include). Collections of the scriptures need not imply a narrowing process, only that associations are recognized. Nor do they imply that there are no other scriptures, nor that the collection is "closing" or "closed."

Let's put it this way: nobody in the first century would use the word "canon" to refer to the scriptures, whether a single document or a collection of them. They would simply call them the scriptures. *For us to use the term "canon" is to inject a foreign concept.*

A "closed canon," on the other hand, is a much later concept (at least 3rd or 4th century) and is *per se* about limits. It says either, "These are the scriptures that we *accept*," or more likely, "These are the *only* scriptures that exist—the only ones that God *intended.*"

Closed canons arose slowly. For example, let's review some general history.[34]

The Hebrew canon wasn't finalized until about the 3rd century A.D. On some levels, this was done in response to the Christian acceptance and usage of the Greek scriptures (OT).

Despite some longstanding claims that the NT canon was formed by the early to mid-2nd century,[35] it is now clear that the Roman Catholic Bible was very slow in developing. Although there were varying degrees of canonical development all along the way, this canon took *final* shape between the 4th and 7th centuries A.D. It accepted a somewhat different OT than the Hebrew canon, and it took a long time to settle on the "NT canon." Official councils (like the Council of Nicaea in A.D. 325 and others) discussed such matters, but they did not *decide* the matter so much as *confirm* what was being used in the churches. In the early 4th century, the Roman Catholic canon was still a bit fluid.

---

[34] This review is common knowledge and can be found in a wide variety of resources: basic dictionary articles, books on canon, and the like. Naturally there are some differences of opinions about some details. The purpose here is for a general overview.

[35] The debate centers largely around the dating of a document called the Muratorian Canon or Fragment. The traditional dating (about A.D. 180) has been called into serious question by numerous scholars and for a variety of very specific reasons, moving it instead to the 4th century. For example, Köstenberger and Kruger, *The Heresy of Orthodoxy,* p. 157, speak confidently of "The Muratorian Fragment—our earliest extant canonical list (c. A.D. 180)" with a cryptic footnote that the date has been "disputed" but that it has also been decisively answered, leaving the impression for readers that the challenge is not serious. The primary argument of the book greatly depends on the early dating of this document and refers to it numerous times throughout the book. The book implies that only those duped by the Bauer-Ehrman reading of the NT would question this. However, this handling of the matter is at best misleading since a growing number of canon scholars today doubt the early date for very specific and well-argued reasons. To see those reasons in detail, go to the detailed discussion in McDonald, *The Biblical Canon,* pp. 369-78.

Some 50 years later, signs existed that the boundaries were closing. Until this time, they didn't even have a word for this, since the word "canon" itself was not used for a list of books until Athanasius used it in A.D. 367 (mid-4th century).[36] He distinguished three kinds of books: those that were *"listed"* ("canonized"), those that were *"read-by-new-Christians,"* and those that were *"secret"* (not to be read). This approach would eventually win the day, but not for a couple hundred more years.

The Protestant canon came much later. Martin Luther, in the 1500's, rejected the Roman Catholic Bible's version of the OT, preferring instead the Jewish Hebrew canon, and he also wanted to ban Hebrews, James, Jude, and Revelation. But Luther's word was not final, and Protestant churches debated this for a hundred years or so. Many people don't know this, but when the KJV was originally published in 1611, it included the Apocrypha.

The fact is, the Protestant canon was *not* actually the original canon that existed at the moment the Apostle John stopped writing the book of Revelation (or whatever the last book to be written was). The Protestant Canon did not exist until about 500 years ago.

We Christians have a bad habit of looking at "canon" only in terms of our own faith traditions. There have been, in fact, throughout Christian history, some 30 different Christian canons of one kind or another, *even*

---

[36] Prior to this time the word was used to mean "rule of faith" or something similar, but not for writings of the NT until the 4th century. Köstenberger and Kruger, *The Heresy of Orthodoxy,* pp. 105-106, are misleading on this, leaving the impression (by means of a vaguely written footnote) that the word might have been used to refer to written Scripture as early as the 2nd century. This is clearly not the case, however, as a review of McDonald, *The Biblical Canon*, pp. 50-51 will show.

though there is often substantial overlap. The Orthodox Tewahedo Churches (both Ethiopian and Eritrean) have 81 books in their canon, for example, including the apocalyptic book of 1Enoch, since (in their view) Jude 14 directly quotes it as a sacred prophecy. And there is much more when considering the full history of canons across Christian traditions.[37] We American Christians pay virtually no attention to traditions other than our own, especially American conservative and evangelical groups (from which I hail). Many of us are happily convinced that God had us in mind all along when thinking about what the church would look like when it finally grew up.

Scripture or Canon?

So now, let us ask: What is the Bible? Is it simply *Scripture*, a holy writing whose edges are somewhat undefined? Or is it a *canon* of scripture whose boundaries are fixed and closed?

Christians today want to equate the two, saying each implies the other. But they don't. To claim that they do is to read into ancient texts meanings they did not have. When we look closely at the usage of these words at the time of biblical literature, we see that they are not interchangeable. This is very important to understand: *The Bible as it has been received—whether Catholic, or Greek Orthodox, or Orthodox Tewahedo, or Protestant—is a canon of scripture. Each group's Bible is a well-defined*

---

[37] As an example, a quick look at the article "Books of the Bible" on Wikipedia.org will illustrate: "The Books of the Bible are listed differently in the canons of Judaism and the Catholic, Protestant, Greek Orthodox, Slavonic Orthodox, Georgian, Armenian Apostolic, Syriac and Ethiopian churches, although there is substantial overlap." The differences relate to both OT and NT. See also articles under the Eritrean Orthodox Tewahedo Church and the Ethiopian Orthodox Tewahedo Church.

list, mostly overlapping but with some significant variations.

This reality, then, puzzles Christians. So the question is asked: *Which "canon" is right?* We ask this question because longstanding church doctrine has set us up to focus on a perfect, inerrant Bible that God had planned before the foundation of the world. It is kind of like the old science fiction movie and TV series, *The Highlander,* about people who are born with the incredible gift of being immortal, except that they can kill each other off by lopping off the other's head in a sword fight while repeating: "There can be only one."

Christian communities engage in these kinds of head-lopping contests, having "My Bible is better than your Bible" battles as we all vie for the prime distinction as God's true people, being heirs of the one true Bible which was planned by God from the foundation of the world.

Umm . . . are we serious? Just what evidence is there for this assumption?

1. No Bible on earth claims that God had in mind to produce an "all-in-one" single book and that our job would be to figure out which one was right. This concept is found only in religious groups that read it back into their various Bible texts.

2. No Bible on earth claims that God inspired the Bible. [You should pause, here, to think about that.] I know that this is a startling statement and that it flies in the face of what every Christian is taught. But that is not my problem. The

fact is, no Bible on earth claims that God inspired the Bible. The claim is, rather, that God
inspired every *scripture.*

Here is where the terminology gets crucial. No, this
is not a minor distinction or a quibbling over words. It
rather pulls a cover back that conceals a major blunder
in much current Christian thinking. For these two little
words—"The Bible"—today means for most people, *"The
Book that God Inspired."* (And whether they know it or
not, this is code for *"The Canon of Scripture that God Inspired."*) But there is no claim in *anybody's* Bible that
God inspired—or intended to inspire—a particular canon, any more than he inspired a particular language in
which the scriptures were being written and read.

Engaging in the Conversation

I said from the start that this is a highly complex issue. And my little presentation here is greatly simplified. There is no question that this approach can be up-
setting, especially if we have heard just the opposite all
of our lives.

But let me suggest an alternative. If we were to stop
reading the Bible only from our own vantage-point (as
belonging only to us and our group), and view it from,
say, *the moon,* maybe we could get the point that "the
Bible" is much more than one tradition. If we were to
read the Bible—in all of its canonical variety—as ancient
and ongoing acts of faith in pursuit of a conversation
with God, this would allow us to do two things:

1. It would allow us to identify both with the authors of the documents and with those who
   handed them down, ourselves engaging in the

age-old conversation alongside our earliest brothers and sisters, *none of whom had a closed canon.*

2. It would allow us to acknowledge the real, rugged, and human history of our Bibles (warts and all) without making up strained arguments.

In actuality, within Christian history, the Bible is a broad-based, varied, and ongoing effort, even though "the Bible" has become Christian jargon to mean "The one true book that God gave—and my church reads it!" (regardless of whether one is Roman Catholic or Protestant or something else).

This battle for ownership of "the one true Bible" is not only a mistake, it is a dead-end road. When speaking of the Bible among Christians, I suggest that the phrase "the Bible" is not best understood in an *exclusive* sense, as if it denoted "the one true canon intended by God." Instead, "the Bible" should be used in a more *general and inclusive* sense to refer to the full historical gamut of canonical efforts by communities of faith.

"The Bible" should no longer be seen as merely a particular canon owned by a particular group: not as only "the Protestant canon" or as only "the Roman Catholic canon" or as only any other privately-owned or idiosyncratic canon. The most important question is not *"Which one is right?"* The question is rather: *"How do we use them?" How can we effectively utilize the various canonical evaluations, judgments, and efforts over the 2,000 year history of the Christian faith in our ongoing desire to communicate with God?*

105

I suggest that reading the Bible can be a bad thing if we draw from it that our "one-true-canon" somehow proves our Christian group to be the chosen group over another (e.g., Protestant vs. Catholic, or vice versa). But reading the Bible in "canonical conversation" (i.e., as faith in pursuit of God, handed down to us in various collections of sacred texts) can be a wonderful thing if it helps us to focus not on the letter, but on the Spirit which gives life.

The 4th Thing

The fourth thing that everybody ought to know about the Bible *is just whose idea the canon was. The fact is, there is no evidence or claim that God initiated this. In fact, the processes of canon can be clearly traced, and in great detail, as a human enterprise: a result of communities of faith searching both for God and for control, and sometimes not distinguishing the two.*

It turns out that "canon"—including every current-day effort to define and defend a particular canon—is both an effort of faith and a form of ownership: a way of domesticating ancient holy writings for our own religious purposes. The fact is, we still don't have the Bible like we want it, as every effort we make to nail it down and define it—and to regulate how it is interpreted—demonstrates. After centuries of such efforts, we are still so busy summarizing, conflating, and substituting doctrinal phrases for it at every turn (as we saw in chapter 3), that we don't seem to appreciate that such efforts are part of the continuing struggle to participate in the larger, ongoing conversation that the various canons of the Bible represent.

106

Of course, that is not to say that God cannot or does not work with and through the various canons, as he does with all things in jars of clay. For it is within those various canons that the "scriptures"—the writings deemed holy by faith communities for centuries—are described variously and lavishly as coming through the breath of God and as moved by the Holy Spirit of God.

The more we can focus on reconnecting with the essence of "Holy Writings," and the less on equating them with a particular canon, the better.   It might sound strange to us, but learning to think about the scriptures in terms of the broader canonical conversation apart from our own provincial arrogance (in which we think *we* have the right Bible and *we* are the right people and *we* are the right ones to decide all of that) would be good for us.

How do we do that without throwing away what is good about our own identity? Next chapter, I will share with you what I call a "7-Tier Universe of Canon," which explores a responsible way of reading the Bible in "canonical conversation" without becoming exclusivist or perhaps even belligerent about it.

Until then, I leave you with two questions:

1. "If God never promised a particular canon, then why should I read the Bible at all?" And related to this

2. "Should the canon be open?"

We'll pick these up next chapter.

5
Should the Canon
Be Open?

For the last couple of chapters we have shown that *scripture* and *canon* are two different things and should not be equated. Whereas scripture is "sacred writing" bearing the stamp of God, it implies nothing about canon. A closed canon, on the other hand, is by definition a "closed collection of sacred writings" and assumes that all documents in its collection are scripture.

Last chapter, we demonstrated that a wide variety of "canons of scripture" have developed over the last two millennia: the Roman Catholic, Greek Orthodox, and Protestant collections (otherwise known as "canons") are only three examples in the midst of about three dozen more. Most Christian canons are pretty much the same at their core, and yet on the fringes of those collections there is sometimes great variety. Furthermore, we have pointed out that all of these "canons" (or collections) are the result of faithful efforts on the part of various faith communities in search of a conversation with God. Thus, the various collections are what these faith communities have accepted as being their "Christian scripture" or "Bible."

Although it is common for believers within each of these faith communities to view their own collection as "the Bible"—i.e., the true form of the Bible, or the one true Bible that God has inspired—we showed in the last chapter that there is no claim or evidence from any sacred text within any of these Bibles that God had in mind creating a single collection of scripture as "the only true and right Bible."

And so, we ended the last chapter with the following two very understandable questions:

1. If God never promised a particular canon, then why should I read the Bible at all?"

2. Should the canon be open?

These two questions will help us show the 5th thing that everybody should know about the Bible.

Why Read the Bible?

So let's begin with the first question: "If God never promised a particular canon, then why should I read the Bible at all?"

First and foremost, we read the Bible, in all its variety, for the same reasons it was written and collected: as an act of faith in pursuit of a conversation with God. Just in case you have misunderstood what I've been doing in the past few chapters, thinking maybe that I've been "attacking the Bible," you couldn't be missing my point more. I'm not attacking the Bible; I'm trying to take it so seriously, in fact, that I refuse to put words in its mouth, even when that makes me, and my closest friends around me, uncomfortable.

The Protestant Bible—even when seen as one of several collections of ancient Holy Writings—is specifically that: a collection of ancient scripture. As such, it is an extremely important witness in the larger effort to interact with God. Despite what some want to think, the various canons are not arbitrary, shot-in-the-dark lists. As we have been seeing, "canon" is more than a *thing* or an end *result;* it is a pursuit, a longing, a dream—yes, still *in process.* In a very real sense, the pursuit of canon is an act of faith, so much so that *the various canons, worldwide, can themselves be personified as living and breathing acts of faith, by diverse communities of faith, over large amounts of time, all in search of a conversation with God.* And we are participants in that pursuit.

Second, we read the Bible to participate in the ancient, yet ongoing, conversation with our faith-community. We are heirs of an ancient conversation, passed down to us from our brothers and sisters before us. But we are not baby birds with our mouths wide open; we are *participants* in this ongoing community effort, taking responsibility to engage in the conversation. To say this more directly: we respect the faith, opinions, and decisions of those who have preceded us, including the efforts of our own parents; but we do not honor them by blindly following them. To honor them, we engage them for our own times. We might even challenge or disagree with them, as we hope our children will engage and challenge what we leave behind for them. We do not want offspring who merely mimic us, but who can think for themselves.

The Bible, as a painstakingly derived collection of ancient texts, makes it possible for our broad-based, time-extended community of believers to carry on a conversation not only with each other now in the present, but also across generations, all as we continue to seek a conversation with God.

Third, we read the Bible so that we might be challenged and changed as human beings. This, of course, is the desired result of all of the efforts at canon. In conversation with God, how can we be transformed into something beyond ourselves? In this effort, we might engage in, but we are not primarily concerned about, heady philosophical or theological debates. Instead, the very purpose of reading ancient sacred texts ("the scriptures") in the first place is ultimately practical; and it is not only about "me," it is about "us" as a faith-community, as it is said:

> *for teaching, reproof, correction, and training in righteousness, that 'the man of God' might be complete, equipped for every good work.*
> *(2 Tim 3:17)*

God did not put us here to play "king on the mountain," to see who has the "right" Bible, who goes to the "right church," or who can say, "We thank you, God, that we are not like these other groups." If we have disagreements, that is all just part of the conversation. But our every reading of "the Bible"—as it has come to us in various canons of the scriptures—must give way to a larger concern: What is possible for us—for me!—if we exist in conversation with God through faith in Jesus Christ and through the power of the Spirit of God?

Should the Canon Be Open

Our second question is related to the first: "Should the canon be open?"

Actually, since a canon is the product of a faith-community, a canon is either open or closed depending on the community, and that might vary from one generation to the next.

When Martin Luther challenged the Roman Catholic Canon, the faith community that walked away from the Catholic church debated the extent of the canon for a hundred years or so. But in the end, it was a somewhat different canon. Anyone who accepts and uses the Protestant canon, accepts by default that a "canon" both comes into being and exists by the acceptance, use, and will of the community and thus can be changed by the community. In fact, it is actually quite hypocritical for those who use the 66 book Protestant canon to hold that canon is forever closed and cannot be altered, or that it cannot exist in other forms. The very Protestant Bible itself is a testament against such a notion.

Should-a-Coating the Canon

All of this actually helps us to realize the essence of canon. It is tradition held high. Canon doesn't start in the 15th or 6th or 4th or 2nd centuries A.D. This is the biggest mistake that Christians make when they start talking about canon: they *should-a-coat* it. What books *should* be included? What rules *should* be followed? Was everything included that *should* have been included? Was everything excluded that *should* have been excluded?

In the process of this kind of thinking, a huge assumption is made about the nature of a closed canon in the first place: that it *should* exist, that only particular books *should* be selected, and that "there can be only one" correct canon.

This is unwarranted. The process of canon starts long before this. The issue is not really about rules and what *should* be there, as if someone has predetermined what should be there. Canon is about community acceptance. When a story that someone tells is adapted, is retold, is written down and becomes sacred to a faith-community, that is the very essence and process of canon. We see this when Isaiah quotes Exodus and adapts the "water in the desert" theme, and when Paul adapts it in 1Cor 10. We see it in Luke 4 when Jesus quotes Isaiah and adapts the texts before him for his own situation. Whenever *sacred story* is adapted to bring renewed life, we see the process at work.

If one wants so much to believe that "the biblical canon" is a pure result of God's initiative, even when there is no such inner biblical claim to such a thing, then there is a lot left to explain. On the other hand, if one chooses to deny the value of canon altogether, there is just as much to explain. *The canonical process is natural and ongoing. It is the process of tradition becoming scripture, and scripture being used and adapted in the life of a faith community.*

It is this tension between "no explicit claim" and the "natural process of faith communities" that not only allows but demands something different from the standard assumptions and explanations about canon.

For my part, I suggest a seven-tier universe of awareness about canons. This is how I personally approach the subject: seven concentric circles of ever-expanding focus.

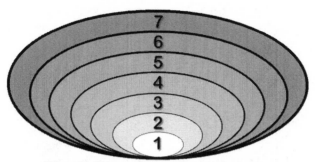

The 7-Tier Universe of Canon

A Seven-Tier Universe of Canon

Starting from the level of greatest focus and moving outward:

1. First, I personally accept the *Protestant Canon as my starting point.* I inherited it at childhood as "The Bible" of my faith-community. Even if I have different opinions from others about the exact nature of this collection of writings or how to interpret or apply it, I can still accept, respect, and engage in lively interchange under this umbrella as "the Bible."

2. Second, I acknowledge *the other Christian and Jewish canons* of the world (more than three dozen of them) as the result of the faith and struggles of millions of people who have gone before me and who now live around me. I include these as the larger definition of "the Bible." The *Apocrypha* contains both valuable spiritual insight and important information; it helps me to think not only about the biblical canon of my own faith community, but also

115

about my world. And so on with other Christian and Jewish canons. Along these lines, I personally hold the study of ancient Greek and Hebrew as a spiritual discipline, not merely as an academic exercise. The study of these languages is a vital means of getting at the many ancient texts mentioned in items 1-4 especially.

3. Third, I then acknowledge that there are *countless other Jewish and Christian documents,* both ancient and more recent, which are based upon, react to, or are influenced by more widely accepted texts, though not generally a part of any current group's "canon of scripture." The *Shepherd of Hermas*, the *Didache*, the *Gospel of Thomas* and other early Christian writings do not have to be in the Protestant or Catholic canons for me to read and teach from them as ancient Holy Writings. The *Dead Sea Scrolls* (found in Israel) and the *Nag Hammadi Scrolls* (found in Africa) are also worth my reading for informational, historical, and spiritual purposes. I can read them, learn from them, teach them, and be inspired by them. Philo of Alexandria, Josephus, and books known as the Pseudepigrapha: all of these are religious books based on biblical texts from which a great deal can be learned about religious history and experience. Philo, for example (a Jew who wrote before Paul) was considered a "Church Father" by some early Christian writers! The Mishnah and Talmud are full of insight. And this doesn't even begin to touch the hem of the garment. The writings

of Augustine, the "church fathers," Marcion(!), St. Thomas Aquinas—and so much more.

4. Fourth, the *wider world of Greek and Latin documents* from the biblical time period: Homer, Thucidides, Herodotus, the moral philosophers, ancient novels, and so much more.

5. Fifth, I look to the various *academic disciplines* around me—biblical and theological studies, world literature, history, science, philosophy, archaeology, and so on—realizing that they all have varying degrees of "canons" from which they operate. And they all are on "scientific, historical, and spiritual quests" of sorts, seeking answers to life's mysteries.

6. Sixth, although I am not an active participant in other world religions, I extend my respect to the *various religions of the world and to their canons* of scripture, knowing that they also explore and experience spirituality in ways I have not and do not. These are special collections ("canons") to which I show respect.

7. Seventh, I reserve an important place for the value of *personal and practical experience* of my own daily life and to that of everyone around me. Like everyone else in the world, I see things through my surroundings and am therefore conditioned by those things, and people, and situations, and events in ways that I can only *try* to understand.

And so you have my 7-tier universe of canon. As you can see, it is not closed.

I am not at all one who sees faith in conflict with or as a judge over science, or history, or of any other category. I take great solace from the fact (not theory, but fact!) that my brothers Paul, John, and Apollos; and my sisters Priscilla, Lydia, and Phoebe; and even my Lord Jesus . . . not one of them ever gave a second thought to the concept of a "closed canon."

Christianity not only *does not need* a single closed canon to survive and thrive, *it has never had one* (even though whole groups of us live under the delusion that we are the ones who have it)! From where I stand, I have put forward a high view of the *scriptures*, and I view *the scriptures* and *revelation* as intertwined. I respect it, I respect the process of it, I respect the widespread witness of the many intertextual conversations, and I am attempting to participate in those conversations.

Above all, I have not put words in the mouth of the scriptures to make them say things they do not actually say. When we start doing that (putting words in their mouth) we overstate our case, and then we lose our case.

The Margins

I am very aware that what I am presenting is so different from the norm that for some it borders on being scandalous. So allow me just a bit of transparency.

An underlying factor for me is my years spent in the study of what is called "comparative midrash" and other forms of intertextual examination of ancient texts. In plain English, this is the study of how ancient texts "talk" to, refer to, allude to, echo, or utilize one another. I not only have read mounds of technical theory about it, I spent months-at-a-time for years in ancient Greek and Hebrew texts pursuing it. I still do.

I am not presenting myself as some great scholar; I am saying I was ushered into something unbelievably special. Through my personal reading of such texts,[38] I came to see that scripture and canon are literally *acts* that ancient communities of faith *did or performed—* slowly, deliberately, and even subconsciously; and it all took place in the margins, the reinterpretations, and the reapplications of earlier texts: *that* is where scripture, yea canon, begins and stirs, *not* in A.D. 367 with Athanasius using the word "canon" for the first time about a group of books. So, when Isaiah, Matthew, and Paul grab hold of a text and wrestle it (and won't let go until they are blessed), this was not merely a list of prophecies; this was *engaged conversation—*the earliest processes of canon in bits and pieces.

Every biblical canon exists as the best expression of a faith community's attempt to carry on a conversation with God. This is a primordial pursuit. It is that community's best attempt to see, touch, and know God; both to listen to and talk to God. It is not merely the desire to experience God; but the longing to be experienced by God: to know and to be known. *It is not so much about the particular list of books as it is the conversation among them. A biblical canon emerges and thrives as both revelation and reflection. Canon **is** conversation.*

Canon is not merely a thing produced and done-with. It is a process. Slow moving. Powerful. Unstoppable.

---

[38] Certainly I was also influenced by specialists like Donald A. Hagner, James A. Sanders, Lou H. Silberman, and a great many others, but they should not be blamed for what I write here.

Like a great river, sculpting, carving, moving, re-shaping the community; and yet shaped by it.

To speak of a "closed canon" is to speak of a dying community, that place where canon has become *thing.* Congealed. Settled. Dead.

Canon is not *thing*, but *act.*

The 5th Thing

The fifth thing that everybody should know about the Bible is this:

> *Canon is (ongoing)* **act***, not (static)* **thing***.*
> *It is an* **act** *of faith that pursues revelation in a context of conversation.*

Canon is a living, breathing, community performance *(act),* not a solitary monument to past ideas or efforts *(relic).* It postulates a focused, highly selective, yet (in practice) somewhat fluid, body of literature—deemed as the scriptures—as a context for conversation with God. It proposes a common framework for community discernment. It preserves and organizes faithful pursuit for generations yet unborn.

And to everyone who asks: "Where is God in this?" I respond: If we cannot see God in this, perhaps we are too busy trying to co-opt and control it.

6
"Jars of Clay"
and Inspiration

We are talking about the nature of the Bible, a book (or various versions of a book) that I have called an act of faith put together by various communities of faith in pursuit of a conversation with God.

Hide and Seek

When I was in the early days of my graduate theological education, I had three professors who lectured on three specific topics: one on canon, one on inspiration, and one on hermeneutics. When I approached any of the three teachers with interdisciplinary questions about text, canon, and inspiration, each one would respond, "That course is taught by Dr. so-and-so." This runaround was inspired by political reasons as much as anything else. It was a hot potato that no one wanted to hold.

Despite many good points, one ugly truth about Christian schools and churches, today, is that genuine "conversation" about important topics is generally discouraged. On the whole, Christian communities do not "think and discuss." Instead, they have "statements of faith" that must be accepted and adhered to, and often they must be signed. Sometimes, one's livelihood and ability to feed his or her family is dependent upon adherence to such statements.

Many topics are "understood" (which means they are "required") without making the list. For example, there is a litany of correct answers on hot topics like abortion, evolution, prayer in schools, women in ministry, gay rights, or other things.

Top of the List

But one topic nearly always makes the top of the list: the Bible as the Word of God. Often, this is accompanied with comments about inspiration, inerrant original autographs, infallibility, and the like; and this is a script so well ingrained, that even to raise questions about it is considered either a cousin of heresy, or heresy its very wicked self. (I brought this up in chapter 3.)

Inspiration is the usual translation of the Greek word θεόπνευστος *(theopneustos)*, which makes a direct claim about the nature of "every Holy Writing" (πᾶσα γραφή *pasa graphē)*. The word *theopneustos* occurs once in the NT (2Tim 3:16), making a rather general claim; but I pointed out earlier that other texts are often brought to bear by current interpreters to help fill-in the blanks left by this concept. Especially important are the following two terms:

Terms and Definitions

The term *Infallibility* occurs nowhere in any canon of the Bible but starts showing up in creeds of the emerging Roman Catholic church with respect to the certainty of Scripture in all matters relating to the salvation of humankind.

The term *Inerrancy* also occurs nowhere in any canon of the Bible; but it also occurs in no church creed or document until the late 19th century. That is shocking, actually, considering that now, in many conservative Christian circles since the mid-20th century, it has very nearly reached the status of the 4th person of the God-head! This term is used in various ways, but it is popularly and very widely used to claim that

1. the Bible (almost always meaning the Protestant canon)

2. in its original autographs (meaning the original manuscript of each biblical document)

3. is without any kind of error in anything at all, including doctrine, science, psychology, politics, chronology, history, or memory by the author—or anything else.

4. This is often extended to include spelling and grammar.

5. Just as often (but not always), this particular focus tends to depreciate the role of the human authors in writing or producing what later became "biblical documents."

The amount of literature on this topic is staggering, and this is not an attempt to survey it. But this much needs to be understood by everyone: *Infallibility and Inerrancy are not biblical terms. They are theologically developed concepts that are used to dictate how the Bible is to be read and applied.*

I suggest this is exactly upside down. *Instead, the biblical term **Inspiration** ought to be defined not only by what some people think a few texts say, but also by what actually occurs within the phenomena of the ancient writings.* In other words, the various biblical texts must be allowed to stand on their own two feet, especially as seen through the biblical phenomena. By phenomena, I mean all of the details of texts, including how early biblical writers quoted and used earlier biblical texts, what we learn about texts from textual variants of manuscripts, textual interrelationships, and so much more that can only be seen by comparing Greek and Hebrew manuscripts.

And so I suggest that the Bible, in all of its canonical splendor, is best seen as "scripture in jars of clay."

Jars of Clay

I've already hinted at this back in chapter 4, but let's go deeper now. Paul helps us with this if we will but remove the veil from our eyes; a veil put there by years and years of religious debates and haggling over technical terms not even found in the scriptures. In a greatly under-appreciated text, the apostle Paul lays out for us the difference between the "written code" (on the one hand) and the proclaimed message of God brought through the Spirit (on the other). It is here that Paul clearly urges us to distinguish between the message of God (i.e., the *logos tou theou*—the preached Word of God) and the container it comes in. It is then that the Lord who said, "Let there be light" will bring that light into our lives.

Paul calls this message a treasure—not just some old thing that he carried around, but a *treasure*—wrapped in a body of death:

But in jars of baked clay, we have this treasure,
it is God's and not ours, this power beyond measure. (2Cor 4:7)

Paul pleads with his readers, saying, in essence:

Although I am given to human frailty, affliction, despair, and faltering in a body of death, the message of God is its own best witness—not the fact that I am bringing it to you in my weakness.

Honestly, you need to stop reading this right now, and go read 2Cor 2-3. Not just once but several times. For this much becomes clear: whether speaking directly of human weaknesses or of the stone into which the commands of God were first etched, don't confuse the message with the container.

Paul loves and quotes the scriptures profusely. But he knows the difference between the written code and the message now proclaimed through the life-giving Spirit. This is not about an "OT vs. NT" battle. This is a way of seeing the scriptures in relation to the message of God. Paul is telling us, *Don't confuse the message with the container.* Paul would have been horrified to discover that his own letters would eventually be read the way some Jewish leaders read Moses. He would undoubtedly write the following about many today:

For to this day, when you read the "new covenant," that same veil remains un-lifted. Yes, to this day, whenever my letters are read a veil lies over your minds. But when one turns to the Lord, the veil is removed. Now the Lord is the Spirit, and where the Spirit of the Lord is, there is freedom.

I am not writing an anti-Bible statement, here. This is an appeal that we learn the difference between the message of God that gives life, and the container it comes in. The Bible—in its various canonical forms—is scripture in jars of baked clay.

This is a great picture, actually—the Bible as "scripture in jars of baked clay." And it is technically very accurate. For it is exactly how the scriptures were carried early on.

This is what Yahweh of hosts, the God of Israel, says: Take these scrolls, both the sealed and unsealed copies of the deed of purchase, and put them in a jar of baked clay so they will last a long time.

That's Jeremiah 32:14, where God is making a promise that, although he is punishing his people for disobedience, he will eventually bless them. Here is a promise that property will be bought and sold once again in the land they are now losing. These scrolls were used to demonstrate the power of God far beyond the sacred page.

The Dead Sea Scrolls give wonderful witness that ancient scrolls, written and rolled, kept in jars of baked clay, helped to protect them for many years. But they were still just jars of clay. These are all precious! But in the end, the baked pottery breaks, the ink fades, the papyrus and leather scrolls deteriorate into dust. Like our human bodies, they die. There is a difference between the message and the container.

Papyrus 26

Take for example the cover of this book. It shows a picture of a badly decaying manuscript. If any of our own letters or papers were in this kind of shape, we would throw them away. And yet here it is, 1,400 years later, adorning the cover of a book.

So, looking at the cover, what do you see? Just another old manuscript? Look closely, perhaps with a magnifying glass. What do you see? Tattered edges; letters across the page, some clear, many not; the texture of the old papyrus, the naked papyrus strips crisscrossing, holding together this ancient "paper;" numerous holes in the page; and what appears to be miniature wrinkles running up and down the page. On the one hand, you see something sturdy enough to last for centuries, still somewhat intact; on the other hand, a delicate piece, falling apart. You wouldn't want to pick this up with your hands!

This ancient manuscript is Greek Papyrus P26, also known as "Bridwell Papyrus 1."[39] It is owned by the Bridwell Library of the Perkins School of Theology, which has made agreements allowing high-resolution photos of this manuscript to be displayed, both front and back (recto and verso), on the website of the *Center for the Study of New Testament Manuscripts.*[40]

When you go to this website and look up the manuscript, you find also a single page description of the name, date, contents, dimensions, and other things. So we learn that P26 is dated at 600 A.D., and that it is a fragment of Rom 1:1-9 (on the front side) and Rom 1:9-16 (on the back), with several verses illegible because of manuscript deterioration (this is the view showing on our cover).

---

[39] The image on the cover and the excerpt in this chapter are used with the generous permission of the Bridwell Library Special Collections, Perkins School of Theology, Southern Methodist University.

[40] http://www.csntm.org/Manuscript/View/GA_P26

The one-page description gives the details, none of which may seem interesting or useful to a casual reader. And then, at the very bottom of that one-page description, there appears a very small, almost unnoticeable, bald note:

"Interesting or significant material: none."

Of course, the "none" is speaking technically and transcriptionally about potential scribal errors or comments or textual variants or even about unusual penmanship or other distinguishing marks. So, from the standpoint of someone who works with ancient manuscripts, there is nothing extraordinary here in the technicalities of this manuscript.

And yet, even for those who work on such manuscripts, this is more than extraordinary. This is breathtaking! For here there is lingering, hovering almost, the presence of a scribe, hunched over a table, writing letter by letter, reaching now for more ink as he copies word by word, letter by letter, from another manuscript, or perhaps as he hears it read aloud in a scriptorium alongside other scribes. It has been 550 years since the original letter was dictated by Paul to another scribe, an amanuensis (personal secretary), sitting in a similar way, writing down the words for someone else to read.

Our scribe was copying something that was already five-and-a-half centuries old. Why would anybody give this kind of time to something so old and out of memory? Such things as painstakingly writing such letters in the first place, or copying them letter by letter throughout hundreds of years, or even (now) photographing and preserving them are not done by people who can't find anything else to do. These are acts of faith and joy and love on one level or another, a sense of both wonder and obligation to both academic and faith communities which hold such texts dear.

But as much as we cherish the manuscripts themselves, the wonder has just begun. Look closer, now, at the front cover of this book, right in front of the title word "Inspiration" (and at the top left of the picture below). You will see two fairly legible words in capital letters: ΠΓΟϹ ΥΜΑϹ (*pros humas*) "to you,"

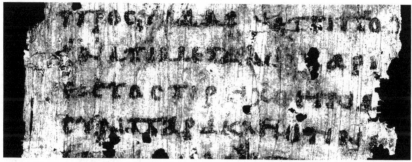

the last two words of Rom 1:10. Then moving down three complete lines you can now see this word: ϹΥΜΠΑΓΑΚΑΗΘΗΝΑΙ taking up the whole line (as much of it as exists) and missing the final two letters due to the corruption (deterioration) of the manuscript. This word is *sumparaklēthēnai* from the word *sumparakaleō*, and it occurs only one time in all of the NT—right here in Rom 1:12 where Paul needs it. And what does it say?

> *[...always in my prayers asking that I might be granted, at last, good passage by the will of God to come]* **to you,** *for I want with all of my heart to see you that I might impart some spiritual gift to you that you might stand, all so that* **I might receive encouragement together with you** *through the*

> *mutual faith we share with one another, you and I.*
> *(Rom 1:10-12)*

Stop reading the words. Stop looking at the deteriorating manuscript and listen to the passion, not of the scribe five-and-a-half centuries later faithfully copying, but of the one he honors through his labor. For now we sense something more hovering near: the spirit, not merely of a dutiful scribe, but of a passionate father—the apostle himself. Paul's heart is on the line, here, and even though the page is crumbling and the ink is fading, the gentle rhythm of that ancient and original heartbeat can still be felt by anyone with the sensitivity to receive it.

Listen closely, for with these words uttered above, Paul is just *beginning* his fervent expatiation. For this is the self-same text in which he says he can't wait to go to Rome to proclaim his gospel:

> *For I am not ashamed of the gospel message, for it*
> *is God's power for salvation to everyone who be-*
> *lieves. (Rom 1:16)*

It is right there on the cover! You can see it at the bottom surrounding my name, preserved in this very old manuscript, now worn and faded and with holes that upon closer examination look like lakes on the landscape of a satellite image.

It is one thing to cherish the manuscripts and to handle them with all the care our latest technology can lend us. This is, of course, a good thing! But we should never mistake the perishable container (whether first drafts lost forever, or later revisions now in our care, or faithful copies made 600 years later) for the message. The so-called "original autographs" were no less vulnerable to the ravages of the centuries than this small fragment from about 600. Indeed, this piece, and many others like it, proved the more durable.

And no, I am not missing the point about the so-called perfection of the original autographs—a theoretical figment of the theological imagination of the many who would force me to accept things not even claimed in any precious text or manuscript of anyone's canon.

The Bible, as we have inherited it—in whatever tradition and with whatever canonical collection—is scripture in jars of baked clay (canon). We may value highly the baked clay, but it must not be our focus. These words were spoken, and then written down, and then later copied, and then still later copied again by our scribe onto this manuscript, and then preserved, and then catalogued, and then photographed, and now reproduced for you and explained—acts of faith all, in pursuit of a conversation with God.

Defining Inspiration

For Paul and other early Christian writers, this was sufficient as a definition of inspiration, for it was all that was given: God at work through ancient texts. Yes of course, "men moved by the Holy Spirit, speaking," and so many other similar declarations, all of them boiling down to this: *God at work though ancient texts to fill the lives of individuals and communities of faith.*

But I wasn't born yesterday, and I know that others will insist on more. So, I suggest that if we simply cannot sleep at night without convening a conference to define all the meanings of words that don't even occur in the texts of our Bibles, then we keep at least four things in mind as minimal criteria:

1. *Definition:* No definition can be accepted which ignores the clear difference between scripture and canon.

2. *Interpretation:* No text must be made to say more than it actually says. (E.g., "scripture" does not imply "canon" or "bible.")

3. *Phenomena:* No doctrine of inspiration is acceptable which is contradicted by the evidence of the phenomena of the scriptures (i.e., all the details within ancient holy writings).

4. *Inclusiveness:* No explanation of inspiration is acceptable which does not account for and include all the evidence.

Quite frankly, I understand and can appreciate the good motives of the many who feel a need to make "statements of faith" about such things. And yet, speaking for myself, I am not only unmoved by the provincial nature of the end results of both the Roman Catholic *Dei Verbum* and the Evangelicals' *Chicago Statement on Biblical Inerrancy,* I am also somewhat put off by it all.

On the one hand, these are useful statements for showing the contemporary currents of thinking by some. But when these become (whether intended or not) mandatory or "canonical" filters through which ancient texts must be read (or else one is considered "suspect"), such statements become straightjackets for reading the Bible.

On the other hand, if these Christian groups wish to add documents to their canons, I suppose they have every right to do so. At least the Roman Catholics are forthright about what they are doing. But just how honest is it for some Evangelicals or some conservatives to maintain the notion that "the canon is closed" and then wrap it in an invisible protective outer layer which is then enjoined upon all? It just moves us all one more step away from the texts we hold dear, and from each other—unlike Paul who proclaims in a simply marvelous little throwaway line that we might seek, instead, "encouragement together" with each other through the mutual faith we share with one another—you and I.

I suggest that the simpler approach is the better approach.

The 6th Thing

The sixth thing that everybody ought to know about the Bible: *The Bible as we have it in its various canonical forms is scripture in jars of baked clay. Inspiration is God at work though ancient texts to fill the lives of individuals and communities of faith. And there is a difference between the message and the container.*

We love the texts. We care for them and treat them with great respect. But we don't worship them, and we don't construct theories that turn them into something they are not. We worship God through the Lord Jesus Christ as we are continually encouraged and empowered by the Holy Spirit. We change our lives, we touch others. We respect the container (the various canons and the many texts, whether so-called "originals" or 7th century copies). But we ingest and personify the message.

7
"The God
Who Kills Babies!"

In the last several chapters, I have described the various Christian Bible canons as acts of faith, put together by communities of faith, in pursuit of a conversation with God.

Not everyone is happy with this.

Canon, Warts and All

I have a friend—a church historian—who has apoplexy every time I make the statement that "the Bible is an act of faith, etc." He replies to me:

Canon is an act of faithlessness—a cowardly act of disbelief in the power of the Holy Spirit and of a desire to control the lives of others.

Actually he makes a good point, even though I think it is overstated. For any human effort (such as canon) will be fraught with imperfection. And *of course* some of the historical processes of canon are not very flattering, as can be historically demonstrated. People are people: weak, short-sighted, power-hungry, corrupt, selfish, manipulative, domineering (including biblical scholars and church historians today, and preachers and church leaders, and every person who opens a Bible and every person who does not). However, people are also inquisitive, and seek to be just, spiritual, and sincere. Anyone who gives fair assessment to the process of "canonization" of texts has to come to grips with both the good and bad of the process. Saying something is an act of faith does not mean it is pure and perfect.

Today, it has become very popular to be hyper-critical and dismissive of the Bible. *The Da Vinci Code's* criticism, as quoted in chapter 3, is just one of many examples.

This can also be seen in popular speakers like Richard Dawkins, an atheist who revels in taunting Christians for the many inconsistencies and inequities of Christian history.

It is also found in authors like Bart Ehrman, an agnostic professor of NT. Ehrman was converted as a teenager to a particularly energetic fundamentalist form of Christianity. He became a zealous advocate of that doctrine, going on to academic training in the study of Greek NT manuscripts. During that training he became disillusioned with his earlier faith and abandoned it, attempting (it appears to me) to maintain intellectual integrity, becoming an equally energetic critic of the Bible.

Christians often have knee-jerk reactions to such things. But there actually is plenty of room for criticism against Christians and even against some of the processes that helped shape our current Bibles. We should not be afraid to face—and we certainly should not defend— the inequities of our own past.

A Mean Spirit

But what I want to deal with right now is this point: a lot of the criticisms today are simply mean-spirited, second-guessing ridicule. It reminds me of Leo Tolstoy's book, *War and Peace*, when assessing Russia's failure to defeat Napoleon:

And it is of this period of the campaign—when the army lacked boots and sheepskin coats, was short of provisions and without vodka, and was camping out at night for months in the snow in weather two degrees below zero, when there were only seven or eight hours of daylight and the rest was night in which the influence of discipline cannot be maintained, when men were taken into that region of death where discipline fails, not for a few hours only as in a battle, but for months, where they were every moment fighting death from hunger and cold, when half the army perished in a single month—it is of this period of the campaign that the historians tell us how Miloradovich should have made a flank march to such and such a place, Tomasov to another place, and Chicagov should have crossed (more than knee deep in snow) to somewhere else.

The Russians, half of whom died, did all that could and should have been done to attain an end worthy of the nation, and they are not to blame because other Russians, sitting in warm rooms, proposed that they should do what was impossible.[41]

From our "warm rooms," it is easy either to blindly accept the form of the "book" which has come down to us, or to ruthlessly second-guess the motives of every person to have touched its pages through the centuries.

---

[41] Book 14, chapter 19.

Communities of faith, some of whom demonstrate a fanatical naiveté about the Bible, might be encouraged to a more fully nuanced view of the Bible and to more completely take in the facts of history along with the actual claims of the scriptures. It is one thing to be people of faith, but even the ancient scriptures encourage us to be reasonable about it.

But to the critics, some of whom are like raving lunatics, I would ask: "How simplistic and shallow can you be in your criticisms? For in many cases, you are a mirror image of those you revile." There are plenty of things to be critical of in Christian history—plenty of inequities, plenty of horrors. Even today! But are there no such horrors outside of Christianity? No inequities within the critics' camp? It is one thing to doubt or decry religious history, but common sense should encourage us to be reasonable about it.

Whether believers in God or not, are we really, as intelligent human beings, that inept when looking at ancient texts, unable to judge them from within their own contexts *as* ancient texts? Imagine, for example, two thousand years from now, how our descendants might evaluate us (assuming humanity is still around and is capable of evaluating its own past). Will they praise us for overcoming injustice? Or for having the will to properly manage the earth's resources? Will they honor us for resolving problems relating to population, homelessness, social and financial stability? What about poverty, world hunger, disease, and war? And what about our legacy in theology and philosophy? Will these be seen as major contributions or minor footnotes best forgotten?

Will our distant relatives praise or ridicule us for such things? Did we help to chart a way for solutions? Or did we merely add one more layer of human self-absorption—like a mound in a lost and forgotten city? Will they dismiss and condemn us with the same ease we wave off the efforts of our own predecessors.

It is amazing, for example, that critics of the Bible who self-righteously proclaim "I don't want a god who will kill babies!" are usually also outspoken pro-choice advocates. Hmm. Well, this talking out of both sides of their mouth sounds more opportunistic than concerned about little babies. And let's get something clear: I don't care about either the pro-choice OR pro-life band-wagons, here, so I'm not advocating or criticizing either position. That is not my concern. I am pointing to the hypocrisy of those Bible critics who yelp about "a god who kills babies" and then who support legalized, at-will abortions. It sounds like self-centered hypocrisy to me, unworthy of serious consideration.

Upgrading the Conversation

The harshest critics of the Bible want to discredit any value of "the Bible as canon." They want a different canon, and they want to decide what's in that canon. And they want to replace it with what? Science text books? Atheism handbooks? It is a desire to depict spiritual pursuits as little more than ancient cave paintings; an intention of stripping the world of a religious or spiritual consciousness and to base concepts like "ethics" and "morals" on the grown-up grounds of atheistic philosophy and pragmatism.

And this comes to a head in no better place than the so-called battle between science and the Bible. This is billed like a WWE wrestling match: "Either Science or the Bible!" Or maybe like Listerine taking on gingivitis. What a dumb debate this is! I'm sorry, but I'm also quite serious: it is a dumb debate!

Oh, how Christians have helped to set this up! And so, disagreeing with many of my Christian brothers and sisters, I would argue in favor of pure, unbridled scientific research. I *want* my kids learning it!

Perhaps you agree with me. Perhaps not. But I wish to say this to all, not wishing to pick a fight, but to propose that this question does not determine whether one is Christian. For those who might disagree I would simply ask: Do you believe in Christ? So do I. Do you hold a high view of the scriptures? I have *at least* as high a view of the scriptures as you do. Do you have an opinion that the Bible should be used as a science textbook? You are welcome to that opinion. But I don't want you teaching my kids!

On the other hand, against many atheistic-type scientists, I would argue that the longstanding processes of canon AS acts of faith, by communities of faith, in search of a conversation with God, are valuable efforts worth continuing. And such scientists have made no contributions that have deterred me from that deeper understanding.

It would be helpful if readers on both sides of the argument would upgrade their part in the conversation. I don't have to be an atheist or a Christian to believe in the value of the pursuit of science—or theology.

Facing Some Facts

And it begins with Bible readers facing some facts. The fact is, there are some individual things in our Bibles that make no sense to us in the 21st century:

1. Like how to handle a fallen bird's nest, or the requirement, in the same law book that holds the 10 commandments, of a railing around your roof, in Deuteronomy 21.

2. Or a man with two wives.

3. Or a captive wife.

4. Or executing an unruly son. (What parent hasn't thought of that?)

5. Or, human slavery.

6. Or animal sacrifice.

Now, be honest—when is the last time you sacrificed a chicken to anything but your own taste-buds? The mere concept of animal sacrifice is actually repulsive to us. This was not just an OT or Jewish thing; it was practiced everywhere! The question is *why*?

Here's what we should be asking: *Why didn't the Jews practice human sacrifice, including child sacrifice,* like the Canaanites did whom the Jews were told to wipe out (including children)? Or like the Aztecs, who—to dedicate their temple—sacrificed 400,000 human beings in the first few months—including babies? Or *cannibalism*, like tribes in the West Indies—including babies? Or *head hunting* like people in China, India, Nigeria, Nuristan, Borneo, Indonesia, the Philippines, Taiwan, Japan, Micronesia, Melanesia, New Zealand, and the Amazon Basin, and among certain tribes of the Celts and Scythians of ancient Europe? Why didn't the Jews do these things? And why not the Christians?

There are simply some things in the Bible that don't make sense to us in our 21st century context. The Bible is not primarily about these things, but they are in there just the same. So we just close our eyes and don't see them: a flat earth in which the sun literally moves through the sky, slavery, bigamy, polygamy, sexism—to us, in the 21st century, most of these are actually either ridiculous or horrifying.

Ancient Texts

Now, how do I say this strongly enough? Instead of shouting, let me whisper this:

> These are ancient texts;
> we need to look at them
> in their ancient contexts.

They are not current-day science books, or money manuals, or political primers, or gender handbooks, or courtship guides. And they should never be used as such. We find principles in them that help us with all kinds of things, but these texts were not written for those purposes. To *ever* use the Bible as a current-day science textbook, or even a gender handbook, is a huge mistake—one that contradicts and violates the very nature of the texts.

Let me put it this way: it is just as possible to develop a **biblical doctrine of handling slaves** as it is a biblical doctrine of the Lord's Supper. Why is it that no church anywhere today supports slavery? At least part of the answer is that *we recognize that these are ancient texts that include some things we don't accept.*

Let us move on, as Christian communities, to more significant questions about our Bibles. How did individual texts function in their own times? Why did they endure? Why were they passed down? Why were they constantly being adapted and reapplied to new situations? (They were, you know!) How did they change and why? What are the larger, overriding concerns for social justice, forgiveness, faith, joy, endurance, and ultimate meaning? These are the kinds of questions we should be asking, for these are the questions which caused the texts to be saved in the first place, passed along, repeated, and adapted for new situations. That is the canonical process in action; and in these questions the search for God can be seen everywhere!

Instead of defiantly criticizing texts out of context for ridiculous things we don't know anything about (as some critics do); or, as some believers do, touting the "unchangeability of texts" (which is not at all supported by the evidence); or hiding behind artificially manufactured theories about so-called "original autographs" (which we don't have and will never see)—instead of all of this, *we need to learn that the key issue is the adaptability of texts to new situations.*

The most important question that faces Bible readers today is not whether we have the right Bible! Nor is it listening to some Bible critic yelp about "a god who kills babies."

The real questions are: "Why were those texts kept in the first place? How did they function in community? And how do we apply ancient documents—for centuries regarded as the scriptures—to what we face today?" The answer is *adaptability:* the continuing search for a con-

143

versation with God. That has always been the key issue. It was then. It is now.

The 7th Thing

The seventh thing everybody should know about the Bible is that *the various documents of the Bible must be read first within their ancient contexts; then they must be applied today according to the principle of* **adapta-bility**—the same principle that has kept these texts alive and relevant for millennia.

We need to be honest and energetic about all of this. Next chapter we'll ask, "What does seeing the Bible as ancient collections mean?" Instead of letting our own past, or even the critics, dictate how we see the Bible, we'll chart a new path. That's our next step.

8
The Bible as
"Collections"

In the last chapter, we talked about how both Bible believers and Bible critics view the Bible. In this chapter we'll focus on the way the NT is structured, and why, and how that both helps and hurts the way we read it every day. We'll also consider some alternative structures, and why that can open our eyes to new ways of understanding.

Ways of Reading the Bible

Have you ever found yourself in a mess and needed help?

That spinach-eating hero of us all, Popeye (the sailor), finding himself trapped in a cave, stumbles upon a magic lamp. Out comes the genie, who says:

I'm the genie from the lamp.
I come from the nowhere, I go to the no place.
You ask it, and I give it.
You want something?

Yes indeed. "You want something?" is the single greatest description of how the Bible is seen today. The popular movie *"The Secret"* comes right out and says it: "Tell the universe what you want. It's the universe's job to give it to you!"

Let's compare two prominent ways of reading the Bible.

1. "What's in it for ME?" This is the hallmark of current-day Bible reading. The Bible is one big glob, and I play hopscotch all through it, looking for solutions to my problems. It starts with me and ends with me—it's all about me.

> *Basis: The Bible is My Personal Guide.*
> *Goal: How God Will Bless Me.*

2. "What does God REQUIRE of me?" This was a prominent approach of previous generations and is still around. In this approach, I still play hopscotch, but this is much like a massive scavenger hunt where we look for commands, requirements, and "how-to-instructions." Here, it's less about what I *want,* and more about what I'm supposed to *believe and do* as part of the church.

> *Basis: The Bible is a Blueprint.*
> *Goal: What God Requires.*

We might all have these two questions, but I'm talking about dominant ways of reading the Bible. Of course, there are other ways of reading, but these are very popular. So, let's compare them.

Parts Is Not Parts

Please don't miss that both of these ways have the approach that "The Bible is the Bible." You know, it's like the old KFC commercial where a customer walks into a fast food place and asks, "What part of the chicken is in your chicken sandwich?" To which the clerk responds, "Parts is parts." That's how a lot of people see the Bible: every part of the Bible is still the Bible, so what difference does it make? God wrote it all; who cares about things like author, date, location, and all that stuff. It really doesn't matter. Texts are not really distinguished for the types of material they present. We might pay lip service to things like authorship, date, context, history, literary style, and so-forth. But actually, they don't make any real difference.

For a couple of centuries now, this kind of reading is well known as "pre-critical-reading" of texts. Everything is governed, in fact, by the goal. If I'm looking for *what I want*, I'll read the texts in such a way as to find it. If I'm looking for *commands to obey*, I'll find those too, sometimes in places that aren't even about what I'm looking for.

Now there's nothing wrong with looking for help or wanting to be obedient. The problem is when we don't really listen. It's like being part of a conversation in which we do all the talking.

Today in the 21st century, it is unthinkable, irresponsible, and just plain inexcusable for us to read ancient texts without asking fundamental questions, like who was the author, the audience, the occasion, the type of literature, and so on; or even more sophisticated questions about literary elements and style. This is not just something to do; it has a bearing on how we apply the material to our everyday situations. Let's put it this way: if you handed me "hand-written letters" from your dear departed great-grandmother and asked me to read them, you'd make sure that you filled me in on some background to help me understand who she was, where she lived and why, what her life was like, why she wrote these letters, and so on. You wouldn't even think about it, you'd just tell me all that stuff.

The point, here, is about reading texts for what they are. For example, all my life I've heard that the phrase, "[The LORD] sits enthroned above the circle of the earth," in Isa 40:22, proves that ancient Jews believed in a "round earth," not a flat earth like almost everybody else at that time. So I guess Rev 7:1, "I saw four angels standing at the four corners of the earth," means the earth is a box? The reply comes back that "the LORD sitting above a round earth" is literal, and "angels standing on a flat earth" is obviously not. How do we know this? Because we can't have the Bible reflecting a flat earth; that would contradict some of our views of inspiration![42]

I'm not trying to be condescending here, even though some may take it that way. I'm trying to point out why we should read texts for what they are. Why should I take God "sitting" above "the circle of the earth" (whatever that means) more literally than the angels "standing" on a flat one? Just maybe these are both poetic descriptions meaning "the whole earth."

When reading Leviticus, Ruth, Luke, or Revelation, do we read them all the same? Or is it helpful for us to realize we are dealing with four different types of writing: Law, ancient story, Gospel, and apocalyptic writing? Are the Gospels really best used as storage bins from

---

[42] A couple of people actually responded to our message board making this very point. They were furious that I would dare suggest that the Bible reflected a flat earth! For them, making such a statement denies the inspiration of the Bible. In other words, their view of inspiration was being contradicted by specific texts, and so we should know that such cannot be the meaning of said texts. This is called "getting your theology straight before reading the Bible."

which to reconstruct the real, so-called "life of Jesus," or does Mark tell a unique story from the others, and John from the rest? Is the book of Revelation really like reading a literal newspaper of the future? Or is it best read in light of the numerous other highly symbolic Apocalypses that existed in and around its own time?

There are many ways in which we all instinctively read the scriptures using some "common sense." In most churches today, women don't wear head coverings to fulfill a religious purpose. Nor do we build a parapet, or railing, around our roofs as required in the law.

Collections

For hundreds of years, now, we have known that our Bible—the Protestant canon, not officially decided until the 17th century—is made up of various *collections of literary types*. We find different types of writing: legal instruction, religious history, prophetic and apocalyptic utterance, various kinds of poetry and wisdom literature, private and public letters, Gospel treatises, and sermon collections—to mention a few. If we know these literary types exist but pay no real attention to them, or act as if it does not matter that we read Genesis and Daniel and Mark and Philippians the same way (to find what's in it for me, or what God requires of me), then we are misreading them.

Besides literary types, a second example would be *collections of document groups*. The premier example in the ancient Hebrew scriptures is the Torah, the first five books, Genesis to Deuteronomy (in Greek known as the Pentateuch). The completed work was produced in five scrolls, but all five were intended to stand together, one scroll leading to the next. That is why it is important to read Genesis as part of the whole, as part of the more focused literary purpose of the five scrolls. When an energetic soul reads so as to fight a battle against scientists, or to build some scientific case that is not at all part of the purpose of the writings in the first place, then these texts are being misread.

A third example of collections can be seen by comparing *the alternate groupings of the Hebrew with the Greek scriptures.* Various NT writers talk about the Law and the Prophets (Mt 7;12; 11:13; 22:40; Lk 16:16; Ac 13:15; 24:14; Jn 1:45; Rom 3:21—curiously not in Mark), and Luke has Jesus say:

*These are my words which I spoke to you while I was still with you, namely that it was necessary that all things written in the law of Moses and in the prophets and psalms about me might be fulfilled."
Then he opened their minds to understand the sacred texts. (Lk 24:44)*

Some say this reflects a similar grouping with the completed Jewish canon after the 3rd century A.D.: Torah, Nebiim, and Ketubim (Law, Prophets, and Writings). But that is over-reading this text. Actually, the wording, here, supports only two groupings, since the prophets and psalms are listed together. Even so:

1. Both the Hebrew and Greek writings of Jesus' day included **collections of the Law**, though not all were identical. The Samaritan Pentateuch, also coming from before the time of Jesus, offers the same five books but with a somewhat different text.

2. Both the Hebrew and Greek writings of Jesus' day included **collections of the prophets**. However, neither the books themselves nor the collections were identical. The Greek scriptures, translated at least a hundred years before the birth of Jesus, reflect numerous differences from the Hebrew, especially in the book of Jeremiah. There are also many other differences in text-form, in document shape, and even in additional books found in the collections.

Of course, it should be understood that there was no single "master collection" of Hebrew or Greek scrolls at this time, and various locations might have more or different books than other locations—like any library would have a variety of books. But at the core was the Torah collection, and also Prophets.

All of these were seen and read as the scriptures, and the early church (mostly Greek speaking) gravitated more and more to the Greek scriptures. Even the NT writers quote the Greek scriptures most of the time.

Now, with all of this in mind, it is fair to say that the scriptures read by the earliest Christians were different from what we now have, not only in language, but also in format, order, and availability. And if we know these things, but then act like they have no bearing on how we should read ancient texts today, you can be sure that we are misreading them.

The New Testament

This leads us to consider Christian writings and the manner in which our NT canons have been handed down to us. As we now have them (from tradition), they are arranged topically and somewhat arbitrarily as follows:

1. The Gospels
2. The story of church beginnings
3. Two collections of letters
4. The Apocalypse

This traditional order of the NT is a logical grouping, with longer books tending to come first in each group. But it is not without its problems. This order encourages the notion that Matthew was the first written NT document and that Romans was the first written of Paul's letters. (They weren't.) It also, unfortunately, separates Luke from Acts, and John's Gospel from other writings bearing his name. Additionally, Paul's letters are not in the order they were written, nor are the Gospels.

Although the arrangement of the NT documents is not a life and death issue, it can be helpful to look at them in alternative arrangements, such as the following "Collections Order," which (although not perfect) is somewhat *chronological*, and which helps to show the development of thought in early Christianity as well as preserving the integrity of related groups. You should be aware that "dating" many of the NT documents precisely is not possible, so the following discussion reflects a fairly standard understanding among the majority of NT scholars.

Keeping in mind that anything can be debated, **Paul's letters** are likely the earliest written documents we have of what is now the NT. 1Thessalonians is likely the first letter of Paul's we have, coming from around

A.D. 50. *Traditions* about Jesus' life and teachings circulated in preaching and other oral forms (and maybe in some written forms) for at least a quarter of a century, if not more, before the Gospel of *Mark* was written.[43] *Matthew* and *Luke* both used Mark and other material they had to write their own stories, and yet all three of the Gospels were uniquely written stories of Jesus, meant to be read from beginning to end, much like a movie is meant to be watched from beginning to end. Although people today tend to mash the Gospels alto-

Pauline Collection 1	Petrine Collection	Jewish Collection
1 Thessalonians (50-51)	Mark (70's)	Matthew (80's)
2 Thessalonians	1 Peter	Hebrews
Galatians (54-55)	Jude & 2 Peter	James
Philemon (55)		
Philippians (56)	**Helenistic Collection**	**Johannine Collection**
1 Corinthians (56)	Luke/Acts (80's)	John (90's)
2 Corinthians (57)	Hebrews	1, 2, & 3 John
Romans (57-58)		Revelation
Pauline Collection 2		
Colossians (??)		
Ephesians (??)		
Titus (??)	**A Possible Representation**	
1 Timothy (??)	**of "Collections"**	
2 Timothy (??)		

gether (or chop them up into bits) in order to reconstruct the so-called "life of Jesus," the Gospels were written as individual treatises, stories all, and were meant to be read as whole stories from beginning to end in their own rights.

---

[43] Accurate dating of these ancient documents is notoriously difficult. The dates offered here represent standard scholarly opinion and are certainly debatable at nearly every turn. Dating can certainly affect interpretation.

I don't know of anybody today who would take all of the different movies about Wyatt Earp and try splicing them together to form one accurate "real story of Wyatt Earp." The result would be nonsense.

But somewhere along the line, Christian people at large got the notion that that is the way the Gospels are supposed to be read. I don't mean to paint everybody with the same brush, but in this case, this is a pervasive practice. If you don't believe me, you should do your own little test. Watch and listen to how nearly everybody treats the Gospels.

We just throw them into a blender and read them all as one "thing." So now, most Christians have no idea what Mark's story is, or Luke's, or Matthew's or *John's*; or that they even have a story! And besides (according to entirely too many people, even to this day) who cares about what the author of Matthew thought anyway, or of any other Gospel? The Holy Spirit wrote them all, so what difference does it make? Let's just put them all together and find out about the real story, the whole story of Jesus.

In many popular readings of the Gospels, it is common to depreciate the human role in all of this. But if we are to believe in the Gospels at all as scriptures, then apparently God did not devalue the human role. The humanness of these documents is everywhere to be seen if we but take the time to notice.

The truth is, despite obvious similarities and connections, each of the Gospels has its own story-line and flavor and could just as well be grouped with other documents. For example, Mark, which focuses vibrantly on the gospel message and discipleship, is traditionally associated and grouped with the material of **Peter**.[44] Matthew was written to a community of Jewish believers who had been ousted from the Synagogues after the destruction of the Temple. Other documents that are especially Jewish (like **Hebrews** and **James**), could be grouped with Matthew. **Luke-Acts** is a two volume work, intended to be read together as a single story of the Holy Spirit's actions in the life and teachings of Jesus and the life of the early church and the apostles, especially Paul, who by the end of Acts is, through the power of the Spirit, acting very much like Jesus. The Gospel of John was very likely the last written of the four Gospels and was very different in order, style, and message from the other three. It was also associated with a community of believers given to the message and style of its founder and main teacher (**1-3 John, Revelation**).

In many ways, these groupings represent different styles or emphases in earliest Christianity, sometimes different messages, depending on the audience, time written, the authors, and the issues being faced by the readers.

Naturally, this grouping could be adjusted, changed, or even challenged. Hebrews, for example, might go better with Luke-Acts because of the style of Greek it uses and its Hellenistic style of argumentation. The so-called "Petrine Collection" could be challenged altogether. And more.

Of course, all of the Gospels can and should be studied together, side-by-side, if done properly and not simp-

---

[44] Of course, many will date 2Peter as the last written document of the NT, coming from the 2nd century. And this makes an odd connection with Mark, the earliest of the Gospels. But this is an illustration.

ly mashed together. Unlike the books of Genesis through Deuteronomy, the Gospels are not the final product of a single editing hand; there is no theme or plot that ties them together. They are separate treatises (not letters) meant to be read for their own sake. Luke and Acts are meant to be read together, as a single story.

Several of Paul's letters (**Colossians, Ephesians, Timothy, Titus**) are often judged as much later (see Pauline Collection 2 in the chart above). Even if you don't like this suggestion or agree with it, you need to know about it. And there is so much more that illustrates diversity.

To ignore these types of things when we are reading them means we will fill in all the blanks with our own agendas. Sometimes this means we will completely twist texts out of context to make them say what we want or need them to say either because of our pre-existing theology or because we are not paying attention to the texts right in front of us. Or maybe both! A truly high view of scripture will see the scriptures for what actually happens within them.

Do not misunderstand. I am not suggesting that we can ever read the NT without bias or presuppositions. The point is rather about reading with awareness of such things. Nor am I suggesting that we need to change the order of OT and/or NT. The traditional arrangement of the Bible is fine, as long as we realize there is nothing holy or heaven-sent about it. It is topical and somewhat arbitrary. But looking at the various canons of the Bible in alternative formats, as illustrated above with the Protestant canon of the NT, can help to broaden our perspective to view all documents contextually within larger collections and possible associations. There are other ways this could be done as well.

The 8th Thing

The eighth thing that everybody should know about the Bible: *The Bible is made up of a great deal more diversity than is normally recognized or admitted. As it stands now, it is put together in a topical and somewhat arbitrary order, lending to the notion of a uniformity that is more artificial than natural.*

When it comes to the Bible, "parts is *not* parts." Reading one part is not necessarily the same as reading another part. Reading our canon of the Bible—that widely diverse collection of ancient scriptures—is not something best left to whims or fancy or preconception or elaborately made theories about what the Bible is. Reading the Bible is rather a skill to be learned over time. Looking at our Bibles as collections of diverse literary types and documents, from a wide variety of times, backgrounds, and authors, and directed toward an array of situations and circumstances can help us to see this point.

Looking at the Bible in alternative formats and arrangements can help us to see relationships between documents we might otherwise miss. It can also help us "grow up" in our view of the Bible so that we might recognize that different types of literature require specialized and nuanced reading; so that we might get past pre-critical readings of the Bible to something more fitting to the nature of the documents we have right in front of us.

The point is not that we have to be scholars to read the Bible; the point is that we all should at least be students of the Bible, ready to learn.

If we're not willing to do that, what does that say about us? If we want something, or if we want to know what God requires of us, there is, of course, nothing wrong with reading the Bible. However, reading the Bible is not primarily about *what is in it for us*, or about *what we are required to do.* It is mainly about something far greater.

And so next chapter, we're going to ask what far greater thing the various documents of the NT are really about? Or stated another way, "What was the *real* canon of the earliest church?" You might already know. But then, you might be surprised.

9
The Earliest
Christian Canon

During the last eight chapters, we have been talking about scripture, canon, Bible, and inspiration, and we have covered quite a bit of territory.

This chapter will be about the real "canon" of the earliest church (by which I mean the church of the first couple of generations). Hopefully this will bring everything together to a sort of summit. It will not only offer an alternative to what is typically taught on the subject, it will also set the stage for the volume that is to follow.

In the previous chapter we talked about being thoughtful readers of the Bible and we compared two popular reading approaches: "What's in it for me?" and "What are we supposed to believe and do?" These may both be fair questions within certain contexts, but seeing the Bible *primarily* as "My Personal Guidebook" or as "A Blueprint for Right Actions" should not dominate our reading of the Bible. The first makes us self-centered and the second makes us read Jesus the way the Pharisees read Moses.

The Question

So, in contrast to these two approaches, in this chapter we are going to ask a simple question that is also straightforward: *"How did the earliest Christians read the sacred texts?"* We are always wanting to know everything about what the earliest Christians believed and did; so since *we* read the Bible, it seems like a logical and sensible question to ask: "How did *they* read the sacred writings?" That ought to tell us something about their view of what the sacred writings are and what they are for.

We ask this question, not so we can recreate or mimic all of their specific techniques or approaches. That would be absurd. They lived in a different time and culture from ours, and it's not their culture that we want to recreate. Instead, we want to look into what led them theologically.

This is a much more incisive question and can be asked as follows:

> *What was it that drove them, or led them, or guided them as they read? What was their real "canon"—their real measuring rod—that directed them as they themselves poured over the various sacred writings that were available to them?*

The Focus

We've already seen that they didn't focus on a specific, well-defined, exclusive list of books. So we are not talking about a "canon of documents" as we are accustomed to thinking. (Nobody could go to a book store and purchase a gold-edged Bible or order one from coffeewithjehu.com.) We are talking about how they read their sacred writings (not Bible). And you can be sure that they didn't focus on either of the two questions from the last chapter.

In fact what they focused on wasn't a question at all. It was, rather, an exclamation. Something that for them was all-encompassing, revolutionary, liberating and universal. It was a single, guiding, "canonical" confession: *"Jesus Christ—his name is KURIOS!"*

When Jews and Gentiles came to believe in Jesus as the Christ, their view of the purpose of the sacred writings took a radical turn. From that point on, they saw the purpose of the sacred writings to be *God's revelation of Jesus Christ as Lord.* And their goal in reading the sacred writings was not primarily to find either personal help or right answers, but to *have Life in Jesus as Lord.* Let's spell this out.

Finding Jesus Everywhere

The earliest followers of Jesus gathered to hear stories and traditions about Jesus and his teachings. They also reveled in having numerous Hebrew and Greek scrolls (deemed as holy writings) read and explained to them for many purposes (of course), but especially as pointing to Jesus. These included primarily Greek but also Hebrew documents of the Pentateuch (the five books of Moses), of prophets, of poetic literature, and other books not in our current-day Bibles. They were energetic about and dedicated to finding Jesus throughout these many and varied writings.

Instead of reading sacred texts primarily asking "What's in it *for* me?" or even "What does God want *from* me?" the earliest Christians read their holy writings with one main goal in mind: *to affirm or establish that "Jesus Christ—his name is KURIOS!"*

Unlike others before them, the earliest Christians now saw the ancient Holy writings as God revealing Jesus Christ as Lord and what that meant for daily living. In doing this, they were pursuing one main target: not only to *make sense* out of life, but to *have* life in Jesus Christ!

Judging by what we have from earliest Christian authors, this was an exciting thing, a revolutionary thing: the truth that Jesus Christ was Lord! Those who were capable of doing so—those described by Jesus in Matthew as "scribes trained for the Kingdom of Heaven"—scoured the various holy writings of the day (in both Hebrew and Greek documents) looking for Jesus everywhere in those many and varied texts. Talk about "Bible Study"—this searching of the ancient holy writings was intense!

Examples

Oh—and how—is this easy to illustrate! Reading the many holy texts "Christologically"—to find Jesus—this was the order of the day.

Among the many, many examples are **1Cor 10** where Paul talks about the people of ancient Israel as if they had been baptized and as if they were in the habit of participating in the Lord's Supper. He says:

Our fathers were all baptized into Moses in the cloud and in the sea. For all ate the same spiritual food, and all drank the same spiritual drink, for they were accustomed to drinking from the rock which followed them.

Yes, this is all very interesting . . . interesting . . . until he makes his next statement; and then it is not just interesting—it gets riveting! For he says:

And the rock followed them,
and the rock was Christ.

What? The rock was Christ? And this is even the more amazing since nowhere in our Old Testaments is there any mention of a following rock. That apparently comes from Jewish tradition. Paul even reads *that* Christologically!

Or **2Cor 3** where Paul finds the veil of Moses to be what blinds people from seeing Christ as Lord, the Spirit. Or **Matthew** who over and over says, "This is what was spoken by the prophet" Isaiah or Jeremiah, or another, all referring to Jesus as Messiah. Or **Hebrews**, which finds in Jesus fulfillment of the Enthronement Psalms, namely Psalms 2 and 110, and so much more. Or **1Pet 2** which speaks of Jesus as the stone of stumbling from Psalm 118 and Isaiah. Or the **passion narratives** (the stories of Jesus' last days) which are extended interpretations of prophetic texts like Zechariah and Malachi and others. The NT is literally filled with this: **Mark**, **Luke/Acts**; **John's** writings, all of Paul's writings—all of it! In fact, many of the NT documents are extended exercises in the re-reading and re-application (i.e., *adapting*) of ancient holy writings.

It is right here—watching the NT authors dance with previously written sacred texts—that *adaptability* of ancient texts comes fully into view. For those with eyes to see and ears to hear, this is where texts long ago come to life again in unexpected ways. They are not merely quoting prophecies to be tallied; they are romancing the texts, adapting their applications, and finding new life for new situations. This occurs on nearly every page of what we now call the NT.

The Name Above Every Name

No text does this better than **Phil 2:9-11**, which talks about the name above every name. Ask any Christian group today what that name is and 95 out of 100 will say "Jesus." We even have songs that beat this into our heads.

But every ancient Jewish child knew what the name above every name was—it was not Jesus. It was God's

Hebrew	Hebrew	Greek	
יהוה ➡	אֲדֹנָי =	ΚΥΡΙΟΣ	"You shall not take the name of YAHWEH your God in vain."
YAHWEH JEHOVAH	ADONAI	KYRIOS	
Not Pronounced	LORD	LORD	

You shall not take the name of the LORD your God in vain.

name—Yahweh (Jehovah). And the Jews would not pronounce this name from Hebrew, lest they profane it. When they saw God's holy name, they said in Hebrew, "*Adonai,*" which means Lord. And so, before Jesus was born, when the Hebrew sacred texts were translated into Greek, God's name was translated as *KYRIOS* or Lord. So, in most English translations, when you see in the Old Testament the word "LORD," capital L-O-R-D, you are looking at God's divine name, the name above every name.

Why is this important? Because Early Christians, when reading the old holy scrolls in Greek, understood the word *KYRIOS* or "Lord" as the Lord Jesus.

Let's look closer. Read Isaiah 45—the whole chapter—from the Greek translation and you'll see it. (Yes, that is available in English.) Here's an excerpt:

18 I am, and there is no other,
19 I have not spoken in secret
nor in a dark place of the earth....
*I am, **I am the Lord**,*
speaking righteousness and declaring truth.
20 Assemble yourselves, and come together;
take counsel together, you who are being saved
from among the nations....
21 Then it was declared to you,
***I am God**, and there is no other besides me;*
there is no righteous one or savior except me.
22 Turn to me and you will be saved,
you who are from the end of the earth!
***I am God**, and there is no other.*
23By myself I swear,
"Verily righteousness
shall go forth from my mouth;
my words shall not be turned back,
because to me every knee shall bow
and every tongue shall acknowledge God,
24 saying, Righteousness
and glory shall come to him...."

*25 **By the Lord** shall they be justified....*[45]

Reading this text carefully, we can see that Paul does not merely *echo* this text, he directly *quotes* it saying about Jesus Christ:

Wherefore,
God exalted him and lavished upon him
the name above every name [KYRIOS or LORD],
So that when Jesus' name is pronounced
Every knee shall bow,
and every tongue confess:
"LORD (KYRIOS) is Jesus Christ,"
to the glory of God the father.

Phil 2:9-11 is a short, incredible, and incisive early Christian hymn written by Paul (or possibly quoted by him). I will leave a great deal out, but I want to mention two things:

First, I have a short technical note which is hardly insignificant. Verse 11b reads this way:

ΚΥΡΙΟΣ ΙΗΣΟΥΣ ΧΡΙΣΤΟΣ
KYRIOS IESOUS XRISTOS
LORD (is) Jesus Christ

Yes, it was written in all caps originally, as was everything else. But what is significant is the *order* of the words, placing ΚΥΡΙΟΣ first, emphasizing the importance of the name above all names. English translations anemically place this at the end of the sentence, illustrating how to be technically correct and misleading at the same time.

---

[45] http://ccat.sas.upenn.edu/nets/edition/

So Christians today, reading "Lord" at the end of the phrase as a mere title (meaning "master" or some such) completely miss the point. To call Jesus "LORD" was to acknowledge that the divine name of the Father had been lavished upon him.

Now the point here is not that all the translations have mistranslated the text. I am not advocating that "Jesus Christ is Lord" is an incorrect translation. The point is that a technically accurate translation is still not adequate for this particular text. People read Phil 2:9-11 and think that "Jesus" is the name above all names. Paul would have passed out! The name above all names is the divine name of God—in Greek, KYPIOΣ (or in English, KURIOS—LORD). It is *that* name that was lavished upon Jesus. Although Jesus followed a path of ultimate humility, he was given the ultimate exaltation of the divine Name of God.

Second, looking over Paul's shoulder as he was reading an "ancient text" (ancient even for him) reveals not simply his "interpretive flair" or some slight-of-hand on ancient manuscripts. No, this is a deep reading of the Greek text of Isaiah 45 using highly sophisticated approaches to interpretation which I have only hinted at in this book.[46] And yet such deep readings are awaiting all who would spend time in ancient texts in search of conversation with God.

Similar readings can be found elsewhere, in texts like these: 1Cor 4:4; 12:3; 2Cor 4:5; 1Pet 3:15; and Acts 2:36. And more. And more.

---

[46] Much more is going on in Phil 2 than the teaser I have offered.

Early Christians were avid about this kind of reading; it was at the top of their list. In fact, it was their main way of reading the sacred texts—in search of the LORD Jesus Christ.[47]

The 9th Thing

The ninth thing everybody should know about the Bible: *The authoritative canon of the earliest church was not a set of books. It was a single truth held above all: Jesus Christ is KURIOS.* This truth was the filter through which both sacred text and tradition were read and evaluated for every situation. They did not call it "the canon;" but in our terms, that is in fact what it was.

What If

What would happen if we were to make our "authoritative canon" less a particular collection of books (as important as the various canons are to us—and *of course* they are important!) than an energetic pursuit of Jesus as Lord? This is not a denigration of ancient sacred texts or of the Christian canons throughout history; it is rather looking at life alongside our earliest brothers and sisters *who not only highly valued ancient holy writings without our sense of "canon consciousness," but who also scoured those writings in search of Jesus as Lord.*

What would happen if our churches were places

- **where** "openly thinking together" was actually *celebrated and encouraged* instead of feared, or hedged, or just given lip-service;

---

[47] For more, see chapter 16.

- **where** our church leaders were more concerned about challenging us in *how to* develop critical thinking skills than with *what to think* about safe window-dressing doctrines (leaving us vulnerable to the opposition of outsiders);

- **where** we could read ancient sacred texts together, you and I, in real and open conversation about the meaning of texts on all sorts of subjects (inspiration and canon, women in the church, spiritual gifts, social justice, genetic engineering, you name it);

- **where** finding ways—together—to support one another in our very best efforts would be as much of a concern as finding the meaning of ancient texts;

- **where** our chief concern—yours and mine— could be the Lordship of Jesus in all things, *including* those many times that we will not agree on the meaning of particular texts or their current applications.

Wouldn't all of this be worth at least something?

10
Conclusion

We have now come to the end of Part 1: hopefully a suggestive look at the topic *Scripture, Canon, and Inspiration.* Our goal has been fairly straightforward: to call Christians to seriously reevaluate the book they call the most important book in the world.

Summing Up

In the course of nine chapters, I have challenged some longstanding and extremely popular views of the Bible. I have distinguished between scripture and canon, and I have advocated that the highest view of scripture we can have is one that takes it seriously in all its aspects, not just in terms advocated by longstanding theories about the Bible. I have challenged the notion that a single Christian canon was a divine promise or intention of God, and I have proposed that a broader, more open approach to understanding the reality and function of canon should be taken. I have represented both the Protestant and Roman Catholic Bibles (and all other Christian Bibles) as being canons of holy Christian scriptures, and I have challenged the notion that there is any one divinely ordained canon that was imagined or predestined by God before the foundation of the world—or at any other time. At the same time, I have certainly maintained that, as with all things in jars of clay, God can use any human effort for good.

Above all I have offered a clear vision of the nature and function of the Bible in our time, a vision both born of reason and borne by faith. I have suggested one main principle:

> ***Canon (whether Greek Orthodox, Roman Catholic, Protestant, or other) is an act of faith, by communities of faith, in search of an ongoing conversation with God.***

This is more than a simple suggestion. It is not an attempt to be glib or dismissive or rebellious or anything else that is negative or destructive. It is rather an attempt to be honest and faithful and precise; an attempt to deal faithfully and carefully with the texts we have in front of us; an attempt to state a case for the Bible, without overstating it.

Seeing the Bible in this light could have major implications. It could free Christians from some heretofore constraining views which do not actually fit with the specific elements and phenomena of the Bible. It could fundamentally change the terms and conditions of many concretized conclusions that are based more in technical arguments than in the Spirit of God. It could also give us a better footing for leading a reasonable discussion about the value of the Bible in our times.[48]

---

[48] Coming to me only after the completion of the this current book is the pioneering work of William J. Abraham, Jason E. Vickers, Natalie B. Van Kirk (eds), *Canonical Theism: A Proposal for Theology and the Church* (Eerdmans 2008). The opening piece, "Thirty Theses, " stands in stark contrast to statements like the Chicago Statement of Biblical Inerrancy. I am particularly drawn to Thesis XXX: "All epistemological proposals, like papal infallibility, scriptural infallibility, and the Methodist Quadrilateral, should be treated as midrash, secondary to the primary constitutive commitments of the church as a whole. Hence we need not give up our epistemological theories, **but they do have to be decanonized** if we are to secure the unity of Christians. This is where the rub is going to come hard for many. . . ." (p. 7, emphasis mine, gdc)

What I have not done in this book is to suggest the denigration or dismantling of our Bibles or even to suggest that one is as good as another or that all should adopt all. Canon is all about community.

What I have suggested is rather this: as members of different Christian communities, there is no reason that we should adopt (or continue) a competitive spirit, especially in respect to the fact that we have somewhat different scriptures and many different traditions. **The center of our faith is not the boundaries of our canon nor the edges of our traditions; it is rather the Lordship of Jesus Christ as our various canons and traditions attest.** So, as did our parents and theirs, let us continue to act in faith seeking conversation with God.

Only now, let us do so with less attention or concern for what separates us. Let us, in fact, honor the persistent and sustained efforts of each other as we have sought to converse with God. Where we have broken faith or failed, let us seek forgiveness and call upon grace. And let us be gracious to one another. And then, let us be all the more convicted that through the adaptability of ancient sacred texts we find divine audience and ultimate transformation. And may the gospel, which in seed-form ever awaits, take root and grow in our various communities, that we may be

Neither Jew nor Greek,
neither slave or free,
neither male and female,
neither Protestant, nor Catholic, nor any other:
for we are all one in Christ Jesus.

The First 9 Things

Each chapter has explored one "thing" that people everywhere should know about the Bible. These will serve as a foundation for the rest of this series called: *40 Things Everybody Should Know About the Bible.* Here then are the first 9 things:

1. Christians are increasingly, just plain and simple, biblically illiterate.

2. No matter how much we want to pretend that it can be so, we will never all see the Bible alike.

3. Scripture and canon are not the same thing. In fact, the difference between scripture and canon is the beginning of the conversation about the nature of the Bible, not the end of it.

4. Whose idea was the canon? The fact is, there is no evidence or claim that God initiated this.

5. "Canon" is (ongoing) *act* not (static) *thing*; a living, breathing, community performance; an act of faith that pursues revelation in a context of conversation. To speak of a "closed canon" is to speak of a dying community, a place where canon has become thing.

6. When it comes to the sacred texts, there is a difference between the message and the container. The Bible as we have it is scripture in jars of baked clay. Inspiration is God at work though ancient texts to fill the lives of individuals and communities of faith.

7. The various documents of the Bible must be read first within their ancient contexts; and then they must be applied today according to the principle of adaptability—the same principle that has kept these texts alive and relevant for millennia.

8. The Bible is made up of a great deal more diversity than is normally recognized. As it stands now, it is put together in a topical and somewhat arbitrary order, lending to the notion of a uniformity that is more artificial than natural.

The authoritative canon of the earliest church was not a set of books. It was a single truth held above all: *"Jesus Christ—his name is KURIOS!"*

PART 2:
Engaging in
the Conversation

ΔΙΑΛΕΚΤΟΣ

(dialektos)
Discourse
Acts 2:8

Hearing in our own language.

In Acts 2, the word *dialektos*
is used for a specific human language or dialect.
In classical literature, it also was used
for *discourse, conversation,* and *discussion*—
a talking with one another in a common language.

Introduction
11. What's Wrong with Da Vinci?
12. Canon
13. Scripture
14. Law & Prophets
15. The Word of God
16. The Name Above Every Name

Introduction

Part 1 is big picture; Part 2 is detail and depth. This approach encourages both general and specific discussion. Part 1 could be used as a the basis for a class; Part 2 as reference material, or as the basis for a more advanced class. In fact, Part 2 helps provide the "meat" from which Part 1 was derived. Part 2 is not generally light reading.

The idea of providing two related Parts was motivated by two things: (1) a desire to provide full disclosure (both big picture and depth) so that anyone can see the bases for my claims; and (2) a frustration I have had with some of my conversation partners (not all) who tend to act like their job is merely to read what I have said and then to say, "You and I simply disagree!"—with no effort of any kind to support their own position. It is almost as if they think their position is the proven one and that it needs no defense. They merely want me to know that they're not "buying" what I'm "selling."

Well, here's the deal: I'm not the only one selling something, here. It is not good enough for *anyone* to take a position and then refuse to support it. As Christians, whether we know it or not, the case that some have made for the canon of the Bible represents all of us. And there are LOTS of people that aren't buying it. Even Christians! This cannot be a *closed* subject—and especially not an *assumed* subject.

Let me put it this way: I grew up and came of age in a church tradition that talked really big talk about "speaking where the Bible speaks and being silent where the Bible is silent"; about being willing always to reconsider beliefs based on what the biblical text says; about pursuing the truth of God no matter the cost; about being Christian only, unbound by the traditions of people and churches. Now that's mighty big talk. But it means absolutely nothing unless the people espousing those ideas are willing to put their money where their mouth is.

No matter what your church background, I would guess that we agree in principle: we read the Bible because we believe it is in some way God speaking. The question is, what are we willing to hear?

Part 1 focused specifically on developing the central thesis that any particular canon of the Bible is an act of faith by people of faith in search of a conversation with God. I will now leave that concept in the background. However, I regard this second half of the book as underlying and supporting the first half.

In what follows I will go into a bit more depth about how my position differs from *The Da Vinci Code*, and about the terms canon, scripture, the law and prophets, the word of God, and the name above all names. Especially number 3 (a textual study on the word "scripture") will get quite detailed.

11
What's Wrong
with Da Vinci

A. Opening Summary:

Since my argument is critical of standard approaches to the Bible, some have (quite fairly) asked me to be more explicit in how my approach differs from the *Da Vinci Code*.

The direct answer is: Significantly!

B. Da Vinci Code:

"The Bible is the product of man, my dear. Not God. The Bible did not fall magically from the clouds. Man created it as a historical record of tumultuous times, and it has evolved through countless translations, additions, and revisions. History has never had a definitive version of the book."[49]

C. My Reply:

To be blunt, the above statement is not a contribution of anything, but is aimed at the popular view of the Bible (a view that I, too, have been criticizing in this book). I agree that the popular view of the Bible has left itself open for significant criticism. I would then say that *The Da Vinci Code's* view (above) is equally flawed.

The Da Vinci Code statement is a modish, "playing-to-the-crowds" declaration that both throws out the baby with the bathwater and is inaccurate in its details. It wrongly implies that scripture is equal to the Bible, and it mentions nothing about

---

[49] Dan Brown, *The Da Vinci Code* (Doubleday, 2003) p. 231.

any sustained faithful effort to converse with God. It also completely disregards the question of revelation and scripture.

The Bible, as a collection, is far more than *"a historical record of tumultuous times,"* and although there *have been* "countless translations, additions, and revisions" in the manuscript tradition over the centuries (is that supposed to be a problem?), the statement completely ignores (and is likely just plain ignorant of the fact) of the role and function of intertextual conversations and reapplications that breathe life into ancient traditions and text. Absolutely, the varied manuscript tradition raises questions to be answered by highly trained technicians (and this should cause us great caution in theoretical statements about the Bible). However, this in itself attests to the great amount of attention paid to such manuscripts.

I agree with the final statement: *"History has never had a definitive version of the book."* So what? A rich and varied faith community in continual search of God *never will* have a single definitive version or translation of the Bible.

12
Canon

What does the Bible say about canon?

This may come as a shock to some people, but nobody's Bible has anything at all to **say** about "a canon of scripture." Yes it is true that many will *claim* that it does, but this is yet one more instance when we don't know the difference between "what the Bible *says*, and what we think it *means.*"[50] It is a simple fact that the Bible **says** nothing about canon.

Paul (and only Paul) uses the word *kanon* four times in two texts (2Cor 10:13, 15, 16 and Gal 6:16) but not about the scriptures or a list of acceptable scripture documents.

It is amazing, actually, how often and easily the concept of "canon" is read *into* certain texts that have nothing at all to say about canon.

A. Reading Canon into Texts

1. For example, **Lk 24:44** and **2Pet 3:15-16** mention *collections* (prophets and Paul's letters) but are in no way specific, so we cannot tell exactly what is in either of these collections (Did they include Daniel? What about Paul's letter to the Laodiceans (Col 4:16)? How about Philemon? How can we know?);

---

[50] I do not intend this critique, which appears numerous times in this book (see "Interpretation: Say vs Mean" in the index, but especially chapter 3), as dismissive or as denigrating to anyone's motives. It is rather an attempt to provide an incisive description and serious critique of what I consider to be a doomed and counter-productive practice: appending our beliefs to particular texts and assuming that the two are the same thing. I do not believe that this is an intentional practice, but it is often surrounded by intense emotional attachment to the conclusions, as though those conclusions are themselves scripture.

and there are no indications from either Luke or 2Peter that any kind of concern was in vogue to do anything other than recognize that these documents spoke of Jesus in ways not understood by others. It may be that people at a later date who are concerned about canon will use these texts for that purpose, but these texts themselves do not pursue or require a canon.

2. **Rev 22:18-19** says not to add to or subtract from "the words of this book." Anybody who wants to quote this as referring to the entire Protestant Bible should at least read it in the context in which the author, John, has set it. For just a few verses earlier, in **22:6-11**, John clearly shows that these words are about this particular book of prophecy, not about a canon or collection of books. Furthermore, these words stand in the tradition of **Dt 4:2; 12:32;** and **Prov 30:6.** This is a standard way of saying, "This document is from God, so don't mess with it."

This same statement ("don't add to or take away from") occurs in the **Letter of Aristeas** (about 170 B.C.) to claim that the Greek translation of the Hebrew Law of Moses[51] (the Septuagint) *is inspired.* Of course, Christians today don't care about the Septuagint (it's just some old Greek thing), so when they hear about this old tradition, that it was "inspired," they simply dismiss it. They have no investment in either the Letter of Aristeas or the Greek Septuagint (which was originally only the Law of Moses.)

Nevertheless, this tradition, along with the statements in Deuteronomy and Proverbs, illustrates well that such a claim says nothing about collecting the document into some imaginary exclusive list of accepted books (canon).

However, this statement (Rev 22:18-19) very definitely *is a self-claim about the inspiration of the book of Revelation.* There is no question about this, that Revelation presents itself in this manner, ending very much the way it begins: as a claim to be a direct revelation from Jesus Christ (Rev 1:1-2). This is not a

---

[51] The Letter of Aristeas deals only with the Law of Moses. Other Greek translations began to be mentioned along with this in later years.

claim of *canonicity*, rather of *inspiration*. It is interesting, in that light, that the book of Revelation **does not** echo, allude to, or directly quote from any previously written document of what is now the New Testament. (In other words, if any of these documents were considered widely to be "inspired writings" or "scriptures," John does not commend them in any such manner. There could be lots of reasons for that, but it is at least something to think about.) Revelation **does**, however, contain numerous apparent references and allusions (not just similarities) to apocryphal and pseudepigraphical documents widely available at the time. [52]

3. **Mt 23:34-35** and **Lk 11:48-51** are used by some interpreters to suggest a canon from the names "Abel to Zechariah son of Barachiah" which are equated with the first and last martyrs of the completed 3-part Hebrew canon (which ends with Chronicles). However, there are numerous complications with this equation, including that (1) Luke and Matthew don't necessarily agree on which Zechariah is being referred to, or even that it is the same one as in Chronicles; (2) Josephus does not apparently place Chronicles last in his list;[53] (3) no other NT document or early church father reflects such a view (as supposedly is alluded to by Matthew); and (4) the Jewish evidence for closure of a 3-part canon is not solid until the 3rd century A.D. On top of all of that, contextually for Matthew and Luke, the point is not about Israel's scriptures, but about Israel's sad history of faithlessness. And there is more. The issues are actually quite complicated and it is not a safe or smart idea to build a case for "canonicity" on such tenuous assumptions.

4. **1Cor 13:10** "when that which is perfect is come" is used by some as a reference to a future completed Bible. Frankly, this approach is highly motivated by theological concerns to explain

---

[52] See Craig Evans, *Ancient Texts for New Testament Studies: A Guide to the Background Literature* (Hendrickson, 2005), 342-409.

[53] *Against Apion* 1.8: "For we have ... only twenty-two books ... five belong to Moses, ... the prophets ... wrote down what was done in their times in thirteen books. The remaining four books contain hymns to God, and precepts for the conduct of human life."

the demise of tongue-speaking and other gifts of the Spirit (since their revelatory functions are no longer needed once a perfect revelation of the perfect Bible is in hand). Once again, this assumes that a completed canon is on the way and was planned by God from the start. But there are no contextual hints that lead to a conclusion that a canon of the scriptures is either needed or is in view. The text is best explained contextually in other ways (not the least of which would militate against the naïve and inadequate notion that the gifts were primarily revelatory "fillers" until a perfect physical text was assembled).

5. There are also other texts treated in very similar manners. But the issue here is this: the idea of a closed canon by the time of Jesus—or even by the end of the 1st century—is not something that is *advocated by or that rises out of* a study of the texts; it is something that is *taken to* the texts to see if it can be made to fit. In other words, Christians often have a need to prove that the Bible fits the theological agendas that they have come to advocate. It is a zeal for the text much like the zeal found in the NT ascribed to Pharisees (in which they don't engage the text, but wrap it in a theological blanket both to protect it, and to protect themselves *from* it.)

B. How Many Whiskers Make a Canon?

Please allow me to illustrate with an example that is not about canon.

I was sitting in a Bible class on Mark 6:1-6 which says "Jesus was not able to do any miracles" in his hometown because of their pervasive lack of faith. The teacher (not me, I was visiting) asked: "Did Jesus fail?" At this point, the people in the class began reaching for answers in every way they have been taught to do so. One noted that we know that God is perfect, so Jesus couldn't fail. Another noted that the only miracle Jesus could not do in his hometown was to make them believe. Another noted that the dispensation of grace (as contrasted to that of law) meant Jesus was *unwilling* to do any miracles. In other words, as Christians, we are trained not to let the text right in front of us ("Jesus *was not able* to do any mighty sign" and "Jesus *was amazed* at their unbelief") stand on its own two feet, or to interpret it in keeping with the larger contrast in Mark between the authority of Jesus and the hard nature of discipleship. There was no effort to engage the story in the context of Mark; in an unintended way, the concern became that we protect our understandings about God *against* the text. [54]

In the very same way, people latch onto all of the texts named above in a "so many whiskers make a beard" kind of argument (namely, there are so many such texts that they must surely add up to *something* about canon!). However, there is no contextual clue in any of these texts that the later concepts of "canon" are in view. Let's put it this way: if you did not know anything about a "canon" to start with, there would not be anything in any of these texts that would give you even a hint about it. They certainly do say some things about the scriptures; but not one of them is talking about canon.

C. Summary

So, despite the fact that the concept of "canon" is often read *into* certain texts, such a concern for developing or closing a "canon" cannot be shown to exist within biblical texts or outside of them prior to the mid-2nd century A.D. (by the most conservative estimates)[55] or more likely until the 3rd or 4th century A.D. This is now extremely well documented by textual scholars and historians. So, the concern for a "closed canon" is not found anywhere in the Bible or in the literature surrounding it. This is not to say that no processes were underway already by the 1st century A.D. which contributed to a later rise of a "canon consciousness." (I have addressed this matter of the "canonical process " in Part 1 of the book. See the Index under "Canon.")

---

[54] Happily, the teacher did eventually address some of these issues. The point here is not to criticize the teacher or to belittle the people in the class, but rather to point out a common style of Bible reading.

[55] Despite what I consider the circular reasoning of Andreas J. Köstenberger and Michael J. Kruger, *The Heresy of Orthodoxy* (Crossway, 2010). I will address some concerns about this book next chapter.

The bottom line is, the Bible says nothing about a "canon" of the scriptures, closed or otherwise.

13
Scripture

As noted in Part 1 of this book, the ancient Jewish and Christian usage of the Greek word *graphē* (often translated into English as "scripture") implied the inspiration of a document as "a holy writing"; but it did not imply "canon" and certainly not "closed canon."

A. Prelude

In what follows, I will broadly survey the many uses of the term *hē graphē* (pronounced "*hay grah-fay*," and meaning "the writing") in biblical and related literature. I will conclude that, despite scholarly assumptions to the contrary, the use of the term through the 1st century A.D. is consistent: namely, the singular was for specific quotes, and the plural was for generalized and undefined references to sacred texts. I will also argue that "scripture" and "canon" are different, and that it is a mistake to read "scripture" as implying "canon."

B. Preferences

We begin that scripture and canon are not the same. I can't stress enough how important this is. And yet, people get involved in silly *"Yes they are, no they aren't"* arguments over this all of the time. How do we get around such an impasse?

First, we distinguish current from ancient usage. It may very well be true that in popular usage today the word "scripture" is most often used for a bound Bible (hence, a closed canon). So, they say, "I love scripture" as they are holding a Bible in their hands. In such a case, it is clear that scripture, canon, and Bible all mean the same thing. But the question is not about current popular usage or whether it is appropriate to impose current popular definitions onto ancient texts.

Of course it's not OK!
(Despite the fact that people do it all the time!)

Here is a simple phrase that every Bible student should memorize as a kind of "prime directive":

Avoid personal preferences
when reading ancient references!

The real question in front of us is how the word was used in ancient texts at the time of the origins of Christianity.

C. Legwork

Second, we stop making claims without doing some basic legwork in our own Bibles. This does **NOT** mean pulling out a Bible dictionary and especially not a one-volume "Study Bible" with notes at the bottom (please don't do that!), because both of these works are notorious for stacking the deck by throwing "scripture" and "canon" into the same hopper and discussing them as if they both mean the same things.

Instead of that, we (at the very least, every one of us who fancies himself or herself—in any sense—a Bible teacher) should at least do some of our own spade work before we look at anything else. And frankly, all you need to do to see this for yourself is to look up the word "Scripture" in a decent English **concordance** of the Bible (the true workhorse of any serious Bible student) and simply take the time to read through all of the texts as you keep notes. You will see that, in the Bible (Protestant or Catholic), the English translation "Scripture" is essentially not in the OT (except for maybe two or three times, depending on the translation you use). In the NT it predominantly is used in fulfillment texts.

Just by doing this simple little exercise—if you are paying close attention (and if your English translation does not get in your way)—you will see that, in the Bible, the word for "Scripture" **seems to be used in the following patterns:**

Singular Texts

1. *In the singular it most often seems to refer to a single text or passage* (e.g., "Have you not read this scripture?" Mk 12:10);

Pervasive Witness

2. *In the plural it seems to refer to a general, undefined group of texts* (e.g., "Paul . . . argued with them from the scriptures," Acts 17:2; or "Apollos was well versed in the scriptures," Acts 18:24);

3. *With the word "all" or "every" the word seems to be a general claim for the pervasive witness or nature of scripture* (e.g., "things about himself in all the scriptures," Lk 24:27; "Every scripture is inspired," 2Tim 3:16);

4. *In the singular, three examples in John use "scripture" to refer to texts that we do not have* (e.g., ". . . the scripture says, 'Rivers of living water will flow out of his heart,'" Jn 7:38; see also 7:42 and 20:9).

Now, some English translations might make this more or less difficult to see. However, no English translation should block the fact that not one of these is about the *boundaries* of sacred texts; instead, they are about the *nature, character, and witness* of sacred texts—all of them!

When we see the declarations about "all sacred texts" or "every sacred text," it is important that we ask whether the word "all" or "every" is attempting to be specifically (1) *exclusive* (to define the *outer limits* of scripture), or rather (2) *intrinsic* (to declare the *inner nature* of scripture). It is not enough to read our assumptions (or even our theological pet peeves) into the texts; we need to have specific contextual clues for interpreting those texts.[56]

---

[56] Naturally, there is no such thing as a presupposition-less reading of anything, and I am not here touting the pristine nature of "historical-critical readings" of texts. Nor do I have any sympathy for approaches today that delusive-

Using such contextual clues, these texts are witnessing to the inner nature, the divine authority, and the usefulness of the sacred writings for the proclamation of the gospel—not a concern for the outer limits.

And all of this is available to anyone doing even basic legwork in the texts.

D. A Deeper Look

Basic legwork is a necessary step, but it's not enough. So, *third, after such a preliminary perusal, we then journey deeper for a look at the actual Greek texts*—you know, to see how the **Greek words** are used, not only inside but outside of our Bibles.

Now this step gets more sophisticated and whether some like to hear this or not, some special skills are required. The more we know about biblical languages, the better; and the more we know about the differences in study tools and how to use them, the better. For example, if you have a KJV and some experience with Strong's Concordance, or Thayer's Greek lexicon (dictionary), that may be better than having nothing at all, but why would anyone *choose* that? Forgive me, but even though a horse and buggy is better than walking everywhere, who really wants a horse and buggy? That is not an "elitist" statement, or that I don't like horses—it is just a fact.

Not everyone takes kindly to this. Not so very long ago, I was teaching a class on a NT book when, right in the middle of class, one of the students jumped up, ran upstairs, fetched a Strong's concordance, and came back to class. I was genuinely thrilled to see this kind of excitement and wanted to encourage such energy. Within a few minutes, this person began making some comments that clearly went beyond the limits of the resource in her hands. An attempt on my part to suggest how such tools can

---

ly assert that historical-critical concerns are of no value. The point I am after is that there is clearly a difference in careful readings of texts and haphazard readings.

benefit us was not considered an act of kindness. Sometimes, we use such tools as a way of supporting our conclusions.

It is important to have the right tools for the job at hand and to know how to use them. A Strong's Concordance is fine for basic work. But for this type of work, as a bare minimum, we need an up-to-date and comprehensive Greek lexicon (dictionary) and a comprehensive Greek concordance for both the OT and NT, not to mention access to the Greek texts of both the Septuagint and the NT. Besides these primary tools, other Greek study tools (like "word study" tools) can come in handy down the road (just don't start with these).[57]

With all of this in our hands, the idea is to *do as much of our own work as possible before we entertain even one judgment or opinion of anyone else.* We certainly want to consider what others say, too; just not right at first. We keep notes all along the way and then write up what we find. Such studies can take hours, days, weeks, or even months, depending on the topic and time we have. But that is the adventure and lure of Bible study—right?

So, following now are my own personal efforts on this topic written specifically for you at this time.

E. Outside the NT Documents

1. Classical Usage

My own experience with Bible students doing word studies is that we don't really care what the "classical" usages are; we just want to cut to the chase and see what the word means *in the Bible!* But that is a mistake, and I hope to demonstrate that, especially for the word "scripture" in the Bible.

---

[57] Naturally, there is a whole lot more that could be said about this, and of course, good Bible software will give you all of this. For a list of such things, go to http://www.bibledashboard.com and click on the Greek Help Center.

So, by going to the internet we can utilize the "open source" (free) resource of the *Perseus Digital Library* to look up words in ancient Greek literature.[58] By going to the following website

http://www.perseus.tufts.edu/hopper/resolveform?type=exact&lookup

and by typing in the word *grafh*, we can look up the word γραφή (*graphē*) to see how it was used in secular Greek works of many kinds with all of its variety of senses. So, here is a summary from that resource, having deleted all the particular sources:

> **I. Drawing: 1.** *Drawing, delineation, outline, painting, the art of drawing or painting.* **2.** *That which is drawn or painted, drawing, picture;* also of embroidery. **3** *Painting, rouging the cheeks.*

> **II. Writing: 1.** *Writing or the art of writing, registration,* writing of treaties. **2. a.** *That which is written, writing, written documents, letter,* spurious *documents, false statements; of published writings, book, written law, contract, copies of judgments delivered in court;* **b.** *catalogue, list, return, price-list;* **c.** *inscription;* **d.** *MS. reading.* **3.** [in the LXX and other Christian literature] *the Holy scripture, also of a particular passage or text.* **4** *Medical prescription.* **5.** *Record-office, archive.*

> **III. Law Term: 1.** *Bill of indictment in a public prosecution.* **2.** *Criminal prosecution in the interest of the state; appear before the court in a public prosecution, either as prosecutor or prosecuted.* **3.** *Generally, an ordinary public action, opp. to special.*

Now, I show all of this detail, not because it is particularly mesmerizing, but because, if you will take the time to read every word of it, it shows that the basic meaning of the word *graphē* is not "scripture." As a matter of fact, that is a relatively minor application of the word. As with all words in all languages, this word was used in a wide variety of ways; it is always *context* (not personal whim) that helps us know how to apply the words in a particular occurrence.

---

[58] Of course, every *real* scholar will use *The Thesaurus Linguae Graecae* (TLG) Digital Library of Greek Literature. For a fee of $100 per year, you can too: http://www.tlg.uci.edu/

In other words, we need to know how to use such a listing of words. We are not looking for "what the word really means," we are looking for "how it is used." It would be ridiculous to go running through such a list as above, hijacking whatever "definition" we want so that it supports our position. For example, we could grab-hold of II.2.b "catalogue, list, return, price-list" and say "see, it means *a list* and therefore implies canon!" To which one should reply, "You mean a price-list? Ah, I get it! 2Tim 3:16 should be read 'All scripture is *for sale,*' meaning Paul was probably a book dealer!" (Sorry about the foolishness, but that is exactly what it is when we look at the word "scripture" and say, "Well, I think it implies canon," just because we can imagine it from our current-day definitions, whether we have any supporting contextual evidence or not.)

One thing we *should* note from the above list is **that *graphē* was not used outside of Jewish and Christian circles for "holy writings."** For example, Homer's *Iliad* and *Odyssey* were looked upon by Greeks and Romans with life-long religious devotion, much like Jewish and Christian sacred writings would come to be viewed. This is beautifully described in the writings of Heraclitus "the Grammarian" who lived at the end of the 1st century A.D. and who wrote in defense of Homer against some critics:

> *From the very first age of life, the foolishness of infants just beginning to learn is nurtured on the teaching given in his school. One might almost say that his poems are our baby clothes, and we nourish our minds by draughts of his milk. He stands at our side as we each grow up and shares our youth as we gradually come to manhood; when we are mature, his presence within us is at its prime; and even in old age, we never weary of him. When we stop, we thirst to begin him again. In a word, the only end of Homer for human beings is the end of life.*[59]

---

[59] Homeric Problems 1:4-7, as quoted from the English translation by David Konstan and Donald A. Russell, *Heraclitus: Homeric Problems* in Writings

All of this beauty and religious devotion, and yet Homer's works are not called *hai graphai*, "the scriptures"—not because they weren't regarded with such a status, but because the word *graphē* was not used that way outside of Jewish and Christian circles—even at the end of the 1st century A.D. As we shall see, the Jewish and Christian practice grew out of the Greek Septuagint for the Jewish and (especially) Christian sacred texts.

2. Old Testament & Apocrypha

So next, using a concordance for the Greek Septuagint, we find over 40 occurrences of the word γραφή (*graphē*) in the Greek OT and Apocrypha. Aside from three occurrences in the Pentateuch (see below), and one in Ezekiel, all others are in relatively late texts: 1-2Chronicles, Ezra, Nehemiah, Psalms, and Daniel. Sirach, 1-4Maccabees, and 1-2Esdras also have a good sampling.

Right off we must notice that nearly all of these instances in the OT carry the classical sense of "writings" in some general or specific sense. And this helps us to remember that the word "scripture" is an English translation (by way of Latin) that is assigned in specific contexts. **There is no special Greek word that means only "scripture."** So then, a close look in the OT and Apocrypha reveals that there is not a particularly sharp distinction between the "writing" sense and the "scripture" sense. Sometimes, it is hard to tell the difference.

For example, when the words *hē graphē* ("the writing") first appear in the Greek text of the Law of Moses, it is simply delicious! Our text is **Ex 32:16** and causes one to hallucinate that this might have affected later uses of the word in this very sense, even though it is technically a standard use of the term in the sense of "writing." Actually, the Greek is a fairly literal translation of the Hebrew text, and both are set forth in a poetic way:

from the Greco-Roman World (Society of Biblical Literature: June 30, 2005), p. 3

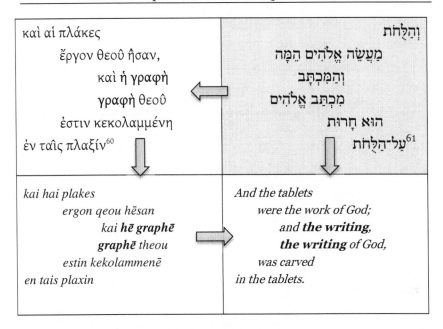

καὶ αἱ πλάκες
    ἔργον θεοῦ ἦσαν,
        καὶ ἡ γραφὴ
        γραφὴ θεοῦ
    ἐστιν κεκολαμμένη
ἐν ταῖς πλαξίν[60]
	וְהַלֻּחֹת
	מַעֲשֵׂה אֱלֹהִים הֵמָּה
	וְהַמִּכְתָּב
	מִכְתַּב אֱלֹהִים
	הוּא חָרוּת
	עַל־הַלֻּחֹת[61]

kai hai plakes
    ergon qeou hēsan
        *kai **hē graphē***
        ***graphē** theou*
    estin kekolammenē
en tais plaxin
	And the tablets
	    were the work of God;
	        *and **the writing**,*
	        ***the writing** of God,*
	    was carved
	in the tablets.

The second and only other appearance of *hē graphē* ("the writing") in the Greek Pentateuch is in **Dt 10:4**:

And he [the Lord] wrote upon the tablets,
according to (just like) the first writing
of the ten words (commandments).

κατὰ τήν γραφηὸ τήν πρώτην
(kata tēn graphēn tēn prōtēn)

So then, in the Law of Moses the words *hē graphē* ("the writing") occurs three times, but in only two texts, both texts stating specifically that the Lord God wrote the words on the tables of stone. This act by God is literally called "the writing." Technically, this is exactly how any other place would refer to an "inscription," so there is nothing special about this. On the other hand, the very context—that God himself is writing this, and it is

---

[60] Septuaginta: With morphology. Stuttgart: Deutsche Bibelgesellschaft, 1996, c1979, S. Ex 32:16

[61] *Biblia Hebraica Stuttgartensia: with Westminster 3.5 Morphology.* Stuttgart; Glenside PA : German Bible Society; Westminster Seminary, 2001, c1925; morphology c2001, S. Ex 32:15

called the *graphē of God*—shows that if this is not a holy writing of some kind, it is hard to imagine what is!

In the second of those two texts (Dt 10:4), the phrase, "according to the writing" (*kata tēn graphēn*) is used to mean "just like the first writing."

However, this exact same phrase (*kata tēn graphēn*, but now with the meaning "according to the authority of the named written document or text") shows up in five later texts of the Greek Septuagint (not always included in English translations). Each instance is singular and refers to a particular text in the named document:

GROUP 1

1Chr 15:15   "as commanded of Moses by the word of God
              according to the writing"

2Chr 30:5   "They had not kept [the Passover] in great numbers
              according to the writing"

2Chr 35:4   "**according to the writing**
              of David King of Israel . . . and Solomon his son."

1Esdr 1:4[62]   "**according to the writing**
              of David King of Israel . . . and Solomon his son."

2Esdr 6:18[63] "**according to the writing**
              of the book of Moses"

In the Greek Septuagint (LXX), there is no distinction in phrasing between any of these uses just listed (remember, in the 1st century A.D., the LXX was not a single book or document, "it" was not actually an "it," but rather originally the Law of Moses, and then gradually a general reference to the various sacred scrolls and texts used by Greek speaking Jews and Christians).

---

[62] Equals 2Chr 35:4. 1Esdras is in the Apocrypha, parallels sizeable portions of 2Chr 35-36, all of Ezra, part of Nehemiah 7-8. Dates from 2nd century B.C.

[63] 2Esdras 1-10/11-23 is Ezra 1-10/Nehemiah 1-13.

However, what we soon find out is that the phrase is identical to three (and only three) NT texts normally translated something like this:

GROUP 2

Js 2:8   "If you fulfill the royal law,
  according to the Scripture (sg)"[64]

1Cor 15:3 "Christ died on behalf of our sins
  according to the Scriptures (pl)"

1Cor 15:4 "he was buried and was raised on the third day
  according to the Scriptures (pl)."

The first (Js 2:8) is singular and (as is typical) is followed by a specific quote from the Law of Moses (Lev 19:18). The next two (1Cor 15:3, 4) are plural and are general references to unspecified texts or documents.

Comparing Groups 1 and 2 naturally raises the question of why the exact same phrase is translated differently in the two groups. Sometimes context requires such a thing (remember, good translation is not a paint-by-numbers process, but is contextually driven). But in these cases, the answer is not a very reassuring one: *it is because of the preconceptions of the translators as to what is "scripture" and what is not.*

This can be seen in the *New English Translation of the Septuagint* (NETS),[65] which translates Group 1 as follows, in the same order as listed above: (1) "prescription"; (2) "prescription" (with a footnote "scripture"); (3) "writing"; (4) "writing"; and (5) "scripture."

The point is not that the translations are wrong. They are in fact all perfectly fine as far as what is possible. However, the

---

[64] "Scripture" will be consistently capitalized by some English translations (e.g., NKJV, NASB, NIV, The Message) and not by others (e.g., KJV, RSV, NRSV, NJB, REB).

[65] *A New English Translation of the Septuagint*, by the International Organization for Septuagint and Cognate Studies (Oxford University Press, 2007). This excellent tool is available online at the following address: http://ccat.sas.upenn.edu/nets/edition/

first three have the same translator, and the last two have the same translator. Each of the two translators chose either to *translate* as "scripture" (2Esd 6:18) or to *suggest* "scripture" (2Chr 30:5) in one of their texts. Now why would that happen when we are dealing with exactly the same phrase in every text (namely, "according to *tēn graphēn*")? The answer appears to be in the source to which each of those two references points: the Law of Moses. (By this pattern, 1Chr 15:15 should also suggest "scripture" in a footnote.) But the other two texts, translated one each by the two translators, refer only to the *"writing* of David."

So, even in this fine new resource, it appears beyond doubt that the inconsistency in translating this phrase is based on a decision of exactly what is *later* to be classified as "scripture."

This gets even more disconcerting when one looks at the premier Greek lexicon of the NT (BDAG) and finds for the word *graphē* that all of the above texts (in both groups) are listed for *"the singular as a designation of Scripture as a whole."* [66] That doesn't fit the above translations at all! So we find, here, an illustration of the truth that all translation is interpretation.

Let's be doubly clear: **there is nothing about the word *graphē* itself that makes it mean "scripture/Scripture" rather than "a writing," a "sales list," or a "medical prescription."** Such translation decisions are dependent entirely on usage and context—and, of course, the translator. So, when we see the same usage and the same contextual supports for a word across various texts, we need to ask why they are translated differently. Sometimes, translational variety can add to readability; but here we are dealing with whether something was thought of as "sacred text" or not, so this is worth some extra attention and detail.

---

[66] Frederick W. Danker, *A Greek-English Lexicon of the New Testament and other Early Christian Literature* (University of Chicago Press, 2000), p. 206d. (Commonly referred to as BDAG.)

Let us press this point a bit more. For we will soon discover that in all cases in our literature, when in Greek the article is present (as in *hē graphē,* "the writing"), some kind of writing is being referred to as an authoritative document or inscription, perhaps even with sacred overtones. And yet the article need not be present to refer to such a writing (although that is rare).

Here are some direct examples: **1Esd 1:4/2Chr 35:4** speaks of "the writing [scroll] of King David," and **Dan 10:21** has someone in human form say, "I am to announce to you what is inscribed in [the] writing [scroll] of Truth" (*en graphē, alētheia*—no article). Both of these documents were seen as carrying the authority of the one having written them. And again: **2Chr 24:27** "the writing [scroll] of the Kings"; and **2Chr 30:18** "they ate [the Passover] contrary to what the writing had specified." In Daniel, the handwriting on the wall (directly from God) offers a tantalizing and recurring use of "the writing" in **Dan 5:6, 7, 8, 9, 15, 16, 17, 24, 25,** and **26.** Although it is clearly not referring to a document, it is just as clearly a message from God. Jeremiah the prophet is the subject of **2Macc 2:4** and "the writing" he had produced there. Similar uses are found in **1Macc 14:27** and **48.** Finally, **4Macc 18:14** (written just prior to Paul's first book) talks about "the Isaiah writing which says..." and then is followed by a specific quote—exactly the format we will find often in the NT.[67]

Now, when we immediately jump up and say, "The very last example should be translated as "scripture" (because it refers to the book of Isaiah), but not the rest, because none of them is part of the canon (meaning *our* canon)"—we assume our case, muddle the terminology, and force the texts to say what we want and need them to say to protect (or at least to fit) our preconceptions about an early (1st or 2nd century) canon of the OT.

---

[67] I'm moving freely between texts found in both the OT and the Apocrypha to show that there is no difference in how the texts are used or viewed in either one. Indeed, it is unlikely at this stage (i.e., at the time of Jesus and the early church) that they would have drawn hard and fast distinctions between many of the writings, especially in the writings outside of what we know as the Law, and even those called the Prophets.

But the real question for the above group of texts is whether any of the writings referred to carried any sacred overtones or connotations *for those writing or being addressed.* If they did, then for them, the *Scroll of Truth* or *the Scroll of King David* or *the Scroll of the Kings* functioned as ancient holy texts. And in that case, why should they not be translated "scripture" like the others (unless by "scripture" we mean a particular canon—which, as I've tried to say already, is a no-no)?

So then: **The word "scripture" is not a word in *any* ancient text; it is an English *translation* of the word *graphē* (by way of Latin *scriptura*, which simply meant "writing")[68] based on whether translators believe it is referring to "scriptures." However, the definition of "scriptures" varies. Far too often, translators read later decisions about *"what is in the OT or NT canon"* back into all of these texts—all of which were written prior to the time of the existence of a canon.** (If you are getting dizzy, here, you are getting the point!)

A focusing note: It needs to be said right here that within ancient texts (biblical, apocryphal, and other), there is a long-standing and rich tradition of texts calling upon, echoing, alluding to, or directly quoting previous texts for both authoritative and sacred purposes (sometimes the two being the same thing). For example, Isaiah quotes, enhances, and reapplies earlier "water texts" from Exodus and Numbers; Nehemiah 9 appropriates themes from Deuteronomy 9; and there is so much more. It is pervasive, actually, since this is part of the intertextual DNA of sacred texts.

But what we are talking about here is this: **at what time did particular passages, documents, or groups of documents start being called *graphē* in the sense that they were thought of as "sacred texts," and exactly what did being *graphē* entail?**

---

[68] The Latin Vulgate translated Ex 32:16 discussed above ("the writing, the writing of God") as "Dei scriptura quoque Dei erat sculpta in tabulis."

So, in the previous pages, we have noticed some tendency in this direction, especially in the later, more peripheral texts (Chronicles, etc.), not so much in the Law of Moses, or even in that group called the Prophets. We found three very savory texts in Exodus and Deuteronomy about the very *graphē of God*—which could be highly suggestive for later uses of the term. However, we must use caution about this suggestion, since there is no obvious overflow from that to other texts.

Although there are some legitimate questions about translation practice in all of these texts, it is not until the 3rd and 2nd centuries B.C. that *graphē* starts to be used more widely in the sense of a "sacred text." Whether this is the same as what different translators today mean by "scripture" remains open.

3. Aristeas

And so from about 170 B.C. comes the **Letter of Aristeas**, written to give the account of the origins of the Greek Septuagint and to claim that it was an inspired translation—a claim that would be oft repeated and that Christians would universally accept. In section 155, the letter uses *graphē* in the singular to introduce quotes from Dt 7:18 and 10:21:

> *Wherefore, the one speaking exhorts us also through the scripture (dia tēs graphēs—sg): "Remember the Lord . . ."*

As we will see, this will be a standard and basic pattern for using *graphē* to refer to a snippet or passage from a document. We already saw this above in 4Macc 18:14 (which is actually later in time, just prior to Paul). Some cite the Letter of Aristeas as an example of *graphē* meaning "Scripture as a whole,"[69] but the reference is clearly to a single text or quote.

4. Philo

Philo of Alexandria holds the distinction of being the most significant early witness of Hellenistic Judaism at the time

---

[69] BDAG p. 206.

of Jesus and Paul about whom Christians today will say (at the mention of his name): "Who?"

He lived 15 B.C. to A.D. 50, which means he was an older contemporary of Jesus and Paul. He wrote massive amounts of commentary on the Law of Moses in Greek, finishing his writing as Paul was getting started. Highly trained in Greek philosophy (but probably unable to read Hebrew), Philo's works (filling 900 pages in a popular English translation)[70] provide an important witness of biblical exegesis in Hellenistic Judaism at the very time of Jesus and Paul. He wrote prodigiously—and almost exclusively—about the Greek Pentateuch (five books of Moses).

It is very common for commentators and study books to simply repeat the information found in each other about Philo's use of *graphē*. But if we are going to stay on track with our own study of the word, then we need the right software, or to get our hands on the complete Philo Index.[71]

Doing so we find that in all of his writings, Philo uses the word *graphē* ("writing") 56 times and with a wide range of classical meanings. Of these, Philo is represented as using the word to mean "the holy writings" only 22 times. However, we are going to contest two or three of those, for it is right here that we run into a problem. It is common for all who write on Philo—including his most recent translators and commentators,[72] and

---

[70] The popular edition of Philo is *The Works of Philo Complete and Unabridged,* New Updated Edition Hendrickson Publishers (August 1, 1993), which reproduces the original translation of C. D. Yonge of 1854-55. This is not, however, the current standard in Philo studies, that honor going to the 12 volume "Loeb edition" which includes the Greek text side-by-side with a "new" English translation and a full volume index: *Philo,* in the Loeb Classical Library (Harvard University Press, 1929-41, with supplements added in 1953, and an index in 1962; fully reprinted 1985). A new Philo translation and commentary series was launched in 1995 under the name of *Philo of Alexandria Commentary Series (PACS)* as listed at http://www.nd.edu/~philojud/38.htm.

[71] Peder Borgen, Richard E. Whitaker, Ronald Skarsten , *The Philo Index: A Complete Greek Word Index to the Writings of Philo of Alexandria* (Eerdmans, 1999).

[72] My point in this footnote is entirely that *it is common in current works on Philo to assume that scripture/scriptures/Scripture are interchangeable for Philo.* For example, it is clear that the "Loeb edition" translators treat singular

including standard reference works like BDAG and TDNT[73]—to use "scripture/scriptures/Scripture" interchangeably for *graphē* in Philo when he is referring to sacred texts. However, this practice deserves a closer look.

To that end, and keeping in mind that the word "scripture" is an English translation (by way of Latin), I shall (for purposes of accuracy), avoid that translation in favor of "writing(s) and text(s)." So, how does Philo use the term *graphē?*

1. The majority of the times that Philo uses *graphē,* it does not refer to "holy writings," but is used in the standard classical meanings as follows:

a.	Painting, Picture, Design	17 times[74]
b.	Writing, Treatise, Records	9 times[75]
c.	Legal Enactments, Table	5 times[76]
d.	List	1 time[77]

---

and plural as identical. They go back and forth in their translation between scriptures or Scripture. Sometimes, Holy Scripture is capitalized, sometimes not. The most recent commentary on Philo is David Runia, *Philo of Alexandria: On the Creation of the Cosmos According to Moses* in the Philo of Alexandria Commentary Series (Brill, 2001). This is a phenomenal work and I will surely appear as a flea on an elephant's back arguing about the definition of a mere word. Even so, Runia jumps over the phrase "the sacred scriptures" in *Opif* 77 (p. 284) with nary a comment (apparently assuming that all readers know what these are and how Philo uses the various phrases?), and on page 20 he assigns to Philo that "the powers of the individual exegete [are] limited when confronted with the *riches of scripture* (*Opif* 4-6 my italics)," even though "scripture" is never used in this section. Runia is after something quite different than the definition of the word "scripture" and, in fact, never discusses the word *graphē.*

73 BDAG p. 206 and TDNT I:749-61. See below under "New Testament—General" for more on this.

74 *Decal* 1:33; *Spec* 4:55; *Cher* 11, 104; *Post* 113; *Agr* 168; *Ios* 87; *Mos* 1:158, 287; *Mos* 2:74; *Virt* 51; *Prob* 62, 94; *Legat* 148, 151, 365; *Prov* 2:17.

75 *Abr* 11; *Her* 167—quotes Ex 32:16 verbatim; *Ebr* 11 *tēs graphēs* "our treatise"; *Migr* 34 great quote showing personal inspiration; *Somn* 1:1; *Mos* 2:40 (Aristeas tradition), 51; *Legat* 276 handwriting. As will be seen below, it will be disputed that four other texts likely belong here.

76 *Decal* 51—*tēs mias graphēs* "the one set of enactments," referring to the commandments 1-5 of the ten commandments; *Sacr* 71 judgment-bar; *Post* 38 indictment; *Conf* 14—this is a damaged sentence; *Mos* 2:203.

77 *Flacc* 185

2. When Philo wishes to use *graphē* to mean sacred books or sacred texts, he adds the word "sacred" to the word: so he says "sacred writings" *(hieras graphas)*—usually with an article, always in the plural (with one exception, see #3 below). In context, some of these refer to specific texts or documents; others appear to refer to texts in an undefined manner.

   a. *hai hierai graphai*   5 times[78]
   b. *tais hierais graphais*   4 times[79]
   c. *en tais hierais graphais*   3 times[80]
   d. *en hierais graphais*   2 times[81]
   e. *tais heirotatais graphais*   1 time[82]
   f. "holy scriptures" Greek unavailable   1 time[83]

   It is sometimes claimed that these phrases refer to the entirety or whole of scripture,[84] but this is at best imprecise or an overstatement since "whole" or "entirety" can imply boundaries. It is rather that these phrases refer to "the scriptures" in an undefined manner.

3. In only one text does Philo use the singular *graphē* with *hieras* to mean "the sacred text" (*tēs hieras graphēs*) and this is referring specifically to Ex 36:1-4.

4. In four texts, Philo uses *graphē* with the adjective *rhētos* ("literal") to mean "the literal meaning of the text" (*tēs rhētēs graphēs*). Two of these are plural and two are singular, and they all refer to the "literal meaning" of texts.

---

[78] *Abr* 61; *Congr* 34; *Decal* 8; *Opif* 77; *Spec* 2:134.

[79] *Decal* 37; *Her* 286; *Spec* 1:214; *Spec* 2:104.

[80] *Abr* 121; *Congr* 90; *Fug* 4.

[81] *Her* 106, 159.

[82] *Abr* 4

[83] *QG* 3:3

[84] BDAG p. 206.

a. This is where the plot thickens, because Philo's translators are not consistent with these four texts, as shown here from the Loeb edition:

i.   sg: *tōi rhētōi tēs graphēs*[85]   "by the literal text of the **scriptures**"
ii. sg: *tēs rhētēs graphēs*[86]   "from the literal text"
iii. pl: *hai rhētai graphai*[87]   "in the **scriptures** read literally"
iv. pl: *en tais rhētais graphais*[88] "in the literal history"

b. The question about these texts is not whether they are referring to or discussing the texts of the Pentateuch (of course they are); the question is the specific meaning of the word *graphē* in these cases. Is Philo, in these four instances (unlike all other times), using *graphē* to mean "sacred text" without the term *hieras* ("sacred")? Or is this a standard classical use of the term in the sense of "writing"?

c. Evaluating each text, it rather appears that the first two (being singular and essentially parallel) are concerned with the *"literal nature of the writing";* that the last two (being plural and parallel in all respects) are focused on *"the literal account";* and that all four phrases are focused on the *"literal sense"* of the texts being commented on rather than on the "holy" nature of the texts.

d. The wavering translations of both the Loeb and Yonge editions in these four texts should be taken as a less than clear reference to *graphē* as "scripture" than to *rhētē graphē* ("the literal sense"). I suggest that these texts are not strong enough to indicate a clear instance by Philo of a particular use for "scripture." So, **these four texts are better all translated in the classical sense of**

---

[85] *Abr* 68

[86] *Abr* 131

[87] *Abr* 236

[88] *Praem* 65. Yonge translates this quite differently as "being continually devoted to the study of the holy scriptures, both in the literal sense and also in the allegories." So, "*holy* scriptures," even though *hierais* is absent.

"writing," i.e., meaning "a literal sense," and not in the sense of "sacred scripture."

e. Furthermore, since there are no other texts in Philo in which *graphē* occurs without the qualifying term *hieras* ("sacred") to refer to the sacred text(s), it is not a "given" that any of these four specific texts (all used with the word "literal") should carry the sense of anything other than a standard classical reference.

f. And finally, in any case, regardless how one chooses to translate them, all four of these instances are commenting upon a particular text—i.e., a specific text, not to undefined texts, and certainly not "scripture as a whole."

5. One final text (*Her* 266) is referred to by BDAG (p. 206) as an example of Philo's use of the word *graphē* to mean an "individual scripture passage"; but this, again, is not a clear reference to "scripture." It is rather another use of *graphē* in a classical sense of writing, as both the Loeb and Yonge editions show: "To connect what is coming to what is *here written* ..."

The bottom line to all of this is that Philo does not clearly use *graphē* without a qualifier ("sacred") to refer to holy writings. Only once is the singular used, and it is a reference to a specific text. Philo does not use *hē graphē* in the singular by itself to refer to "scripture as a whole." Although it is widely assumed and stated that, in Philo, both the singular and plural of the word "scripture(s)" are interchangeable and refer to "scripture in its entirety," this case is not established and cannot be taken for granted.

5. Josephus

Josephus is much better known among Christians today, and like Philo, he too was prolific. A Jewish general captured early in the war against the Romans, he wrote after A.D. 70 in defense of the Jewish people, philosophy, and religion. He wrote roughly at the same period as the traditional date of the Gospel of Luke (in the 80's-90's), and in **Ap 1.38** (= 1, 8) he showed a very high regard for Jewish sacred texts. He argued that, unlike Greek religion:

We have not an innumerable multitude of books among us, disagreeing from and contradicting one another, but only twenty-two books ... [five belong to Moses, thirteen to the prophets; and the remaining four] contain hymns to God, and precepts for the conduct of human life.

However, this is not as clear-cut as some have tried to make it. There is plenty of debate about this "list" and it is unwise to take this as representative either of all Jews or even as identical with the later Hebrew canon, closed in the 3rd century. The point here is merely that he argued for his people from a strong sense of sacred texts and spent much of his time rehearsing (re-telling) written sacred texts, interpreting them in the flow of his writing. Even though he is referring directly to and describing the sacred texts of his people (in contrast to the Greeks), he does not use the word *graphē* in this text.

In fact, despite Josephus' vast amount of writing, he only uses the word *graphē* twice.

First we'll note **Ant 3.38** (= 3.1.7) in which Josephus expands the story a bit (as a means of interpretation) of God bringing water from the rock for a grumbling people. The note he adds next is what interests us, for by reading Whiston's[89] translation (made in 1736), Josephus appears to use *graphē* for scripture. It is translated:

Now that Scripture (graphē), which is laid up in the temple, informs us, how God foretold to Moses, that water timid in this manner be derived out of the rock.

However, through a project called PACE (Project on Ancient Cultural Engagement)[90] which specializes in Josephus, we learn

---

[89] William Whiston (trans), *The Works of Josephus* (Complete and Unabridged, Hendrickson: 1987) originally published in 1736.

[90] http://pace.mcmaster.ca/york/york/ (this is the correct address at the time of writing, but it is apparently moving).

that other such references are made in Josephus to documents kept in the Temple (Ant 4:303; 5:61). It has been long judged by scholars that it is unlikely that this use of *graphē* in this text refers to the Pentateuch or other standard "scriptures" at all. It rather refers, perhaps, to "a separate collection of chants made for the use of the temple singers" or even "to a work of the Apocrypha or Pseudepigrapha, such as the *Assumption of Moses*."[91] So, PACE translates this text as follows:

> *A writing (graphē) lying in the temple reveals that God foretold to Moyses that water would thus issue forth from the rock.*

It is clear that *graphē* (without a definite article) is being used by Josephus to refer to a specific text or document. The question is, what kind of document?

And so we have hit yet another instance in which the meaning of *graphē* as "sacred writing" is being decided by the translators on the basis of what is later determined as "scripture," not on what Josephus might have considered, on any level, as "sacred texts." To be sure, the PACE translation as "a writing" is safe in that it technically makes no judgment on the matter. On the other hand, Josephus does not appear to be commenting about some general treatise of only marginal account. Rather, according to Josephus, here is a document that speaks of (1) *God* bringing (2) *water from a rock*, and it is kept (3) *in the temple*. And when this is compared to the other documents that Josephus says were also kept in the temple (mentioned above)— mentioned by the way in the same writing as this one, only a few pages later (Ant 4:303; 5:61)—one wonders just what we might consider a "sacred text"!

Just look at the first one in particular, which talks about Moses reading to the people

> *a poem in hexameters, which he has left behind in a book in the Temple, containing a prediction of what will be . . . .*

---

[91] PACE commentary note 78, on Ant 3:38.

> *Therefore, he handed over to the priests these books, as*
> *well as the ark, in which he also deposited the ten state-*
> *ments that had been written in two tablets, and the Tent*
> *...*[92]

Now, even granting the suggestion that these books may be references to collections of chants or even portions of a book like the *Assumption of Moses*, the question is: what was Josephus' attitude about the writings to which he himself is referring? Clearly these are considered "sacred texts"—or else what are they doing near or in the ark of the covenant? Contextually, for Josephus, there is no reason to consider these documents (one of which was described in Ant 3:38 as *graphē*) as anything less than holy texts—unless we are intent on forcing later judgments about what is and is not "scripture" back onto earlier texts.

The second use of *graphē* is found in **Ap 2.45** (= 2,4) where Josephus is actually reinterpreting the tradition written in the Letter of Aristeas. To show the gravity of Jewish philosophy, he repeats the tradition about the origins of the Septuagint as an inspired translation. However, he especially enhances the part that Ptolemy Philadelphus himself acquired "the books of the sacred writings" (*tais tōn hierōn graphōn biblois*) for the express purpose of "learning our laws" (noting that Ptolemy would not have done so had he been negative toward it). This strongly emphasized the importance of Jewish sacred texts.

In this text, as in Philo, the same two words are brought together—*hierōn graphōn* ("sacred writings")—and so specifying that these are *sacred* writings, but now as the *books* of the sacred writings. Again, there is no emphasis on what the boundaries are, whether just the Septuagint as in the Letter of Aristeas, or more. The use of the phrase is undefined as to quantity.

Now it must be emphasized here that Josephus refers to holy writings quite often—just not as *graphē*. This continually comes out in his polemic in **Ap 1:54** (= 1, 10) when he defends himself as an able spokesman, saying he himself should know the story

---

[92] PACE translation, Ant 4:303.

up-close, since as a highly trained priest, he translated directly "from the sacred writings (*ek tōn hierōn grammatōn*—pl). Here the word is not *graphē* but *grammatōn* (another word for "writings").[93]

One more text will help to illustrate something of Josephus' regard for and use of texts: **Ap 2.201** (= 2, 25, although again, not using *graphē*). Here, Josephus extols the superiority of the Jewish law pointing to the high requirement for morality and purity shown in the clarity of the stations of men and women:

> *for, it says, "A woman is inferior to her husband in all things." Let her, therefore, be obedient to him; not so that he should abuse her, but that she may acknowledge her duty to her husband; for God hath given the authority to the husband.*[94]

This text is useful not only for its standard way of quoting a specific text ("it says"), but, like James 4:5 (see below), we no longer have record of such a text as quoted. This is all the more reason to understand that Josephus does not likely have a "Bible" that is identical to the closed canon in the 3rd century.) But there could be other sources for such texts as well.[95]

In summary, it is safe to say that *graphē* (whether singular or plural) is not a favorite word of Josephus, although he is extremely interested in the special nature of the sacred texts of the Jews. It seems clear contextually that both times he uses the word, he is referring to sacred texts (whether all of those texts

---

[93] Cf. Ant 4.196 (= 4, 4) For the laws being "in writing."

[94] As read in Whiston. Cf. with Ant 4.219 (= 4, 15).

[95] Another thing that must be considered here is exactly what Josephus considers "sacred text." James C. Savage notes: "Josephus understood the sacred writings to include more than just the written biblical text: Sadducees, not Pharisees, accepted only the written part. The Pharisees also accepted the *Paradosis* of the Fathers—traditions handed down from at least the time of John Hyrcanus—as equally authoritative and binding; indeed, even more so than written scripture." *Josephus: Jewish Historian and Translator of Sacred Scripture* (PhD dissertation [for Ellis Rivkin] Hebrew Union College–Jewish Institute of Religion, Cincinnati, Oh., 1993), pp. i and 362-67. We will come back to this work below in the last section on the Gospel of John.

were later in anyone's canon or not). When he used the singular, he was referring to a particular document; and the plural, to sacred texts in an undefined manner. Even when he uses the word with "sacred" (only once), he wraps it in the blanket of "the books." Josephus (at the end of the 1st century), does speak of some boundaries of those books, but it is not decisive, or even the focus. The focus for Josephus is on the superiority of Jewish religion over the Greeks.

6. Summary

Ok then, we're now right in the middle of our word study, and already we've come across several major questions:

1. Is the definite article significant when used with *graphē*?

2. Is there a pattern of usage of *graphē* when in the singular and when in the plural?

3. What are the guidelines for translating *graphē* as "writing" and as "scripture"? Should this be guided by later decisions about canon?

4. When *graphē* is translated as "scripture," should "Scripture" be capitalized? Sometimes? All the time? Ever? Whether it is or not, do these mean the same thing?

5. Do any of the uses of *graphē* studied so far indicate a concern for what is "in" or what is "out"? Is this word used contextually to indicate an exclusive list of books or to imply boundaries in any way?

F. Inside the NT Documents

1. General NT

Coming now to the NT documents, and continuing our own face-to-face acquaintance with occurrences of the word *graphē*, we now need a complete Greek concordance to the NT, or software that does the same. Using either, we find that the word

graphē is used 50 times in the Greek NT, and although it is difficult to tell all of this from English translations, the following are
some guidelines that we may draw out of those occurrences. In
other words, what follows is drawn from the finished study of
the occurrences in the NT, and they are put up front for ease of
reading. Of the 50 occurrences of the word γραφή (*graphē*) in
the NT, the word

1. always refers to *sacred writings,* not to any of the
   other classical usages (this is striking and may very
   well arise out of the Septuagint use of the term as re-
   viewed above);

2. always occurs with the *definite article* ("the") or some
   defining qualifier ("holy" Rom 1:2; "prophetic" Rom
   16:26 and 2Pet 1:20; "every" 2Tim 3:16; "another" Jn
   19:37. There is one exception to this "rule": 1Pet 2:6
   "it stands in sacred text" *periechei en graphē*_i, followed
   by a quote from Isa 28, Ps 117, and Isa 8. Incidental-
   ly, this phrase is exactly the phrase for the *Scroll of
   Truth* in Dan 10:21.); [96]

---

[96] Even the exception is instructive for the stated "rule." First, it is most
common in the Septuagint for *en graphē*_i to refer to "in writing" as in "put
something in writing" 1Chr 28:19; 2Chr 2:11; Ps 87:6; Ezek 13:9; Sirach
39:32; 42:7; 44:5; 45:11; 1Macc 12:21. Even so, Dan 10:21 uses this exact
phrase to announce what is "in [the] Book [Scroll] of Truth." So, while there is
a precedent for this usage of *en graphē*_i in the LXX, there is also manuscript
evidence that some scribes may have corrected the text here to read (1) *en tē*_i
*graphē*_i ("in the writing"), which is exactly the pattern noticed above for NT
usage of the word. The alternate text (called a variant reading) is found in P (a
9th century ms) as well as the Majority Text (which means this reading is found
in the majority of all of the 5,000+ Greek manuscripts. The Majority Text is
also the text which was used by the translators of the KJV. There is a second
variant reading in some manuscripts: (2) *he graphē* ("the writing"—again, exactly what we might expect from all other usage) in some late minuscule manuscripts, including 1739 and Latin witnesses. (3) The reading above—*en graphē*_i
("in writing")—is supported by P72, a 3rd century papyrus manuscript, as well as
the major 4th and 5th century uncial manuscripts ℵABC (Sinaiticus, Alexandrinus, Vaticanus, Ephraemi Rescriptus) and some later manuscripts of this
tradition. The point of this note is not to suggest that current Greek editions
are incorrect, but that the "rule" stated above—that *graphē* in the NT always
occurs with the definite article ("the") or some defining qualifier—may be supported by the scribes who felt a need to make the alteration. It is what one
would expect in the NT.

3. most often refers to a *specific passage or text* when used in the singular;

4. always refers to an *undefined group of texts or documents* when used in the plural (unless further defined by "law" or "prophets").

In other words, rarely if ever (I will argue "never") do NT authors say "scripture (sg) says" referring to a group of books. The pattern is clearly that the plural is used for "the sacred texts."

Now, with this summary in mind, I want to once again call your attention to the fact that some highly respected works claim a widespread use in the NT and elsewhere of the singular "scripture" for "the whole of Scripture." Because I am directly challenging that claim, we need to look at it a bit closer. Actually, my demurrer can be stated like this: *A more careful examination of specific texts will show that there is much less a witness for the singular "Scripture as a whole" than is currently presented.*

A leading example of what is normally presented is the article on γραφή (*graphē*) in the highly esteemed *Theological Dictionary of the New Testament* (TDNT), which spends six pages or so arguing for the collective use of the singular term "Scripture"—for example stating that for Gal 3:8, 22 it is "quite inconceivable that Paul should have in view an individual text"; that for Js 4:5 this "must surely be with reference to Scripture as a whole"; that for John's usage throughout "there can hardly be any doubt whatever that ... we are to think of the unified totality of Scripture," and that "it is impossible to take" 1Pt 2:6 and 2Pt 1:20 "in any other way" than a reference to the OT as a whole.[97]

Now when we add to this the testimony of the "standard" lexicon for NT Greek, the *Greek-English Lexicon of the New Testament and other Christian Literature* (BDAG), such claims become very formidable—especially since they essentially agree. Of course, BDAG is a much more concise dictionary (not an en-

---

[97] TDNT I:749-61. I do not intend a wholesale negative assessment of this resource. Only of the apparent presuppositions that mar this particular article. For the quotes just given, see pp. 753 and 755.

cyclopedia), so all of the texts of the NT are listed according two main categories. According to BDAG, here are the meanings of the 50 occurrences of the word in the NT:[98]

a. individual ***scripture passage*** (12)
b. ***scripture in its entirety*** (38)
 α. the pl. *hai graphai* ["the writings"] designates collectively all the parts of Scripture [18]
 β. the sg. as a designation of Scripture as a whole [20]

Now, add to all of this that the article ends by quoting from the *Dictionnaire étymologique de la langue grecque:*

"Scripture" in the early Christian period always means the OT, and only after some passage of time was this term used in ref. to the writings of the NT. etc.[99]

With this kind of weight, why would anyone want to challenge it?

And so we all in unison recall the proverb, "Fools rush in where . . ." Or perhaps it is more like the visitors to Jurassic Park being advised to proceed cautiously.

And yet, how does one *not* proceed? For unfortunately, it appears that these articles are flawed to one degree or another by an underlying presupposition about canon. For example, (1) the TDNT article (on *graphē!)* makes numerous references to canon reflecting a particular set of presuppositions about it, even sporting a whole section titled "The Early Christian Canon" [100] and treating the two concepts as though they are intertwined. (2) It also appears that (for this article) the way we know that *graphē* means "Scripture" (instead of just "writing") is if it refers

---

[98] BDAG p. 206. This is a direct quoting of major sections, with original emphasis kept in-tact. The numbers on each line are added. Although there were some minor changes between the 2nd and 3rd editions, they are essentially the same.

[99] BDAG p. 206d. The French dictionary was published in 1968 and is available at http://www.archive.org/details/Dictionnaire-Etymologique-Grec

[100] p. 756.

to a canonical document. (3) The claim that *"'Scripture' in the early Christian period always means the OT"* implies a finished OT.[101] And (5) finally, even the language of the BDAG article of *"the designation of Scripture as a whole"* lends the notion that there is such a thing as a completed whole.

In contrast to this, instead of reading such texts while assuming a completed "whole" for the OT (as these articles tend to do), or assuming a one-volume, 66-book Bible (as many Protestants do by default), it might be helpful to imagine a variety of rooms in various locations (not all locations necessarily the same as another), each stocked with one or several or many individual scrolls rolled and neatly stacked on a shelf with sides to hold-in the scrolls. Then, while writing, scribes of NT documents (authors) would nearly always speak

1. in the *singular* if they wanted to point to a particular document or passage in a scroll: "the sacred text says" or "this sacred text says" or "it says" or "it is written" or something similar meaning "this particular text";

2. in the *plural* if they wanted to refer to several scrolls or make a general undefined reference: "the sacred texts" or "according to the sacred texts" or "holy texts" or something of that nature.

In other words, they did not think of "the Bible," as if they had a completed whole; they rather thought of "texts" (whether passages or documents) in terms of a large number of individual scrolls, some a well-defined collection (like the Law) and some not well defined at all. Even the collection called "the Prophets" is not entirely defined, either by books included, or by a particular text being used, or by a given order.

The following account from 2Macc 2:13-15 gives a sense of what a collection of books might have been like and reminds us

---

[101] Even if that is not the intention. Clearly the point of the quote was that NT documents were not called "scripture" until later. But we can't talk about "the OT" without implying that the canon is closed.

that scrolls were considered precious, and they were often unavailable to many:

> *Now these things are told about in the public records as well as in the annals of Nehemiah. It is also said that he established a library and collected scrolls about the **kings as well as the prophets**, and the **scrolls of David**, and **letters of kings** about offerings involving vows. In this same way Judas [Maccabeus] also brought together all the **scrolls that had been lost** on account of the war which had befallen us, and they are with us now. So if you find yourself in need of them, send those who might take them along for you.* [An early example of interlibrary loan!]

Another good example is the collection of books by the Qumran community, which (at the very time of Jesus and Paul) included manuscripts from all OT documents except Esther, many documents of the Apocrypha and Pseudepigrapha, and other documents, many of which the community itself apparently authored and considered as additional scripture (such as the Temple Scroll at the very least). In fact, these "new" documents, produced by the community, reveal that the sectarian agendas of the community guided all interpretations of so called "standard texts" (from our viewpoint). It must also be remembered that they did not refer to these texts as "OT" or "Apocrypha and Pseudepigrapha" and it is improper to speak of a settled canon in that community, since it is clear that the Qumran library only included what would have been considered sacred texts useful for their pursuits and agendas. This was not a "secular library" and all documents were kept and copied in keeping with the religious and sectarian ends of the community.

Again, the point here, in both of these cases, is not about a striving towards a closed canon of some kind (although some try to read such texts in that manner), but a collection of a wide variety of highly coveted (precious) scrolls considered sacred by those collecting them. Having such collections does not mean they had any sense of a "canon consciousness," as if they ever had a thought "we need to be whittling these down to just the right books that God has already decided." Nor can it be supposed that all such collections of this kind would have been identical with each other.

So then, although this may all come across as extremely gnat-straining to some people, the question, here, is fundamental and quite basic: **How does our own Bible use the term that is often translated as "scripture"?** And when we learn that the answer is: *"The Biblical documents use the term quite differently than we do!"* we should be concerned about this.

The reason this can be difficult for 21st century English readers to see is our own very imprecise use of the term "Scripture" to mean not only the whole completed Protestant Canon, but *only* the completed Protestant Canon or texts found in it. We then impose that meaning (consciously or not) onto the texts we read.

It would help us to discern a more biblical connotation of the word if we were to substitute the words "sacred writing(s)" or "sacred text(s)" for the word "scripture(s)"—both for all of the texts (discussed above) and for the NT texts. **It is not that the word "scripture" is wrong (of course not!), or that I am proposing a ban on its use (again, of course not!).** But keeping such a substitute in mind could help us check our own baggage.

With all of this in mind, each text in which the word occurs should be reevaluated as to usage. That is what we have been about so far, and now we will give attention to NT texts (albeit inadequately and hurriedly). And because of all of the baggage attached, I will (as a personal discipline) use the word "scripture" sparingly.

2. Specific NT Texts

Several specific texts stand out and deserve special comment for how *hē graphē* is used as a singular.

a. Paul (& Peter)

We will begin with **Paul**, by all accounts the earliest Christian writer.[102] **Gal 3:8** "The sacred writing (*he graphē*) foreseeing that God justifies the Gentiles by faith" refers specifically to Gen 12:3 which Paul is unpacking by way of numerous other texts (Gen 15:6; Dt 27:26; Hab 2:4; Lev 18:5; Dt 21:23). The main subject is Gen 12:3 all along (that is to say, Gen 12:3 is being exegeted by using the other texts), and the issue is "promise vs. law." So, in **Gal 3:22** "The sacred writing (*hē graphē*) consigned all things to sin"—even though it is a personification (surely, God is speaking ... to Abraham!)—is specifically the same text as quoted in 3:8: the promise to Abraham. There is no contextual call to force upon this a notion of a "whole (canon of the) OT."

Rom 1:2 ("holy writings" *graphais hagiais*) is not singular, but plural; but along with **2Tim 3:15** ("sacred books" *hiera grammata*—also pl), these are the only texts in the NT that qualify the writings in the way Philo routinely did, and Josephus once (of his two uses of *graphē*). Even so, the plural use of *graphē* signaled such an "undefined" quality even without the qualifier.

Other Pauline texts using *hē graphē* (singular, and often said to be designating "Scripture as a whole") are clearly introducing specific texts. For example: **Rom 4:3** is a classic case: "For what does the sacred text say? 'Abraham believed God ...'" (Gen 15:6). Frankly, this is so straightforward and classic, it is baffling how this can be taken as "scripture as a whole"—unless it is being read into it. The same is true for **Rom 9:17** (Ex 9:16); **Rom 10:11** (Isa 28:16); and **Gal 4:30** (Gen 21:10).

Even **Acts 8:32** (Isa 53:7) should be read this way:

Now the passage of the sacred text (periochē tēs graphēs) which he was reading was this: "As a sheep led to the slaughter...."

---

[102] Of course, there were certainly earlier "Jesus traditions" both oral and written, and some of those end up in the Gospels (and some in Paul) one way or another. However, I speak of completed documents which we now have.

This is clearly not a reference to "scripture as a whole," but to the sacred scroll of Isaiah the prophet, from which he was reading (Acts 8:30). The very same is true of **1Pet 2:6** which is not only singular (*he graphē*), but then quotes the very text it is talking about (Isa 28:16).

In **2Tim 3:16-17**, "Every sacred writing or text" is singular and should be translated that way, as it matches every singular use found in the NT. As with other similar texts ("holy" **Rom 1:2**; "prophetic" **Rom 16:26** and **2Pet 1:20**; "another" **Jn 19:37**) this text as a qualifier ("every") and helps to form the guideline stated earlier. This does not refer to some imaginary "whole of scripture," nor is it a statement for a collection of books or a canon any more than any other use of the singular term. "Every" is actually undefined and unlimited. The focus is on the inner nature: the inspiration and usefulness of every sacred text for very specific purposes: "instruction, reproof, correction, discipline in righteousness, to bring the 'spokesperson for God'[103] to complete preparation."

This practical purpose is to be compared to the similar kinds of goals stated in **Rom 15:4**, which, after quoting a specific text (LXX Ps 68:9)[104], notes that

> *whatever was written long ago was written for our instruction so that through patience and through the encouragement of **the [sacred] writings** (tōn graphōn—pl) we might have hope.*

Once again, these writings (being plural) are undefined and unlimited. What they included or did not include beyond the text just quoted prior to this comment (LXX Ps 68:9) is not specified. That is not Paul's concern. To assume a specific OT canon and to read that into this text actually puts limits on the text that it

---

[103] Literally, "man of God," which is used also in 1Tim 6:11 to describe Timothy's role. This is a phrase used for Moses, Elijah, Elisha, David, and others, all clearly prophets speaking on behalf of God, especially in 1-2Kings.

[104] In the Psalms, the LXX numbers are often one less than in English. So, LXX Ps 68 is English Ps 69.

does not support. This is, instead, a general comment about the value of sacred texts starting with a specific text. The focus is on their intrinsic usefulness and applicability, not on their extent or limits.

b. James

Turning now to **Js 4:5-6,** this text offers a special challenge when it quotes two texts in a context of warning against friendship with the world: [105]

> *Or do you think the sacred text (he graphē) says in vain,*
> *"The spirit which he has caused to dwell in us craves to the*
> *point of jealousy, but he gives the more grace." That is*
> *why it says: "God opposes the proud, but he gives grace to*
> *the humble."*

It is well-known that we have no outside record of the first quote (said to be *he graphē*), and so some (including our sources above) suggest that this is a general reference to the "whole of Scripture." If so, it is extremely awkward, for according to what tradition or standard does the "whole of Scripture" (whatever that is supposed to mean) make such a specific and obtuse claim?

This problem is compounded when seen in the light of **all six unknown quotes in the NT:**[106] **Jn 7:38**; 1Cor 9:10; 2Cor 4:6; Eph 5:14; **1Tim 5:18**; **Js 4:5**—all of which utilize standard practice for quoting a specific resource. Are we to understand that these are all "general references to Scripture as a whole"? If so, they are all very specific summarizations and all completely different. No, these are all specific quotations of resources now lost to us, or unrecognized by us. (Compare this with Josephus Ap 2:45 cited above.) Furthermore, it is not even clear that a written text is always the source, since the author might be quot-

---

[105] Js 4:5 is translated differently by various translations (e.g., KJV and NIV vs. NRSV) due to a somewhat vague text. But the point for us now is not the precise meaning so much as the manner of quotation.

[106] English translations sometimes make it difficult to tell that a now unknown resource is being referenced, but these are recognized and clearly marked in NA27 (see the copyright page of this book) on 806.

ing an early Christian hymn (as in Eph 5:14) or other possible popular aphorisms (as perhaps, 1Tim 5:18b). We may be tempted and tried and oft made to wonder why it should be thus all the day long, but as it says: "We'll understand it all by and by."

As for Js 4:5, it is clear that this text follows a very specific pattern for quotation, with all the right elements (definite article + *graphē* + direct quote) it is more natural to conclude that James refers to a specific text or resource that he (and his readers?) knew but that is now lost to us.

This is not at all different from the OT and Apocryphal patterns we looked at earlier. Regardless of how much angst this causes those who want to make sure that only books in our canon are called *"he graphē"* there is no reason to treat this text (or any of these texts) differently than the standard usage.

c. John

(1) This brings us, finally, to the Gospel of **John** which has 12 occurrences of the word *graphē* (more than all the Synoptic Gospels combined), all of them (with three possible exceptions—see below) in line with the standard usage already laid out. However, it should be noted for John, that normally, just because he does not name the source or give a specific quote, does not mean that no specific reference is in mind. So then, **Jn 2:22** is referring very specifically to the whole context of Ps 69 which was directly quoted four verses earlier (69:10 at Jn 2:17);[107] **Jn 5:39** is plural and is a typical general reference to undefined "sacred writings"; **Jn 13:18** quotes Ps 41:10; **Jn 17:12** speaks of the "son of destruction" compared to "children of destruction" in LXX Isa 57:4 (cf. thematically Ps 41:9);

---

[107] It is not uncommon for NT quotations to pull from the larger context when quoting a specific verse from the OT or other texts. For example, Psalm 69 is quoted or alluded to in John at least in Jn 2:17; 15:25; and 19:28. However, even this list is not sufficient, in that it does not take into account other possible subtleties to be found within texts—see more on this below under (d) Jn 20:9. Furthermore, Psalm 69 is quoted or overtly alluded to in eight other NT documents—which means this was a popular Christological Psalm among early Christians.

Jn 19:24 quotes Ps 22:19; **Jn 19:28** once again quotes Ps 69, now verse 22 (cf. above at Jn 2:22); **Jn 19:36** quotes LXX Ex 12:46 as a reference to the Passover lamb (cf. Ps 34:21); and **Jn 19:37** specifically cites Zech 12:10. All of these uses are as one would expect from other uses in our literature.

(2) **Jn 10:34-35** deserves special attention. This text mentions three important phrases that are sometimes confused by readers:

> *Has it not been written in* **your law**, *"I said, you are gods!" If he called those people gods, to whom the* **word of God** *came (and* **the sacred writing** *[hē graphē] cannot be nullified!)—then how dare you say: "You blaspheme!" when I—the one whom the Father sanctified and sent into the world—say: "I am the Son of God!"*

"*Your* law" (actually LXX Ps 81:6, which shows that this is not a reference to any special category, but rather to "your sacred writings") is not a repudiation of the law of Moses, but a statement that "even *you* accept this as authority." The "word of God" is not at all referring to some imaginary completed canon of Scripture here, but points directly to the "*I said*"—the word that God spoke! The claim that the sacred writing (*graphē*—sg) cannot be "nullified" (destroyed, torn down, ruined) is a clear reference back to the specific quote from LXX Ps 81:6 and to its authority. So (says Jesus), the authority of the quoted sacred writing not only shows that God spoke to *them;* it shows that he now speaks "*in me.*" This is not a "general reference to scripture as a whole," as advocated by some.

(3) **The Quotes of "Known Conclusion":** Three texts in John deserve special attention because they are different from all other uses we have seen anywhere in any text by any author. This usage represents a new direction in the use of the term, a direction that will be picked up, enhanced, and developed by later Christian writers—all the way down to today. I will call these the quotes of "known conclusion" and they are found in **Jn 7:38, 42; and 20:9.** Let's set them out to see them clearly:

Jn 7:38 *As the sacred text (hē graphē) says, "Rivers of living water will flow out of his heart."*

John 7:42 *Did not the sacred text (hē graphē) say, "The Christ comes from the family of David and from Bethlehem, David's home village"?*

John 20:9 *For they did not yet understand the sacred text (hē graphē), "It is necessary for him to rise from the dead."*

Problem: none of these quotes exists anywhere in our literature—even though they are all specifically called *hē graphē*.

Clarification: We peeked at the first quote already in the previous section; but if you look up the last two in your Bible you will see that they are both translated as "indirect discourse," not as direct quotes, as above. Indirect discourse would look like this: *Did not the sacred text say that the Christ would come from Bethlehem, etc.?* Actually, I agree with that practice and that the last two are better translated as indirect discourse.

However . . . I want to make a point right here, and that is why I translated them all as direct quotations: **(1) all three texts have *hē graphē*; (2) all three texts set up their quotes essentially the same way; and (3) not one of the quotes exists in our literature.** Regardless how we end up translating the texts, these similarities should at least cause us to look more closely at them.[108]

In standard approaches, these three texts are seen as distinctive because the first is said to be an unknown scripture, and the last two are said *not* to be specific quotes, but *general summar-*

---

[108] The presence of ὅτι ("that") in the last two is of little consequence. I could offer a long footnote here discussing the details of direct and indirect discourse in translation, but I'll spare you. See instead the detailed discussions in Daniel B. Wallace *Greek Grammar Beyond the Basics: An Exegetical Syntax of the New Testament* (Zondervan, 1996), pp. 454-457; A. T. Robertson, *A Grammar of the Greek New Testament in the Light of Historical Research* (Broadman Press: 1934), pp. 442 and 1027-32.

ies of "scripture as a whole."[109] As I have continually noted, this language is objectionable and should *at least* be stated as *"general summaries of an undefined nature."* With that stipulation, it is certainly possible that such exceptions in usage of the singular of *graphē* can occur. If that is so in these cases, then these texts are exceptions to what we have been seeing from all the other texts and authors. It is certainly possible, and I do not want to imply that exceptions cannot occur.[110]

However, I am going to suggest an alternative to the standard explanation, namely, that none of them is a reference to "Scripture in general" (and certainly not to "Scripture as a whole"—since there clearly was no whole!). It is fine if interpreters go searching for specific texts that might apply; however, that is not the point of these quotes. **Instead, these are references to known conclusions (i.e., widely shared traditions) about the topic at hand, all of which have become well-known by the author and readers, almost to the point of being a proverb or at least a general truth widely accepted. And John called these *hē graphē*.**

An illustration of this would be someone today saying

I believe in disciplining (but not abusing) children, since **the Bible says** *'Spare the rod and spoil the child.'"*

Or perhaps:

*"**The Bible says** 'Cleanliness is next to Godliness.'"*

Now, most people know that neither of these quotes is found in the Bible. But they believe the principle is taught. It is a widely shared conviction, a "known conclusion." This is not a summary of the whole Bible, nor is it designed to cause one to think of any

---

[109] Once again, BDAG p. 206 and TDNT on *graphē*, but this is also standard in the commentaries.

[110] As a matter of fact, it is these texts in particular that help interpreters to feel justified in generalizing this perceived usage for other texts, where *hē graphē* is said to refer to "Scripture as a whole." I have tried to show that such an approach is based more on assumption than on paying careful attention to details of texts on a broad range.

particular verse or collection of verses. This is not, for example, equal to the plural uses of *graphē* we have seen over and over again, such as in the phrase, "according to the scriptures." It is not even as specific as Heb 2:6: "Someone has testified somewhere"! In other words, the quote is not given to make you go tracking down one text or another; **it is rather given for its own sake as itself stating the principle adequately.** In effect, it is taking the place of sacred texts and therefore itself becomes sacred text (written or not). It is traditional interpretation handed down alongside the written text representing written text.

This is not at all unheard of. We noticed earlier that Josephus, for example, demonstrates this throughout his writings by retelling the history of his people from the holy writings: and he meant by this both written and spoken text.

> *Josephus understood the sacred writings to include more than just the written biblical text . . . The Pharisees also accepted the Paradosis of the Fathers—traditions handed down.*[111]

Christians today don't want anything to do with the Pharisees (at least in theory), so my suggestion will sound to some like sacrilege. But it is not sacrilege. It isn't even non-biblical. In fact, *paradosis* is a perfectly good word used twice by Paul (a former Pharisee) to indicate the body of *Christian teaching* that he himself was handing down (1Cor 11:2 and 2Th 2:15). Note especially the emphasis on oral and written *paradosis* in the second of these texts:

> *So then, brothers and sister, stand firm and grasp onto the **paradoseis** (pl= "traditions handed down") which you were taught **whether by spoken word or written letter.***

Notice: Paul does not distinguish these, nor give more weight to one over the other! The emphasis placed on the oral and written

---

[111] Savage, "*Josephus*, pp. i.

teaching was a part of Christianity from its inception. We will especially notice this when we look at the phrase "Word of God" a couple of chapters from now. So then, by looking closely at Paul's letters, it is clear that this "Christian Paradosis" included things he had received by revelation, from written sacred texts, from his former life as a Pharisee, the sayings of Jesus, early Christian confessions, hymns, and much more.[112]

My suggestion that the Gospel of John is reflecting this use of Christian teaching—in a similar manner as Paul, but with different emphases—is not at all new. It is commonly known, for example, among those who study the Gospel of John with any degree of seriousness, that John and the Synoptics are independent of one another. That is to say, although Matthew and Luke co-opted Mark's Gospel and reshaped it and added more materials to it in keeping with the needs and purposes of each, John is completely independent of the Synoptic tradition. As one scholar on John has written:

All similarities between them can be accounted for by shared tradition, whether written or oral, which John used without access to the Synoptics . . . which does not rule out eyewitness recollection.[113]

The existence of such early and widespread Christian tradition— both oral and written (in many forms that did not survive)—was both pervasive and formative for early communities of faith.

Applying this understanding especially to the three otherwise unknown quotes attributed to *hē graphē* in the Gospel of John can be revealing. However, it is not enough to *suggest* it; it must be *demonstrated*—at least to show the possibility.

---

[112] For a good summary of such things, along with a fine bibliography, see M. B. Thompson, "Tradition" in *Dictionary of Paul and His Letters* (IVP 1993), pp. 943-45.

[113] M. M. Thompson, "John, Gospel of" in The Dictionary of Jesus and the Gospels (IVP: 1992), p. 375.

3. John 20:9 and Shared Traditions

Turning, then, to **Jn 20:9:** this text brings us to a particularly interesting phenomenon in the NT when it states about Peter and "the other disciple" at the tomb:

For they did not yet understand the sacred text that it was necessary for him to rise up from the dead.

oudepō gar	ē̦deisan	tēn graphēn
For not yet	*did they understand*	*the sacred text*

dei	autōn	ek nekrōn	anastēnai
[that] it is necessary	*for him*	*from the dead*	*to arise.*

Very specifically, this is not merely a statement that it was necessary for Jesus to rise from the dead, but that *the sacred text* (*he graphē*) showed that it was necessary.

The question is, does the Gospel of John itself make or build this case? If so, where and how? And, is this the language (especially *dei* and *anistēmi*) used by John to discuss the topic as resulting from *hē graphē* (sacred text)?

a. Words and Phrases

We'll take Jn 20:9 one phrase at a time, in something of a commentary style:

oudepō gar ē̦deisan lit. "For not yet did they understand."

This concept not only *occurs* within the Gospel of John, it is a thoroughgoing *motif.*[114] Furthermore, when it is stated that the disciples "do not understand" in this Gospel, it can be expressed either by *ou ginōskō*,[115] or by *ou oida*[116] as here in 20:9.

---

[114] A motif is a recurring element in a narrative that has some kind of significance for the overall story.

[115] For *ginōskō* see specifically Jn 3:10; 8:27; 8:43; 10:6; and 12:16. For *oida* see Jn 13:7; 16:18; and 20:9. There is a tendency for English translations to render *ginōskō* as "understand" more often than *oida*. For example 13:7 is possibly "You do not *know* (*oida*) what I am doing, but later you will *under-*

This motif appears often.[117] However, when said of the disciples that they did not understand, it is tied closely to being *reminded by the Spirit* after Jesus was raised from the dead or glorified. This motif throughout the story helps to explain the disbelief, slowness, or confusion of the closest disciples in the face of what *readers* can see is overwhelming evidence. However, this is more than "hindsight is 20/20"; it is rather that this is what Jesus said would happen, and the Spirit was given to effect it. This motif also helps to prepare readers for what is supposed to happen to *them.* We'll take each occurrence for the disciples, one at a time:

1. Early-on in the Gospel at **2:22** (Cleansing the Temple), after Psalm 69 is directly quoted, the *Jewish leaders* argued with him. Then it is said that when Jesus was *raised from the dead* (*ēgerthē ek vekrōn*), **the disciples remembered** his promise that he would raise up (*egeirō*) the destroyed temple (his body) in three days. (The reason for "three" days is not stated in John.)[118] So it says that the disciples,

---

stand (*ginōskō*)"; or John 21:17 where Peter felt hurt "and he said to him, "Lord, you know (*oida*) everything; you understand (*ginōskō*) that I love you." Even so, it would be easy to make too much of this since the two words are often used interchangeably. In this Gospel, *oida* occurs 70 times compared to 49 times for *ginōskō*. The two words occur together in Jn 7:27; 8:55; 13:7; 16:18-19; 21:17 (see elsewhere in the NT at 1 Jn 2:29; 1 Jn 5:20; Mt 24:43; Mk 4:13; Lk 12:39; Rom 7:7; 1Cor 2:11; 2Cor 5:16; Eph 5:5; Heb 8:11). Referring to a special sense, Bultmann (TDNT "γινώσκω" 1:711) notes that this word, in addition to its ordinary usage, plays a greater role in John and 1John "than in any other Christian writing" speaking (in some texts) of the relationship "to God and Jesus as a personal fellowship" (e.g., 10:38; 14:11; 17:21, and others). As with all "meanings," such specialized senses are clearly garnered from contexts and not the word itself.

[116] Jn 13:7 and 16:18

[117] Jn 3:10; 8:27; 8:43; 10:6; 12:16; 13:7; 16:18; and 20:9

[118] "Three days" is mentioned in the Gospel of John only twice (both in 2:19-20). No rationale is provided. "Third day" is at 2:1 and is unrelated. It is a fact that no number of days in the OT, Apocrypha, and NT occurs more than "three days/third day" (129 times) except the number "seven/seventh day" (173 times). Next is "first day" (52), "forty days" (31), six (21), two (13), ten (12), eight (9), five (7), and four (6). "Nine days" does not occur. There is special significance to the number 3.

later (when looking back), believed the sacred text (Psalm 69) as well as what Jesus had said about himself.

2. About the middle of the Gospel at **12:16** (Triumphal Entry), after Zechariah 9 is directly quoted, it is said once again that **the disciples did not understand (*egnōsan*) at first,** but only after Jesus was "glorified" (which included the crucifixion, resurrection, and ascension as the divine plan of God, cf. 12:27-33).

3. In **13:7**, when Jesus took up a towel to wash the disciples' feet, Jesus says to Peter: "You don't *know* (*oida*) what I'm doing now, but later you will *understand* (*ginōskō*) it." The point of both is understanding, not that Jesus was hiding his actions so they could not see. Again, the focus is on an understanding that will come later.

4. In 16:18, we find the same paring of words as in 13:7. Jesus prepares his disciples that "yet a little while and you will see me no more." But they are confused: "We do not understand (*oida*) what he is talking about!' But Jesus perceived (*ginōskō*) what they were thinking." The point again is how lack of understanding results in coming to know, for "you will be sad, but your sadness will turn to joy" (16:20).

5. Related to the above four comments, it is explained within the Gospel that the disciples had not yet received the Spirit (**7:39**) who would **remind them** (later) **of all that Jesus had said (14:26)** and would make them witnesses (**15:26-16:23**).

6. So then, at the end of the Gospel, **20:9** is part of the "disciples remembering/being reminded" motif that is found throughout the Gospel.

This motif of "understanding" does not itself carry with it a connotation of "necessity." (This will become clearer below.)

ek nekrōn anastēnai lit. "from the dead to arise."

Specific Terminology: On the one hand, there is actually very little talk in the Gospel of John that uses the specific language of "rise up" and "resurrection" (*anistēmi, anastasis, egeirō*) specifically for Jesus' own resurrection. Most all such language occurs in the first half of the book (in what is commonly called the "Book of Signs," 1:19-12:50).

1. As noted above, **2:19** uses *egeirō* ("raise up") twice when **Jesus promises to raise up himself**. Jesus is said to show zeal for the Temple (Ps 69:10, which is directly quoted), and then Jesus says "Destroy this temple and in three days *I will raise it up*." Although the following is not specifically brought out in John's Gospel, Psalm 69 in its entirety provides the backdrop for this text, speaking of covenant loyalty, rescue, deliverance, salvation, and even not letting *"the pit close its mouth over me"* (69:15). Here is a sacred text that could easily have been understood by early Christians as referring to resurrection. Nothing about *necessity* is stated or implied in this text of John or in this Psalm.

2. In **6:39, 40, 44, 54, Jesus promises to raise up others.** In the last part of the "bread from heaven" story, Jesus says that he (as the true bread) comes down from heaven bringing eternal life. He then promises (four times) that for each one drawn to him by the Father and who eats his flesh and drinks his blood: "I will *raise that one up* at the last day."

3. In **11:23-24, Jesus raises up Lazarus.** Jesus promises that Lazarus will rise from the dead, and he proclaims to Martha: "I am the resurrection and the life." And with a simple "Come out," Lazarus comes out of the tomb.

4. In **20:9** our quote occurs. It is the only text so far that says anything about "necessity."

5. In **21:14**, there is a side comment about "the third time Jesus was revealed since he was *raised from the dead*" (*egertheis ek nekrōn*).

Look at what *does not* occur: we might expect to find clear reference to the resurrection of Jesus using the language mentioned in 20:9, namely, "I rise up, resurrection, or I raise up" (*anistēmi, anastasis, egeirō*). But it is not there. The second half of the Gospel (commonly called the "Book of Glory," 13:1-20:31) does not have the specific "resurrection" terminology *at all* (except in the two incidental quotes at 20:9 and 21:14).

As to what *does* occur: aside from 20:9, only the first and the last (2:19 and 21:14) speak of Jesus' own bodily resurrection. The middle text (Jn 11:23-24) speaks ultimately of Jesus as "the resurrection and the life." However, there is nothing in any of these texts that makes any point at all that sacred texts showed the *necessity* for it. So far, only Psalm 69 has been referred to overtly, but not for the purpose of indicating resurrection. So far, only Jn 20:9 makes this claim.[119]

Pervasive Witness: On the other hand, we cannot leave this topic about the specific terminology of "resurrection" (*anistēmi, anastasis, egeirō*) without acknowledging the absolutely **pervasive witness throughout the Gospel of John to Jesus' own resurrection from the dead even apart from specific words**—the concept is literally woven into the fabric of the entire Gospel (from start to finish) without using the specific terms mentioned above.

Too many to rehearse here, it is sufficient to note that (1) Jesus is from the beginning and from heaven.[120] (2) He continually says: "I'm leaving for the Father," "I'm going to the Father," "Father I'm coming to you," "where I'm going, you (disci-

---

[119] Certainly, John's Gospel is greatly steeped in its reflection upon many sacred texts and ancient concepts (such as Psalm 69). However, much of that is in the background; the Gospel does not appear—so far—to be developing any kind of overt "case" that sacred texts show the *necessity* for Jesus to rise up from the dead.

[120] Jn 1:1-13; 3:33 and others.

ples) can't come," "I'm only here a little while longer," "I'm going back where I came from," and other such language.[121] (3) He says "my hour has not yet come" and then "my hour has now come."[122] (4) He says "I have the power to lay down my life, and the power to take up again.[123] And especially (5) he speaks of his glorification, that the time for his glorification had come, and he prays to the Father "Glorify me!"[124] (6) All of this builds up to the incredibly touching and powerful moment of the already raised but not yet ascended Jesus looking at a distraught woman in obvious pain and speaking her name in Aramaic: "Mariam." And turning around (which can have the double meaning of physically turning and of coming to faith) she replies, also in Aramaic, "Rabbouni" (Teacher). This breathtaking moment is the essence of resurrection—where individuals are personally touched and changed forever.

So then, what started as a limited number of specific texts focused on Jesus' resurrection, ends up as a vast testimonial sea of interrelated phrases, concepts, and allusions. Every part is steeped in reflection on sacred texts; and yet, there is still no effort—so far—to overtly develop a case that sacred texts speak of the *necessity* of Jesus rising from the dead.

dei autōn lit. "it is necessary for him."

Now comes the word (*dei*) at 20:9—translated "it is necessary." It shows up ten times in the Gospel of John, but hardly as

---

[121] Jn 1:18; 6:52; 7:33; 13:33; 16:5; 16:10; 16:16; 16:28; 17:11; 17:13; 20:17; 20:19; 20:26; 21:1; 21:14.

[122] Jn 2:4; 7:30 ; 8:20; 12:23, 27; 13:1; 17:1.

[123] Jn 10:17-18 where the verbs for "lay down" and "take up" are *tithēmi* and *lambanō*—the only use of *lambanō* to refer to resurrection in the Gospel.

[124] See Jn 7:39; 12:16; 12:23; 13:31; 16:14; 17:1; 17:5 ; 17:10. Jesus' glorification in the Gospel of John is very important and includes the betrayal, trial, and crucifixion as much as the resurrection and ascension: it is all one picture, one design by God. And so we find the powerful statement at 12:27: "So now I have a troubled soul! And what shall I say, 'Father save me from this hour'? No! This is why I came—for this very hour! Father glorify your name!"

a motif (rather, as scattered references on a variety of things).[125] Interestingly again (as with the words on resurrection), aside from 20:9, the word only occurs in the first part of the Gospel (1:19-12:50, the "Book of the Signs").

Two uses of this word are of special interest in three closely related "Son of Man" texts:

1. **3:13-14**—At the end of the Nicodemus story, Jesus says, "You're a teacher in Israel and don't know what being born from above means?" He then says: "No one has ascended into heaven, except the one who descended from heaven: the Son of Man. Just as Moses lifted up the serpent in the desert, **so it is necessary** (*dei*) **for the Son of Man to be lifted up,** so that everyone who believes in him might have eternal life." Moses lifting the serpent is an overt reference to Num 21:9, but the comment which follows ("so it is necessary for the Son of Man to be lifted up, etc. . .") is not overtly attributed to any source and may simply look like a comment by Jesus on the action of Moses. As such, the word "lifted up" (*hupsoō*) in Jesus' reply is new to us here in John. It seems to show up out of nowhere in place of the expected words "rise up, resurrection, raise up" (*anistēmi, anastasis, egeirō*) used elsewhere in the Gospel. It occurs only three times in the entire Gospel, standing out, as it were, in a sea of standard language on resurrection (as described above).

---

[125] Jn 3:7; 3:14 ; 3:30; 4:4; 4:20; 4:24; 9:4; 10:16; 12:34; 20:9. In these texts, it is said that *it is necessary* to be born from above, for the Son of Man to be lifted up (indicating the type of death), for John the Baptist to decrease, to pass through Samaria, to worship in Jerusalem (according to the Jews), to worship in spirit and truth (according to Jesus), for Jesus to do the works of the one having sent him while it is day, and to bring the other sheep (not of this fold). This does not mean that no other ways exist in Greek for showing some kind of necessary action. We are following up on the word *dei* in Jn 20:9.

2. **8:28**—A full five chapters later, this concept is brought up again, not with *dei*, but with "lifted up" (*hupsoō*). So, after saying publicly "I'm from above" and "I'm telling you what the Father told me" and "I'm going away" and "where I'm going, you can't come" (8:21-27), Jesus says: "Whenever you **lift up the Son of Man, then you will know that *I am!*"** There is no overt reference to Moses here, as before. Instead, key words here are "lift up," "know," and "I am" (*hupsoō, ginōskō, and egō eimi*). Once again, it looks as though—on the surface—Jesus is merely giving his own comment.

3. **12:32-34**—Another four chapters and we arrive at the last of the three special "lifted up" Son of Man texts. Here we find once again both *dei* ("it is necessary") and *hupsoō* ("lifted up"). So, after announcing publicly that his hour has come, there are two signals of Jesus' authority: (1) a voice from heaven (heard by all) and (2) Jesus "calling out" the ruler of the world, promising to cast him out. What comes next is not a sign of defeat or weakness, but a sign of the beginning of the end for all who oppose God:

> *And so then I,* **when I am lifted up from the earth***, I shall draw all people to me. (Now he was saying this as a sign of what kind of death he was about to die.) Then the crowd answered him, "We have heard from the Law that the Christ 'remains forever'! So how do you say: 'It is **nec-essary** (dei) **for the Son of Man to be lifted up'?** Who is this Son of Man?*

All three "Son of Man" sayings (presented as public declarations) bring us the Gospel's most significant Christological claim: that it is necessary for the Son of Man to be "lifted up."

b. Wordplays and Keys

Let's get serious, now. All three texts (Jn 3:14; 8:28; 12:34) occur only in the Gospel of John. All three are linked together by the word *hupsoō* ("lifted up"), causing them to stand out among the thirteen Son of Man texts in the Gospel of John.[126] The word *hupsoō* ("lifted up") occurs in John only in these texts, and it stands in place of the expected words *anistēmi, anastasis, egeirō* ("rise up, resurrection, raise up"), redefining the central concern as "glorification," and including the death, the resurrection, and the ascension—all three.

So then, Jesus was to be "lifted up" from the earth (to die), which would portend his being lifted up into heaven with the Father. It has a double meaning, and it is all part of the same ultimate reality of being glorified.[127]

How did this happen? The answer is found in Num 21:9 as quoted at Jn 3:13 ("as Moses lifted up the serpent"). Num 21:9 says literally that Moses "stood up" (*estēsen*)[128] the serpent for people to look upon.[129] The word *estēsen* is past tense of *histēmi* ("to stand"), the root word from which comes *anistēmi* ("to rise"). So then, Jesus, in the Gospel of John, interprets the text to mean "lifted up," going from

---

[126] "Son of Man" occurs 13 times in John: Jn 1:51; **3:13-14**; 5:27; 6:27; 6:53; 6:62; **8:28**; 9:35; 12:23; **12:34a, 34b**; 13:31. The texts in bold all have "lifted up" and serve quite literally as the core of the sayings. These do not speak of the resurrection of Jesus in the typical terms. These three texts provide a pinnacle for understanding the glorification of the Son of Man; the surrounding texts provide a basic context of authority, judgment, and resurrection for these three. Jn 1:51 has angels ascending and descending on him as a sign of divine choosing; all the rest have to do with authority, judgment, resurrection, and glorification of the Son of Man and the importance of believing in him.

[127] Two things show that the word *hupsoō* ("lifted up") is used to imply *not only* resurrection and ascension, *but also* the events leading to and including death on the cross: (1) the reference to Moses lifting up the serpent; and (2) the phrase in 12:32 "He said this to show the kind of death he was to die." Not only that, "lifted up" (*hupsoō*) has a different meaning in John than anywhere else. The word "I lift up" (*hupsoō*) occurs 16 times in the NT. The only ones that refer to Jesus as "lifted up" are our texts in Jn 3:14; 8:28; 12:32; 12:34 and also Acts 2:33 and 5:31. **Only John implies that lifting up on the cross portends the resurrection and ascension.** Acts refers only to being "lifted up" (exalted) at the right hand of God.

[128] The Hebrew of Num 21:9 (שִׂים, *sum*) means "to set, establish, place."

[129] This is the same word as Jn 7:37 in which Jesus stood himself up and cried out "Let anyone who is thirsty come to me."

$$histēmi \rightarrow [anistēmi] \rightarrow hupsoō$$

"stood up" → ["arise"] → "lifted up"

(Num 21:9) → **(Jn 3:13)**

By interpreting the text in this way—"Moses **lifted up** the serpent," rather than "stood up"—he thereby reflects a link to **Isa
52:13**, even though it is not overtly quoted. That text says:

> *Behold, my servant shall understand (suniēmi), and **he
> shall be lifted up** (hupsoō) and he **shall be glorified**
> (doxazō) exceedingly.*

These have become key words and concepts in the Gospel of
John.[130] Isaiah 52 is also important in the wider Christological
tradition, including "I am" (v. 6 cf. Jn 8:28); the announcing of
good news (v. 7); the form and appearance of the servant (v. 14),
and the emphasis upon knowing or understanding (vv. 6, 13, and
15).[131]

From this we can see that Num 21:9 is not the main text; it is
only the cover text—a kind of entry text. It actually provides the
hermeneutical key that calls up and unlocks **Isaiah 52**, the true
main text that stands quietly in the background of the Gospel's
claim.

Interpretive wordplays, such as moving between "stood up"
and "lifted up," were actually not that unusual. For example, it
can be seen in 1Cor 10:7 when Paul quotes Ex 32:4 ("People sat
down . . . and rose up") as a means of unlocking and interpreting Numbers 11.[132] Also, a similar wordplay existed in Qumran

---

[130] For "glorify" see Jn 7:39; 8:54; 11:4; 12:16; 12:23; 12:28; 13:31; 13:32;
14:13; 15:8; 16:14; 17:1; 17:4; 17:5; 17:10; 21:19. For "lifted up" see above. For
suniēmi, this word does not occur in John at all. There is only a conceptual link
with the words *ginōskō* and *oida*, as discussed earlier under the motif of remembering. Isa 52:6 *gnōsetai* from *gignōskō* (<*ginōskō*), which in John, as we saw
above, is an important motif in the Gospel of John. The word *suniēmi* occurs at
Isa 52:13 and 15. It is a synonym of *ginōskō*, "to know, perceive, or understand."

[131] Isaiah 52 is quoted or alluded to at least 23 times by all the NT authors
except the authors of Mark, James, Jude, and Hebrews.

[132] See Gary D. Collier, "'That We Might Not Crave Evil': The Structure and
Argument of 1 Corinthians 10:1-13." *Journal for the Study of the New Testament* 55 (1994) 55-75.

texts perhaps two centuries before the Gospel of John was written. 4Q175 (often called 4QTestimonia)[133] is a document which links four messianic texts together based on a word play between the Hebrew words ʿamad / qum ("stand"/"rise").

Dt 18:18-19 I will <u>raise</u> up a prophet (*qum*)
Num 24:15-17 The star of Jacob will <u>rise</u> (*qum*)
Dt 23:8-11 Role of the Priest (enemies will not <u>rise</u>) (*qum*)
Josh 6:26 Evil brothers have <u>arisen</u> (ʿamad)

Once the texts are connected, interpretation ensues between the texts as if they belong together.

The point is not that John copied Paul or the Qumran scrolls; the point is rather that this kind of interpretation (awkward for us) was not new or out of line for them. So then, the author of the Gospel used the word "stood up" (in Num 21:9) as a bridge between "rise up" in the rest of his Gospel (and perhaps the rest of Christian tradition), and "lifted up" in the Isaiah text. In this way, he calls up Isaiah 52, which is the silent partner in the background of all three of these texts (Jn 3:14; 8:28; 12:34). Using Isaiah 52 ("lifted up", "glorified"), he reinterprets the meaning of the resurrection tradition to include the arrest, trial, conviction, crucifixion along with the resurrection and ascension: and it is all part of Jesus being "glorified." The bottom line then, was that for Jesus to be glorified, it was necessary for him to be lifted up.

c. Synoptic Tradition

With all of the above, a particular puzzle remains: why does the Gospel of John go to all the trouble throughout his Gospel to reinterpret the resurrection tradition in terms of the necessity for the Son of Man to be "lifted up," and then at the end to resort to language that he uses nowhere else in the entire Gospel?

For they did not yet understand the sacred text that it was necessary for him to rise up from the dead.

---

[133] Vermes, *Dead Sea Scrolls*, pp. 295-96.

oudepō gar ē₁deisan tēn graphēn
dei autōn ek nekrōn anastēnai.

Admittedly, especially to most English readers, this does not seem all that different. However, it is not the same. Actually, **the statement in Jn 20:9 is closer in wording to the Gospel of Mark** (most likely the earliest Gospel) **than to what is elsewhere in John!** Why?

For this, it is helpful to compare John with the synoptic tradition.

In fact, Mark makes this concept a key element in Jesus' own teaching (**Mk 8:31; [9:9-10;] 9:31; and 10:33**).

*And he began to teach them: "**It is necessary** (dei) or the son of man to suffer many things, and to be tried by the elders, the chief priests, and the scribes, and to be killed, and after three days **to rise up** (anastēnai)." (8:31)*

In the Gospel of Mark, only 8:31 has "it is necessary" (*dei*). Mk 9:9-10 adds something of a side comment and has the disciples asking what it means "to rise from the dead" (*to ek nekrōn anastēnai*). Mk 9:31 and 10:33-34 essentially repeat 8:31, however getting a bit more specific and urgent each time.

In other words, in Mark, Jesus (by his own authority) is presented as the source of the teaching, and there is no specific or overt mention anywhere in Mark's Gospel that sacred texts had anything to say about rising from the dead,[134] let alone after three days.[135] Mark uses *graphē* only three times (12:10; 24; and

---

[134] The point is not that there is no suggestive language in important sacred texts, such as Mk 9:31 "rejected" (*apodokimazō*) and Psalm 118:22 which uses the same word in the "rejected stone" text. It is rather that in the narrative of Mark, Jesus is not calling upon sacred texts, here, for his authority; Jesus is his own authority.

[135] Mark is the only source that says "after three days." Matthew, Luke, and Paul have "on the third day." John does not use either phrase, but has Jesus say, "Destroy this temple, and in three days I will raise it up (*egerō auton*)" (Jn 2:19). Interestingly, Mk 15:58 and Mt 26:61 say that false witnesses brought this charge (Luke abstained on this point), and the Synoptics do not record that Jesus himself said it.

14:49) and the last two are plural, both making undefined references. But even 14:49 at Jesus' arrest ("let the sacred texts be
fulfilled") makes no specific mention of rising from the dead.

Nor does the **Gospel of Matthew** overtly connect the claim
to sacred texts (*tas graphas*—even though Matthew uses these
words four times 21:42; 22:29; 26:54, 56—all plural). Matthew
essentially co-opts Mark's claim about rising from the dead. He
has the same four "son of man" claims[136] (**Mt 16:21-23; [17:9];
17:22; 20:17-19**), and like Mark, he uses "it is necessary" (*dei*)
in only the first of these.

However, Matthew does shift each time to a different verb in
the passive—"shall *be* raised" (*egeirō*)[137]—and also to the phrase
"on the third day." In Matthew's telling of the story, the latter
very likely reflects an accommodation toward the shared Christian tradition as seen in 1Cor 15:3-4,[138] which likely calls upon
Hos 6:2:

He will heal us after two days,
*and **on the third day we shall be raised up***
(en tē̦ hēmera̦ tritē̦ anastēsometha)
and we shall live before him

If Matthew is intentionally alluding to this, it is a move in the
direction of connecting it to sacred text, but it is subtle rather
than overt. The use of "it is necessary" (*dei*) is not presented as
a result of sacred text, as if sacred text is requiring anything.

Now the point here, for Mark and Matthew, is not that the
passion narratives are not deeply rooted in ancient sacred texts
(of course they are); the point is that neither Gospel makes a
specific claim that sacred texts are the source of (or that they
prove) the claim that **"It is necessary for him [the Son of
Man] to rise from the dead."** Even though they both have a

---

[136] Although he changes the first to "him" (referring to Jesus) Mt 16:21ff.

[137] Matthew never uses the verb *anistēmi* for the resurrection of Jesus.

[138] Paul uses the phrase *egēgertai tē̦ hēmera̦ tritē̦* which is the same essential form found now in Matthew.

form of that phrase, and even though they both talk about sacred texts, neither clearly connects these two things (although Matthew has taken a step in that direction).

And so now comes the **Gospel of Luke** repeating the same claim (**9:22, 43-45; 18:31; 24:7, 25-27, 46**). Only now, in 18:31 (which repeats the last of Mark's three claims), Luke introduces the following phrase right at the beginning of the claim:

> *... and all the things that have been written through the prophets about the Son of Man shall come to completion ...*

Luke (in chapter 18) has now connected the *claim* to the *sacred texts* for the first time in the tradition of the written Synoptic Gospels. He next adds an entire section—the famous Emmaus story—which has Jesus essentially conduct a workshop on sacred texts on this very topic (24:7).

> *"Oh foolish men and slow in heart to believe all that that the prophets spoke. Was it not **necessary for the Christ to suffer** and enter into his glory?" And beginning from Moses and from all of the prophets he interpreted for them in all the sacred texts (tais graphais —pl) the things concerning himself.*

The text has now switched from the Son of Man to Christ. And one more switch is getting ready to happen: from the necessity of suffering, etc., to the necessity that sacred texts be fulfilled. So, he meets with a larger group later on and gets even more specific (24:44-47):

> *"These are my words which I spoke to you while I was still with you, namely that **it was necessary** that all things written in the law of Moses and in the prophets and psalms about me might be fulfilled." **Then he opened their minds to understand the sacred texts** (tas graphas —pl). And he said to them:*

> *"So it stands written: that **the Christ must suffer and rise up from the dead on the third day,** and repentance leading to the forgiveness of sins are to be preached to all the gentiles by the authority of his name . . . ."*

All of this, then, sets the stage of the preaching of Paul in the Book of Acts, especially Acts 17:2-3, speaking of the synagogue of the Jews:

> *And as was Paul's custom, he went in with them and for three Sabbaths he dialogued with them* **from the sacred texts** *(tōn graphōn —pl), explaining and setting forth in a clear order that:* **"It was necessary for the Christ to suffer and to rise from the dead.** *And this is the Christ, Jesus whom I proclaim to you."*

What started out as a major emphasis in Mark to show the authority of Jesus *by his own teaching*, ends up in Luke/Acts as a major proof—from the sacred texts (always plural)—for the suffering and resurrection of the Christ: a major step in the direction and emphasis of Paul. For when Paul talks about this concept, he states this:

> *For I handed over to you as of first importance, what I also received: that* **Christ died for our sins according to the sacred texts** *(kata tas graphas—pl), that he was buried,* **and that he was raised on the third day according to the sacred texts** *(kata tas graphas—pl), and that he was seen ... (1Cor 15:3-4)*

Although Paul speaks of what he "received," he mentions nothing about a tradition of Jesus' own teaching on this topic (like he did already in 1Cor 7 about divorce), but points directly to the sacred texts.

The point, here, is not about "which account is right." And it is especially not about conflating the different approaches as if the individual treatments are only meat for the bones of a larger skeleton. (In other words, I am quite uninterested in the tendency to make one Gospel mean what another says. Each must stand on its own feet.) Mark and Luke represent different approaches from each other for different reasons and each one should be left the way it is—and appreciated—for what it offers.

But Luke-Acts clearly stands in the tradition of Paul; and in that tradition, the proof necessary for seeing the suffering, death, and resurrection of the Christ is found in the sacred writings (pl).

d. Full Circle

This brings us back to the Gospel of John. Gone now are the emphases found throughout either Mark (Jesus' own teaching) or Luke (proof by the scriptures). John, in fact, develops an entirely independent strain of this story, based on the necessity (as flowing from Isaiah 52) of the Son of Man to be glorified by being lifted up (both in death and in resurrection).

And then he states in Jn 20:9:

> *For they did not yet understand the sacred text (he graphē) that it was necessary (dei) for him to rise up (anastēnai) from the dead.*

To what does he refer in this rather uncharacteristic summary? Given the fact that John developed such a unique, detailed, and coherent argument for the uplifted and glorified Son of Man; and given the relative scarcity of specific language (on this topic) as found in the Synoptics or Paul (such as the complete lack of uses of *anistēmi* for the resurrection of Jesus); and given that the exact word in Jn 20:9 (*anastēnai* "to rise up"), although nowhere else in John, is a key word used for the resurrection in Mark, Luke, and Acts—given these facts, we should not expect something in John that looks so . . . traditional.

Unless, of course, that is exactly what it is: Christian tradition. And so, a suggestion: John is not quoting the Synoptic Gospels, or Paul, or anyone else. Perhaps he's not even citing a specific sacred text or "scripture as a whole." Perhaps, in 20:9, he is quoting common Christian tradition—known conclusions about Jesus' resurrection.

And how can he use the word *graphē* in this manner? The same way he can use it for the other quotes of known conclusions (or shared traditions) found in Jn 7:38, 42; and 20:9:

> ***Jn 7:38*** *As the sacred text (hē graphē) says, "Rivers of living water will flow out of his heart."*

Jn 7:42 *Did not the sacred text (hē graphē) say, "The Christ comes from the family of David and from Bethlehem, David's home village"?*

Jn 20:9 *For they did not yet understand the sacred text (hē graphē), "It is necessary for him to rise from the dead."*

All of these are statements about the Messiah. His origin, his destiny, his character. Instead of understanding them as "the quotes that time forgot," perhaps these are better understood as references to known conclusions—traditions shared widely—about the Messiah, all of which had become well-known by the author and readers, to the point of each being a truth on its own terms, widely accepted. And these are called by John, *hē graphē*.

This is not like "A stitch in time saves nine."

This is rather "It was necessary for him to rise up."

The one is seen as a helpful general truth. The other is believed as the necessary ultimate truth. They are different.

Such statements are not remembered so that one goes tracking down one text or another; **they are rather given for their own sake as themselves stating the principle adequately.** In effect, they take the place of sacred texts and therefore themselves become sacred text (written or not). In such cases, *hē graphē* in these texts can almost be translated as "sacred sayings": what we all know by reason of widespread witness to be true. Or, recalling what Paul wrote, not distinguishing between the written word and the shared tradition:

*stand firm and grasp onto the **paradoseis** (pl= "traditions handed down") which you were taught **whether by spoken word or written letter*** (2Th 2:15)

Of course, it is common for readers today to throw all of the accounts into a trash compactor and to read what they take out as the Bible. But the Gospel of John defies such reductionism. Taking John on its own terms allows us to suggest that John may be using *graphē* in a way we have not seen before.

4. Summary for the NT

Despite widespread assumptions that *hē graphē* is used in the singular in many texts to refer to "the OT as a whole," this assumption is unlikely. It appears, instead, that the NT uses *hē graphē* in fairly standard and predictable ways either for specific texts (in the singular) or for undefined texts (in the plural). The Gospel of John follows this same practice except in three texts, which might be quotations that are now lost or are general summaries. My suggestion is that they might be quotations of known conclusions. Whatever they are, these three texts represent a type of use not found elsewhere in the NT or in other Greek literature of the 1st century and before.

G. Overall Summary

In English translations of the Bible, "Scripture" will be consistently capitalized by some (e.g., NKJV, NASB, NIV, The Message) and not by others (e.g., KJV, NRSV, NJB, REB). This may seem to be merely a matter of harmless style. On the other hand, simply by capitalizing the word one might read particular meanings and theological opinions into it.

For example, The Message paraphrases 1Cor 15:3 as "Scripture says . . ." (instead of "the scriptures say"). Some will argue that this is legitimate and that "This is what early Christians surely meant." I would disagree with this approach since it can easily imply to current readers the existence of a "canon consciousness," or even a "closed canon"—neither of which is implied by any NT document. This is one more very clear example of not knowing the difference between what the Bible *says* and what we think it *means*.

What is needed is more clarity on the specific use and application of the term *hē graphē* in the NT.

So then, in this study of *graphē*, we have looked at three important steps to avoid reading this term *anachronistically* back into biblical texts: (1) distinguish current from ancient usage; (2) do our own basic legwork using an English concordance; and (3) take a deeper look at the use of the Greek word *graphē* both inside and outside of the Bible. The last step requires some sophistication in the original languages, not to mention quite a bit of patience. It is also not a study one should be satisfied to do alone. Eventually, one needs interaction with specialists in the field and other interpreters to draw final conclusions. In this case, I have engaged in a good bit of conversation with scholars, and I have challenged some standard scholarly assumptions.

Doing so helps us to discover first that prior to the Greek Septuagint (the Greek translation of Hebrew sacred texts), *graphē* was not used in a religious sense. It was through the Jewish translation of those texts into Greek and the handling of those texts (both Hebrew and Greek) that the word began to take shape as representing something more than paintings, writings, accounting lists, and legal documents. Once the word was essentially co-opted for special use as referring to Jewish sacred literature (in both Greek and Hebrew texts), it began to be widely used as such just before the turn of the 1st century A.D. Early believers in Jesus and writers of Christian documents (like Paul and John) kept this usage to refer to the same Jewish literature, especially for the Greek Septuagint (a loose but fairly diverse collection of Greek translations considered to be inspired of God),[139] as the writings intended by God for the Church. And in that context, those writings were considered as both supportive of and subject to *the oral paradoseis* (traditions) and *oral proclamation* of the gospel message of Jesus Christ.

The words *hē graphē* were consistently used by early writers, including NT writers, to refer to a specific text or quotation (if in the singular), or to refer to an undefined plurality of texts (if in the plural). The Gospel of John follows that practice in all but three uses. Those exceptional uses of the singular *hē graphē* are generally understood as either (1) quotes of specific lost texts, or (2) general summaries of unspecified texts.[140] I have suggested an alternative: (3) quotations of known conclusions (shared

---

[139] For more info, see index under "Septuagint."

[140] This language is to be preferred over "Scripture as a whole."

traditions). However they are taken, they are exceptional even for John's Gospel, and all involve otherwise unknown quotes.

From this point, this particular usage of *graphē* would be adopted[141] by writers in the following centuries in which the singular *graphē* would become common for a general or pervasive reference.

1. Hundreds of years later, it would be applied to the completed canon and used as synonymous for the Roman Catholic canon, naturally excluding other books not in that canon.

2. Beginning with the Reformation period, the word in English, "Scripture," was applied freely to the Protestant canon.

3. By the mid 20th and early 21st centuries, the word "Scripture" had come to be routinely used exclusively for the Protestant Bible amid doctrinal formulations (speculations) that God had intended this particular book (the Protestant Bible) all along. (It just took 1,600 years to get to it.)

4. This then is read back into biblical texts as self-evident proof of the case.

In contrast, it may be stated from this study that when NT texts make general statements about "the sacred texts," it is not at all safe to assume that this includes only texts in the Protestant (or even Roman Catholic) canon of the OT. Nor is it correct to think that NT authors even had a word for "Scripture/scripture" that was applied to nothing other than books only in our canon.

A close look will show that the use of the word *graphē* in the NT focused on the *intrinsic nature* of the texts, not on *the external boundaries or limits* of groups of texts.

---

[141] I am not suggesting that the Gospel of John is the start of such a usage. It is merely the first record we have of it.

In the final analysis, NT authors not only do not imply an interest in "a closed canon," their own materials are a testament that their understanding of sacred writings was quite open to growth and expansion.

14
Law & Prophets

It is clear that from about the 3rd century A.D. on that the Hebrew Bible had been narrowed down to 24 books in three parts: Law, Prophets, and Writings (Torah, Nebiim, and Ketubim). Commentators are notorious for reading all the details of this later stage back into specific biblical texts of an earlier time. However, this is not a justifiable practice. The question is, what does the phrase "Law and Prophets" mean in ancient texts prior to the 2nd century A.D.?

A. Important Background

It appears that at least from the 2nd century B.C. through the 1st century A.D., (1) the Law had been set as the five books of Moses (possibly for hundreds of years); (2) the Prophets, as a category, was less settled; and (3) any supposed third "group" was so totally amorphous as to have no designation at all—it was just "other books." That's not really much of a group.

As far as the early synagogue was concerned, the Prophets apparently included (at least) what would later be called the four former prophets (Joshua, Judges, Samuel, and Kings) and the latter prophets (Isaiah, Jeremiah, Ezekiel and the Twelve) throughout the 1st century A.D.

However, keeping in mind that one could not go to a bookstore and buy "The Prophets" as a standardized set of scrolls, and remembering that both Hebrew scrolls and Greek translations were made in culturally distinct settings, then it is not difficult to fathom a time of growing textual variety. All of these flourished throughout this period and continued to be copied and produced without any overseeing agency that established "standards" for keeping them uniform. Add to that a heightened political and religious fervor that could fiercely influence what was written and kept (see, for example, the library of the Dead Sea Scrolls), and we have an environment rife with the potential for textual instability. Such a climate would abruptly change when the Roman general Titus would quash the Jewish rebellion, sacking Jerusalem and the Temple in A.D. 70, and when Christians and Jews would more or less "officially" go their separate ways.[142]

Despite the fact that many current-day authors want to present a very settled and neatly organized emerging biblical canon at this period, the evidence presents a vastly different scenario. One of the clear results of the Dead Sea Scroll discoveries is that the text-form during this time was far more fluid during this period than earlier imagined. As one of the more obvious examples (besides the Dead Sea Scrolls), one need only do an overview of a comparison between the Greek Septuagint Jeremiah and the Hebrew Jeremiah of the later Masoretic Text to see that there are some fairly drastic differences, including a wholesale reordering of whole chapters. This does not necessarily mean in all such cases that the Greek Septuagint changed the text; it might actually reflect an earlier text.

B. Flexibility and Adaptability

Now, with just this small amount of information in mind, it should not come as any surprise that, in the 1st century, the category "the Prophets" might not signify a completely uniform or settled group, especially since this is too early to talk about a closed (or even a well-defined) canon of any kind. For example, Moses, David, and Solomon (including the Psalms and Proverbs) might be included in that group along with Isaiah, Jeremiah, Ezekiel and the Twelve (what we call 12 minor prophets). So, David is called a prophet in **Matt 13:35** (quoting LXX Ps 78:2);

---

[142] On this last point, ancient 4th century tradition supports that Christians fled Jerusalem prior to its destruction (Eusebius, *Ecclesiastical History* III:5). As with most things, scholars have debated the accuracy and ramifications of this report. Whatever the outcome of the debate, it is clear that Post 70 Judaism took radical turns and that Christians were no longer part of it.

and Jesus is said to have called the Psalms "the Law" in **Jn 10:34-35** (quoting LXX Ps 81:6).

Such flexibility is a means of adaptability and extends to other prophets like Enoch the Seventh from Adam, as in **Jude 14**, which clearly refers to this book as a *sacred prophecy:*

> *And it was Enoch the Seventh from Adam who also* **prophesied** *about these men by saying, "Behold, the Lord came with his holy myriads to make judgment ...*

Jude is not merely making an illustration here, or buttering up his hearers like Paul did in Athens, saying "As some of your own poets have said ..." This is *prophecy and judgment* and a picture of God coming in wrath to destroy those who would undermine the faith of others. As if introducing Isaiah the prophet, Jude here quotes 1Enoch in the same authoritative fashion and with the same authoritative force. And as the only directly quoted holy text in the entire short letter, this becomes the central authoritative anchor of the entire message of Jude.

Current interpreters sometimes reel at a suggestion like this—frankly because it flies in the face of preconceived notions of inspiration and of a completed canon. In this view, nothing can be "inspired" or "Scripture" if it is not in our particular canon. (As mentioned earlier, the Orthodox Tewahedo church accepts 1Enoch as part of an 81 book canon based directly on Jude's acceptance of it! But then we know their canon is wrong ... right?). But this approach is exactly backwards—getting our theology in place before we allow the texts to speak. Such an approach must simply be rejected.

The point of this early flexibility must be understood: Jude is not about *canon;* it is about *prophecy*—what was considered and used as inspired "holy writing." So, dispensing with the inappropriate terminology of whether Jude thought anything was "canonical," it is enough to read the book of Jude with the question, "Did Jude consider the sources to which he was alluding (viz., Exodus, Numbers, The Assumption of Moses, Book of Jubilees) and the source which he directly quoted (1Enoch)—did he

consider these as 'prophecy'? Were they authoritative or inspired of God? Did he consider them as 'sacred writing'"?

Given the NT emphasis on the authority of prophecy and the
very specific wording of Jude and the texts alluded to and quoted, one is hard pressed to understand how anyone could say no.

NT writers show flexibility on this. Prophecy was a key element and no one should draw the conclusion that the mention of
"the Law and the Prophets" necessarily signified a neat, closed
list of books. Instead, the situation among early Christians is
just the opposite: there was no apparent move at this stage to
set the boundaries of who was "in" and was "out" as Prophets.
"Prophets" was a category that could be used to include and allow at least some measure of flexibility.

The combination of "Law and Prophets" into a single phrase
was apparently shorthand (at least sometimes) for saying "the
holy writings" in general, which might also have allowed for
much more than we ourselves might expect.

C. Prior to the NT

Specific texts prior to the NT show that "law and prophets"
was not a well-defined group of texts.

Within the Septuagint itself, the prophets (Moses, Elijah,
Isaiah, etc.) were seen as proclaiming God's law to the people—
or they failed to do so (2Kgs 17:13; Neh 9:26; Jer 2:8; 18:18;
Lam 2:9; Ezek 7:26; Dan 9:10; Zeph 3:4; Zech 7:12; 2Macc
2:2). So, prophets and law were seen as related.

But, by at least the mid-2nd century B.C., "the Law and
Prophets" were being put together as a single phrase and used as
the main resource for those who were following God. It is important to note that this phrase appears to include more than
what might be included much later in these categories—the
"shorthand" to which I was referring. Here are some examples.

In **2Macc 15:9** (a document from the 1st century B.C., originally composed in Greek), Judas Maccabeus stirs his army to
battle by "encouraging them from the Law and the Prophets"

and by reminding them of previous victories. It is unlikely that this means he avoided quoting the Psalms or other sacred writings; it is more likely a general reference to sacred writings.

In **4Macc 18:10-19** (a document written during the lifetime of Paul, also originally in Greek) there appears a simply wonderful text about a father who had taught the sacred writings to his children for the purpose of helping them through suffering and other difficult times. A mother says, "While he was still with you, he taught you the Law and the Prophets." In the process of the story, quotes are made from Genesis, Numbers, Deuteronomy, Isaiah, Ezekiel, Daniel, Psalms, and Proverbs (not in that order). This shows that "Prophets" might be used somewhat loosely to include the writings of David and Solomon as a more general reference to "holy writings."

But the best example showing a variety of documents was written a hundred years or more before either of these texts, from about 180 to 130 BC. Here's a quote from the prologue of a book called **The Wisdom of Sirach***:

*As for the **Law and the Prophets and the other books that followed them***: *Because they have brought us so much good that Israel deserves high praise for its instruction and wisdom; and because they require readers not only to come to a personal understanding but then, as lovers of learning, to assist outsiders through both oral and written efforts—for these reasons, my grandfather, Jesus, devoted himself to diligent public lectures on the **Law and the Prophets and the other books of our fathers**. He became so proficient in these that he himself decided to write a manual suitable for instruction and wisdom, so that those who love learning and who pursue such studies might—to an even greater degree—align their daily lives in submission to **the Law**.*

In this text, exactly what "the Prophets" consisted of is not stated; but the phrase "the other books of our fathers" is completely undefined, stating overtly what is sometimes included in

the simple phrase "Law and Prophets." This last part is so undefined as not even to have a designation.

But we must not miss this: *The author had no problem referring to an undefined group of "other books from our fathers"
equally alongside the rest. Rather than showing any interest in
closing a canon, this actually shows the opposite: that at this
time, two general collections of sacred writings were seen as part
of a much larger undefined group of sacred writings.*

D. In the NT

All of this lays the groundwork for the occurrence of the
"Law and Prophets" in the NT.

For example, although the phrase does not occur at all in
Mark, it occurs four times in **Matthew** on the lips of Jesus in
opposition to the Pharisees (5:17; 7:12; 11:13; 22:40) as a way
of saying "this is how the Law is properly understood—*in the
way the prophets read and applied it (not the way you apply it)!*
It is worth noting that 5:17 and 7:12 begin and end (i.e., they
form a kind of interpretive bracket for) the sermon on the mount
showing that Jesus is reinterpreting the scriptures in the tradition of the prophets instead of in the tradition of the Pharisees.

The phrase occurs three times in the Gospel of **Luke** (16:16;
24:27 and 44), the last two on the walk to Emmaus and the Emmaus supper (unique in the Gospels), and with the eleven back
in Jerusalem. The whole story is too long to quote, but here are
some important verses showing that sacred texts are being referred to inclusively and generally in a variety of ways:

> *25O slow of heart to believe all that **the prophets** spoke ...
> 27And starting with **Moses and from all the prophets**
> he explained to them in **all the sacred writings** the
> things about himself. ...*

> *32And they said to one another, "Were not our hearts burn-
> ing within us as he went on speaking to us along the way,
> as he was opening to us **the sacred writings!**" ...*

*44[Jesus said:] "These are my words that I said to you while I was still with you: 'It is necessary that everything is fulfilled that is written in the **Law of Moses and in the Prophets and Psalms** about me.'" 45Then he opened the mind of each of them to understand **the sacred writings.** 46And he said to them: "So **it stands written** that the Christ is to suffer and to rise from the dead on the third day, 47and that upon his name repentance for the forgiveness of sins is to be proclaimed to the Gentiles."*

This is a simply marvelous text, of course; but one that is often subjected to a complete over-reading. Is it indeed the claim of this text (as some say) that in the space of a seven mile walk every single passage or text found within ancient holy writings was named and discussed? And are we really to believe (as some say) that this reference to "all sacred writings" linked with "Law, Prophets, and Psalms" implies a closed OT canon equivalent to the Hebrew Torah, Nebiim, and Ketubim (Law, Prophets, and Writings) of a later period—which, of course, is equivalent to the Protestant Canon? How could we be persuaded by this kind of reading?

Do we not, rather, find (once again) a view of sacred writings that allows an exuberant exclamation: "They simply *all* talk about him!" This is a text that talks about the utter importance of sacred writings as witnessing to Jesus; but this text does not in the least talk about a closed canon. I repeat what I said much earlier: at the time Luke is writing, Christians were not in any mood or mindset to talk of the *boundaries* of sacred texts.

Being finished with Luke, we move on to volume two (the book of Acts). Here we find the same author continuing to use this basic description in the second half of the book, specifically (and only) when dealing with Paul.

So in **Acts**, the phrase may be a bit more literal when used of the synagogue worship to summarize that "after the public reading of the Law and the Prophets," the ruler of the synagogue asked Paul and Barnabas to speak (Acts 13:15). However, the subsequent uses are more general and inclusive, since Paul refers to the Law and the Prophets as the foundation of his own faith (24:14); he then stands before all testifying that he says "nothing aside from what the prophets were saying, and even Moses" (26:22); and finally he received groups of people into his lodging "testifying to the Kingdom of God and persuading them about Jesus from both the Law of Moses and the Prophets, from morning till evening" (28:23). Are we to think that he did not refer to the Psalms? Or even to other texts? That is very unlikely.

Indeed, in the only use of the phrase in the Pauline letters (**Rom 3:21**), for Paul, the Law and the Prophets testify to the righteousness of God apart from the Law, "the righteousness of God through the faith of Jesus Christ for all who believe." This is certainly a general reference to the whole body of sacred writings at his disposal. However, now in Romans, the Law and the Prophets not only proclaim the message of Jesus, *they become secondary to that proclamation, functioning as the supporting cast.*

Even in the Gospel of John, it is said: "We have found him of whom Moses wrote in the Law, also the Prophets, Jesus son of Joseph from Nazareth" (1:45).

E. Prophecy and Sacred Text

Finally, as promised at the end of section 2 on "Scripture," there are a few texts that use the word *graphē* ("sacred text, scripture") tapping into this emphasis on the authority of prophecy.

2Pet 1:19-20 has two phrases that are essentially identical:

"the prophetic word" (*prophētikon logon*)
"every prophecy of a sacred text" (*pasa prophēteia graphē*)

It is clear that the focus is on the intrinsic nature and authority of prophecy and its origins, not at all on any concept of canon, especially when compared to the striking similarities in **Rom 16:26**:

"the prophetic sacred texts" (*graphōn prophētikōn*)

This is also similar to the practical force of **2Tim 3:16-17**, although 2Peter focusses more on the origins and power of a prophetic text because prophets were carried along by the Holy Spirit as the divine agent.

Finally, later in the same document, **2Pet 3:16** considers "all of Paul's letters" (although none is mentioned by name, nor do we know the extent[143] of any) using the same language as to other sacred writings: "as also the rest of the sacred writings" (pl.). However, these sacred writings are also not specified (because that is not the point). Here, the focus is on using those documents by Paul, along with the other sacred texts, for helping with such personal character issues as purity, blamelessness, expectation, awaiting the Lord, peace, patience, salvation, and even the gleaning of wisdom.

Now, it is important to note that this text (2Pet 3:16) does not give a witness to the closing of a canon, but instead to just the opposite. This document indicates that Christians apparently had no trouble accepting Paul's letters alongside other more well established sacred texts. The very fact that collections of sacred texts could exist side-by-side, and even continue to grow before their eyes, shows an openness and readiness to sacred text that was very different from anything that exists today. They show no indication of being bothered by such a concept as the proliferation of sacred writings. The very fact that Christians viewed their message as promised by, and as a hidden mystery of, and contained within, the Greek sacred texts, made this possible.

(As an interesting side note, the statement that Paul's letters are "sacred writings"—on the same level, say, as the Psalms or Isaiah—is much less strongly stated than Jude's authoritative quotation of 1Enoch. However, Protestant Christian interpreters

---

[143] In other words, if (say) 2Corinthians was included in that group, how long was it? Did it look like ours? A good deal of NT scholarship has long questioned the unity and literary integrity of this letter. We simply don't know.

will typically fall all over themselves to avoid every appearance of such an "evil" as this kind of equation.)

F. Summary

The bottom line for all twelve NT occurrences of the phrase "Law and Prophets"[144] is that it generally serves as shorthand for "all sacred texts," not simply two well-defined groups. Nor should it be read in light of later realities about the closed Hebrew canon after the 2nd century. In the first century, the Law is clearly the five books of Moses. But the Prophets are not clearly defined as to number of books, contents of books, or form of text. Even in Lk 24:27-44, the "Law and the Prophets" are set side-by-side with "all sacred writings," including the Psalms.

As to canonical implications, there is simply no evidence from our texts that there was any concern about "closing down" or securing the boundaries of sacred texts. The Law and the Prophets form the foundation for the proclamation of the gospel. But in none of the texts is there any concern stated that only "these or those" texts are to be classified as "sacred writings." Actually, NT authors appear unconcerned with such a thought.

G. Final Note

Having noted all of these things about the word *graphē* ("writing"), in the previous chapter, and now the phrase "Law and Prophets," we must also note that that's not all there is to it. For whether or not these terms are used, the NT documents are *constantly* interacting with ancient sacred texts on one level or another (such as deep conversations that might or might not be visible to casual readers). It is very common for NT texts to be reflecting upon, or echoing, or alluding to ancient holy writings (without necessarily directly quoting them) in a way that might not be at all obvious.

---

[144] Matthew 5:17; 7:12; 11:13; 22:40; Luke 16:16; 24:44; John 1:45; Acts 13:15; 24:14; 26:26; 28:23; Romans 3:21.

15
The Word of God

Perhaps the most significant concern raised to me about the argument of my book is that I may appear to be suggesting that the Bible is nothing more than a human book and that I may be minimizing the concepts of divine revelation or even any concept of the Bible as "The Word of God." I hope that by the end of a careful reading of the book, that is not so much of a concern. Still, it is a subject worthy of address.

I will begin by commenting that much of the difficulty in offering a renewed and thoroughly biblical view of the subject at hand is the need to "undo" many things that have been done before. Knowing where to look and what to keep is half the battle.

I remember being 6 years old, following my dad in the middle of the night across fields, down gullies, through creeks, and in the midst of thickets chasing the sound of two dogs hot on the trail of the bandits of the woods. Finally, we arrived at the base of a big tree, my dad's well-trained dogs barking in a now different way, showing they had indeed treed, not just one, but three large coons.

My dad would not have kept a dog that would have barked up the wrong tree. But as Bible students, that is one of our favorite pastimes.

A. Opening Summary

So, wanting to be sensitive to concerns of my readers (as to whether I am somehow denying the value of the ancient scriptures and of divine revelation), I will now offer an extended and somewhat detailed note on the biblical phrase: "The Word of God" and how it relates to the words "scripture" and "revelation."[145]   I will first summarize my position and then unpack it in a more detailed manner.

In what follows, I will broadly survey the biblical uses of the phrase "The Word of God" (and related phrases), and I will look especially at three texts in 1Thessalonians relating to the "Word of God." I will conclude that early Christians did something new with the phrase "The Word of God." For them, it referred to the preached Message of Christ, or even to Christ himself. However, the Word of God was not about *format* (whether speech, act, or text), but *substance*. This was a perfect message, with the revelation and authority of the Lord as the key elements. This will have implications for the quest for something perfect. I will end by relating all of this to the argument of the book.

B. The Word of God in the Bible

The phrases "Word of God," "Word of the Lord," "Word," and numerous others occur in so many texts and with such interchangeable nuances as to make it impossible to fully survey here. However, I do want to highlight a few things.

1. Use in the OT

In the OT, the key issue in all the phrases and all the occurrences everywhere is the origin and authority of an encounter with God. Whether the reference is to a story, speech, event, or a written document, the concern is the same: it is not the word of some man we are talking about, but "the word **of God**."

Whether . . .

---

[145] γραφή *(graphē)* occurs 91 times in the OT, Apocrypha, and NT, and refers to "holy writings." The words κανών *(canon)* and βίβλος *(book)* occur 18 and 36 times respectively, to mean "rule," and "book." They do not take on their current meanings of "closed canon of Scripture" and "Holy Bible" until much later. In other words, these are all three biblical terms, but they have all taken on special baggage today that Christians tend to read back into biblical texts.

- **Moses** is telling the people "the words of the LORD" that he had been summoned to the ascend the mountain of Sinai (Ex 24:3);

- or **Balaam** is refusing the offer of payment to curse Israel: "I cannot go against the word of the LORD" (Num 22:18);

- or **Moses** reproaches Israel, *"You were disobedient to the word of the LORD your God"* (Dt 26:1);

- or **Ehud** says to king Eglon, *"I have a word of God for you"* (namely a two-edged sword in the stomach— Judges 3:20)

. . . the point is still the same: **God has something to say.**

From **David's** exclamation, *"The Spirit of the Lord spoke within me, and his word was on my tongue,"* (2Sam 23:2) to the **great prophets** who began their books, *"The word of the Lord which came to Hosea"* (or Micah, or Zephaniah, or Malachi), they make it clear that God has something to say. The concern is not how or in what manner or by what means: it is merely that God is talking. Was it spoken? Or written? Or acted out? Never mind. It was all God.

Jeremiah is filled with this: *"The word of the Lord came to me,"* *"Hear the word of the Lord,"* *"The Lord says,"* *"The Lord told me, 'Look now, I have placed my words in your mouth,'"* and so much more. God was speaking through Jeremiah: *"You will be my mouth"* (15:19), and God's message was a *"fire burning in my bones"* (20:9), so that Jeremiah could not *not* speak. Throughout his text, whether the truths and events were spoken, acted, or written (36:2), calling them "the Word of God" (and related phrases) did not focus so much on the *format* in which they were received, but on *fact of being* the message **of God.**

2. Use in Other Literature

This was true of many books from this period of time: one should certainly not think this was unique to the literature in our Bibles that we most know about.

For example, a century or two before Jesus was born, **The Temple Scroll** (for a reclusive group of Jews near the Dead Sea) presented itself as a new Torah, a replacement of instructions for the Temple, the priesthood, and the worship. This book is not offered as an *interpretation* of the Torah, but as itself the new Torah, written in the first person by God himself. As it says: *"You shall do everything as I tell you"* (11QT.XXXI)[146]

Or the book of **1Enoch** which says of itself: *"This is a holy vision from the heavens which the angels showed me: I heard from them everything and I understood."* (1 Enoch 1:2). Jude thought enough of it to make it the central quote of his letter.[147]

Or the **Apocalypse of Baruch**: *"The narration and Apocalypse of Baruch concerning the secret things he saw by the word of God"* (Apocalypse of Baruch 1)[148]

Or the **Psalms of Solomon**, commenting on God's judgment: *"The scattering (dispersion) of Israel was among every nation, according the word of the Lord."* (Psalms of Solomon 9:2)[149]

However, no statement anywhere—inside or outside of anyone's later "canon," is more potent or descriptive than this marvelous statement from the book of **Tobit**:

> For I myself believe the **word of God** against Nineveh
> that Nahum **spoke**, that all these things will be and will
> happen to Assyria and Nineveh. Indeed, whatever the

---

[146] From Geza Vermes, *The Dead Sea Scrolls in English.* 3rd rev ed.

[147] James H. Charlesworth, *Old Testament Pseudepigrapha. Vol 1: Apocalyptic Literature and Testaments.* Doubleday, 1983. People have long argued (anachronistically) about whether Jude considered 1Enoch as "canonical." The real question is whether he considered it a holy writing (*graphē*). The fact is, there is nothing (technically or otherwise) different about how Jude quoted this ancient book from how any other NT writer quoted any other ancient holy writing.

[148] Most likely written by Christians in the first two centuries A.D.

[149] The *Psalms of Solomon* dates from the latter half of the first century (roughly equivalent to the traditional dating of the Gospels). It is a response by pious Jews to the 1st century overthrow of Jerusalem by Rome.

*prophets of Israel (sent by God) **spoke**, every bit of it will happen! Not any part of **all of their words** will fail, and all things will come together at their appointed times. . . . For I myself know and I believe that every single thing that **God has said** will be fulfilled and it will be; and not so much as a single **word** from the **sayings** (words) will fail. (Tobit 14:4)*[150]

The issue in all of these statements from all of these books (and from many more) is that *God has something to say* and that you, as a reader, as a hearer, or as anyone at all, had better listen to it. The issue in all of these is not canon, a set of books, or whether books are more authoritative than speech. The issue is *God is talking. So listen!*

3. Use in the NT

In NT literature, this very same concern is continued, but now it is carried in a very specific new direction; for now the "Word of God," "Word of the Lord," "Word" (and more) are used to show that God has something *new* to say, for now comes *the message of Jesus Christ—preached.* It is the mystery hidden, but now revealed. The message of hearing, of truth, of life. The living word. One NT text above all brings all of these concepts together:

> *You have been newly born, not from anything that dies, but of something that cannot die, through the living and lasting **Word of God**. For . . .*
> > *Everything mortal is like grass*
> > > *and the beauty of its wild flower.*
> > *The grass dries up,*
> > > *the flower falls off.*
> *But the **Word of the Lord** lasts forever!"*
> *This is the **Word** that was announced to you:*
> ***"the Gospel!"*** *(1Pet 1:23-24; cf. 2Tim 2:9)*

---

[150] Based on the text family Sinaiticus, which differs significantly from text family BA.

This is simply an incredible text, for here, all three phrases are brought together and defined as the gospel, the saving message of good news, the living word. And how is this accomplished? Through a deep reading of Isa 40:6-9—which, it turns out, is part of the very text that stands at the base of the gospel message to the whole world:

> *A voice crying in the wilderness:*
> *"Prepare the way of the Lord!"...*
> *and the glory of the Lord will be revealed...*
> **for the mouth of the Lord has spoken!**
> *(Isa 40:3-5; cf. Mk 1:1-3)*

But it does not stop here. This message grew out of the work, teaching, death, and resurrection of Jesus Christ, and of his very *being,* identified as the Lord of all, the Name above all names. The Word of God is even found to be his very name:

> *And his name is called the* **Word of God** *... and from his* **mouth** *extends a* **sharp sword** *... and on his robe and on his thigh the name has been written, "King of kings and Lord of lords." (Rev 19:13-16)*

The new direction of Christian usage and emphasis is so pronounced and so sweeping that every occurrence of the "Word of God" in the NT can be understood in this light. It refers in some way to the saving message of Jesus Christ, which ultimately is the person of Jesus Christ. No NT occurrence of the phrase is used in a way that makes it an indisputable reference merely to the written scriptures.[151]

---

[151] On this point, Kittel writing in the *Theological Dictionary of the New Testament* (TDNT) IV:112 is entirely too exuberant about anachronistically reading "canon language" into texts like Col 1:25 and Heb 4:12. Also, the following NT texts are often read as if a reference to OT texts, but there is nothing in any of them that separates them from the special sense of the Word of God as the message of Jesus Christ: Eph 6:17; 1Tim 4:5; Titus 2:5; Heb 4:12; 6:5; 13:7; even John 10:35 where Jesus speaks of the message of God to original hearers (of ancient holy texts). There is no reason to read these texts abnormally.

"Word of God" in the NT

PAUL	MARK MATT	LUKE ACTS	GENERAL LETTERS	JOHN
Rom 9:6	Mk 7:13//	(Luke 3:2)	Heb 4:12	(John 3:34)
1Cor 14:36	Mt 15:6//	Luke 5:1	(Heb 6:5)	(John 8:47)
2Cor 2:17		Luke 8:11	(Heb 11:3)	John 10:35
2Cor 4:2		Luke 8:21	Heb 13:7	1 John 2:14
(Eph 6:17)		Luke 11:28	1Pet 1:23-25	Rev 1:2
Col 1:25		Acts 4:31	2 Pet 3:5	Rev 1:9
1Th 2:13		Acts 6:2		Rev 6:9
1Tim 4:5		Acts 6:7		Rev 17:17
2Tim 2:9		Acts 8:14		Rev 19:9
Titus 2:5		Acts 11:1		Rev 19:13
		Acts 12:24		Rev 20:4
This Chart Shows:		Acts 13:5	**Your Own Word Study:**	
		Acts 13:7		
logos tou theou		Acts 13:46	Read each text from an	
(hrema theou)		Acts 17:13	English translation.	
//= texts are parallel		Acts 18:11		

Although my statement just above will be seen by some as a denigration of the scriptures, it is nothing of the kind. For even in the OT, where the Word can refer to the written scriptures, it is not to sacred writings for their own sake that the reference is made. The emphasis is always **of God**. In the NT, there is plenty of emphasis on the continued importance of the scriptures, continuing a supportive role to the NT Word of God, living, moving, engaging—the mystery now revealed, the gospel, the truth of Jesus Christ.

This shift is so significant that Kittel can state in *The Theological Dictionary of the New Testament*:

After the coming of Jesus the Word of God or the Word of the Lord has for the whole of primitive Christianity a new and absolutely exclusive sense. It has become the undisputed term for the one Word of God which God has spoken, and speaks, in what has taken place in Jesus and in the message concerning it. From this time on, the term cannot be used of any other revealing event, no matter how authentic and estimable in the religious sense. . . . The revelation which has taken place in Jesus Christ is de-

finitive and unique, and . . . the new age has been inaugu-rated therewith. (TDNT, IV:113)

C. The Word of God in Paul

All of this said, we will now note that Paul uses the language in the same manner, calling it the mystery hidden for ages, but now revealed: the Word of God, of the cross, of truth, of life, of faith, of hearing—they are all speaking of the message of Christ, the gospel.

But instead of wandering around in Paul generally, lets dig a bit more deeply in a single place—the small letter of 1Thessalonians—and get a taste for how Paul used the word "scripture" and the phrase "Word of God" differently, but in concert with each other.

1. Paul and Scripture

1Thessalonians was Paul's first letter and likely the first of all the NT documents to have been written. We see his love and respect of the sacred writings both subtly and overtly. For him, the holy writings were crucial. For example, he refers to the Christ Community *(ekklēsia)*, to election *(tēn eklogēn)*, and to holiness *(hagiasmos)* (1:1; 1:4; 4-12): all of these concepts are rooted deeply within the sacred texts read by the early Christians. Without a deeper understanding of this language from both the Hebrew and Greek OT, these are just technical terms to us.

Although 1Thessalonians is not like, say, Galatians or Romans or 1Corinthians, quoting many texts for interpretation, there are still numerous echoes of the sacred writings, which shows that they were viewed as the bedrock of conversation with God. For example, the reference to those "who don't know God" in 1Th 4:5 is an apparent echo of Ps 79:6, especially when contrasted with Paul's newly coined phrase "God-taught" just four verses later. 1Th 4:9 looks to be an echo of Isa 54:13, in which the context of that part of Isaiah may underlie what Paul is writing to the Thessalonians. Later, when Paul speaks "by the word of the Lord" in 1Th 4:15ff, English readers might completely miss the deeper references to the rich tradition of sacred texts standing behind this phrase and the subtleties of nuance that apparently come with it.

Even more overt is how Paul sees himself in terms of the prophetic texts of (2:4; 3:14; 4:15; and 5:19-22), especially in terms of the call of Jeremiah, including the Jeremiah texts mentioned above. These are not the musings of someone who occasionally would read sacred texts, or who haphazardly buzzed over the top of a few verses here and there and called it "daily Bible reading." Nor was he beginning to walk away from ancient sacred texts because he was now a follower of Christ. These are the words of someone so thoroughly familiar with the holy writings that not only his language but his view of his own identity was shaped by it.

The ancient holy writings are extremely important for Paul in this little letter, even when he doesn't come out and say the word *graphē* overtly.[152]

2. Paul and the Word

Contemporary readers will see that title ("Paul and the Word") and think of Paul and Bible again. But let's stick with Paul, here, for that is *not* what he would say. For actually, when Paul uses "the Word" or the "Word of God" in this letter, he is not referring directly or immediately to sacred texts, but to the saving message of Christ—preached. There are three texts in 1Thessalonians that are begging for our attention about this.

a. 1Th 1:6:

*... you **received the Word** in a great deal of suffering with a joy produced by the Holy Spirit.*

Paul here refers to "receiving the Word," which can have the double-meaning of internal acceptance, but also as the teaching

---

152 γραφή *(graphē)*, the word for Scripture, occurs 14 times in Paul's letters, but not in 1Thessalonians. Rom 1:2; 4:3; 9:17; 10:11; 11:2; 15:4; 16:26; 1Cor 15:3-4; Gal 3:8; 3:22; 4:30; 1Tim 5:18, 2Tim 3:16.

handed down or preached (cf. also Lk 8:13; Ac 8:14; 11:1; 17:11; Js 1:21). This is to be compared to the *paradosis*—teachings or traditions handed down by Paul through preaching and teaching (1Th 4:1; 1Cor 11:2, 23; 15:3; 2Th 2:15; 3:6). When joined with the phrase about imitating Paul and the Lord (committing to a path of suffering), it is fairly clear that "the word" they received was not so much sacred texts as the contents of the gospel they "received," and it included at least the oral teaching about Jesus who endured suffering for the sake of God. These hearers now "received" that spoken message and committed themselves to a life of suffering.

b. 1Th 2:13:

*... once you received **the Word from God***
—namely, the Word which you had heard from us—
you did not take it as something conjured up in a back
*room. You saw it for what it truly is, **the Word of God**,*
powerfully active in you who are believers.

Once again, Paul is not referring to sacred texts, but to the Message (Word) of Christ which Paul had preached and taught. As in 1:6 above, they had received *internally* what Paul had handed down *externally* (the *paradosis,* "the tradition").

But in this text, Paul defines it in more specific terms, which can be shown somewhat literally like this:

logon   *akoēs par hēmōn*   *tou theou*

"The Word [which you heard from us] **from God."**

First, these last two words *tou theou* are in emphatic posi-tion, contrasting "from *us*" with "from *God*": You heard it from us, but you received it from God. God is the author and origina-tor of this message. Paul was only a mediator. [153]

---

[153] The place of *akoēs (hearing)* in the sentence has caused interpreters pause: most take it not as "the word of hearing" but in apposition as "the word which you heard." Either way, it is referring to the preached word—the mes-sage of Christ—not OT scripture.

Second, the phrase *logon ... tou theou* ("Word ... from God") is a bit unusual. One expects *logon* to have an article as well.[154] Of the 21 other times this exact phrase occurs in the NT, all 21 of those times have what is expected,[155] unlike here. So, the addition of the article before *theou* serves to heighten the contrast between "from us" and "from God," as it also tends to strengthen the association with "Word": it is not just any word, but the Word **from God**! This is exactly the emphasis we saw from the OT texts about the Word of God being primarily **of God**.

Now here is a good example of a text that will be greatly understated in a near-literal translation, such as is found (in this case) in the NIV: *"...when you received the word of God which you heard from us."* Although certainly not incorrect, it is somewhat flat, leaving out the emphasis inherent in the inclusion of the article and the placement of *tou theou* ("of God").

In the last part of this sentence, all of this is followed by even more emphatic clarification when Paul uses the contrast: "not as the word of man ... but instead as the Word of God" *(logon anthrōpōn ... logon theou).*

So, the "Word of God" occurs twice in this one verse and is extremely strongly characterized, not as sacred texts, but as the preached message of Christ. It is **from God**, not man. Once again, this is not a battle between formats or delivery systems (as if asking, "Which is better? Preaching or sacred texts?"); this is a focus on the source and authority of the message.

c. 1Th 4:15:

*Pay attention, now, because we are telling you this by a **direct revelation** from the Lord!*

---

[154] "We may add what is almost a grammatical rule: if the noun used with a following genitive is itself without the article, the article is generally omitted, by a sort of assimilation, with the genitive also." in Maximilian Zerwick, *Biblical Greek*, Rome, 1963, p. 59.

[155] Mt 15:6; Mk 7:13; Lk 5:1; 8:21; 11:28; Ac 4:31; 6:2; 8:14; 11:1; 13:5; 13:7; 13:46; 18:11; 2Cor 2:17; 4:2; Col 1:25; Heb 13:7; Rev 1:2; 1:9; 6:9; 20:4;

This is an interpretation by which I tip my hand as to my inclinations. Quite literally the text reads: *"For we say this to you* **by the word of the Lord"** *(touto gar humin legomen en logōi kyriou).* This text has a long history of debate, and scholars have suggested three primary (and exclusive) options:

1. Paul is claiming a direct revelation from the risen Lord.

2. A pre-Pauline Christian prophetic tradition underlies Paul's claim (thus, it is not a revelation, but a tradition handed down).

3. This is but another reference to the "Word" as the message of Christ (thus it is another reference to Paul's gospel). [156]

All three options have things to commend them. However, I am not persuaded by the second option since Paul does not use the "received" *(paradosis)* terminology here as in 1Th 1:6 and 2:13 discussed above. And the tenor of the text seems to be quite different from those, as well as some specific phraseology.

Nor am I inclined toward the third option (although it is stronger than the second), *as an exclusive option,* since it does not appear to me to adequately account for the special circumstances and phrasing of this text over the other NT uses of "Word" to refer to the message of Jesus Christ.

In fact, it appears to me that the third option can walk hand-in-hand with the first in the following manner: *As a revelation from the risen Lord, this is part of Paul's gospel—the message of Christ, the mystery hidden, now revealed.*

This is not offered as a compromise, but as an attempt to make sense of all the elements that need to be accounted for. Throughout this chapter I have myself argued that the "Word of

---

[156] Michael W. Pahl, *Discerning the Word of the Lord: The Word of the Lord in 1 Thessalonians 4:15.* Library of New Testament Studies, vol 389. T & T Clark, 2009 offers a thorough review of the debate and suggests that the "message of Christ" (as found elsewhere in Paul) best explains the usage here.

God" in all NT references is a new emphasis by Christian writers, not to ancient texts (for the sake of texts), but to the message of Christ (whether in speech, act, or text). And now here, in this very first letter of Paul—the first of all NT documents to have been written that we have—Paul appeals to a specific revelation from the risen Lord as, indeed, a part of that larger gospel.

In support of this position, I will now explore several unique features of this particular text. For in this text we get to see Paul

1. interacting on a very deep level with sacred texts

2. as he uses specifically revelatory language to present a revelation from the Lord.

Naturally, this is part of his gospel—which, according to Paul on several occasions, has been revealed to him (cf. Gal 2).[157]

3. Paul as a Prophet

Paul believes strongly in prophecy and now (in 1Th 4:15) takes on the role of a prophet. The *gar* ("for") links what he says here to what he had just said. So now, to back up what he had just said, that believers who have died are coming back with the risen Lord, Paul states that he has a direct revelation from the Lord on that very matter. He does not comment on how or when he had received this message; nor does he specifically say whether he is quoting it verbatim or merely giving a summary. But he does not need to spell out such details any more than any other prophet.

Keeping in mind that classical prophecy was as much (or more) about forth-telling (teaching) than fore-telling (specific time-sensitive predictions often associated with prophecy by modern readers), Paul's "word of the Lord" is aimed to settle the concerns of early Christians worried about the death of loved ones before the return of the Lord has occurred. The translation offered above regards 4:15b-17 to be Paul's setting forth the

---

[157] See Philo Spec Leg 1:214-215 where he parallels the holy scriptures and the holy word.

"Word of the Lord," which was apparently given by the Lord to the very question at hand about those who have already died.

It is worth noting that Paul's wording is unique in all of NT literature; and it is worth considering that this is a claim (in ancient prophetic mode) that the risen LORD gave him the message directly.

a. By the Word of the Lord

In one form or another the phrase *logos kyriou* ("the word of the Lord") occurs nearly 200 times in OT texts, especially in prophets like Jeremiah and Ezekiel, to indicate God's direct message to one or more people. Furthermore, the exact Greek phrase used by Paul, *en logō͵ kyriou*, "by the word of the Lord," occurs only 10 times in five biblical texts:

1. 1Kgs 13:1, 2, 5, 9, 17, and 32 (Jeroboam's folly);
2. 1Kgs 20:35 (Ahab's folly);
3. 2Chr 30:12 (Hezekiah's reform);
4. Sirach 48:3 (Commenting on Ahab's folly);[158]
5. and 1Th 4:15 (the dead in Christ).

In every case, the issue is not so much about time-sensitive predictions as it is about God's instructions for particular circumstances. It is striking that Paul's use, here, is the only occurrence of this prepositional phrase in any NT document (the similar phrase *ho logos tou kyriou* in 1Th 1:8 is clearly used in context to mean the Saving Message of God, not in a revelatory context (unlike here). It is also striking that no other Greek phrase meaning "by the word of the Lord" occurs in the NT.

In every single example listed above, when something is spoken "by the word of the Lord" (*en logō͵ kyriou*), there are serious consequences for not obeying that message. In the context of Paul's letter, his concern was that his hearers stand firm in the face of disappointment and discouragement, and even more specifically, to stand firm in the belief that "Jesus is returning!" – all

---

[158] The apocryphal book of *Sirach* (also known as *Ecclesiasticus*) was written down about 180 years or so before Jesus was born.

in the face of competing beliefs and notions from ancient Roman imperial cults.

b. Divine Revelation

And before we lay this topic to rest, there is one more absolutely delicious morsel to consider. I listed above all of the examples of "by the word of the Lord" (*en logōi kyriou*) in the Greek OT, Apocrypha, and NT. This phrase is a literal translation of the Hebrew phrase *bidvar YHWH* (בִּדְבַר יְהוָה). However, by chance, there is yet one more place in the Hebrew Bible that has this phrase which does not appear in the Greek OT (the Greek text is quite different). The text reads as follows:

> *19 As Samuel grew up, the LORD was with him and let none of his **words** fall to the ground. 20 And all Israel from Dan to Beer-sheba knew that Samuel was a trustworthy prophet of the LORD. 21 The LORD continued to appear at Shiloh,* **for the LORD <u>revealed</u> himself to Samuel at Shiloh <u>by the word of the LORD</u>.** *4:1 And the **word** of Samuel came to all Israel.* 1 Sa 3:19 (RSV)

Is it not at least interesting (striking?) that the Hebrew phrase "by the word of the Lord" is directly named as the manner of the Lord *revealing* himself?

The argument, here, is not that Paul is directly quoting or alluding to any of the OT texts listed above. (He is not on some proof-texting gig.) It is rather that he is using the exact same phraseology as found in these OT texts in order to elicit the same responses. This can only be done by one who is thoroughly accustomed to deep conversations with sacred texts.

As the call to Hezekiah's reform *by the word of Lord* (in 2Chronicles 30-31) resulted in followers of God going around destroying the influences from foreign religions, Paul's hope would be for a complete rejection of any competing claims from the Roman imperial cults (or any other source) for divinity, salvation, or hope in anyone but the risen Lord.

4. That's Just Perfect

In the course of this chapter, I have surveyed the sea of biblical uses of the phrases listed, and I have cast my net into the specific waters of one (likely the first) of Paul's letters. For Paul and all other NT writers (all of whom loved and quoted from the sacred texts), the "Word of God" is not a collection of books, but The Message of Jesus—the gospel.

To be clear, I do not believe that writers of the NT would have hesitated to refer to ancient holy writings as the Word of God. But they would not have confined it to that. Furthermore, whether we are talking about the OT or the NT, the authors *never* used the phrase "Word of God" to focus on the written texts for the sake of it being somehow holier than other forms of God speaking. And they *never* used it to refer to a "closed canon" of books. And even if certain texts in the NT are taken as using "Word of God" to refer to the written holy writings (and I don't think they do), they are not the predominant use of the phrase.

The mistake of contemporary readers is the disregard they have for specific applications of the phrase *in their own Bibles!* In other words, they assume a closed canon, overlay that with mounds of theological theory, apply "Word of God" to it, and then read that phrase in their leather-bound, gold-leafed, thumb-indexed "All about Me" Study Bibles to mean "closed canon" (namely *their* canon)—*and then they disregard how that very Bible of theirs uses the phrase!*

You might not like my approach or solution. So my reply is this: *Do something about this!* Repeating the same old stuff is not working. My book makes a simple suggestion. *Let's pursue the Word of God—the message of Christ. Let's stop concentrating so much on* **which** *canon, and more on* **how to use** *the various canons. Let's stop focusing so much on* **theoretical** *original autographs that we will never see, and focus more on properly applying the texts we* **hold in our hands**.

Many have sought to support the idea of perfect original autographs of biblical documents. But this is both beyond demonstration and a waste of time. I truly do not intend to be rude in this suggestion, but the usual approach is simply barking up the wrong tree. The Word of God is not about *format*, but *substance*. It is the message of Christ, the mystery hidden, and now revealed—whether by speech, act, or text (all of them precious—like the moon reflecting the sun). What is perfect is Christ living and alive: the Word of God in word, and text, and deed. If we want to talk about something perfect, then let's talk about that. But we don't need to theologically manufacture things about a perfect book.

16
The Name
Above Every Name

This topic deserves a lengthy set of detailed notes. Because of
its technical nature, I'll begin with a general overview and then
get more specific as I go.

A. Opening Summary

When I have talked about this in live classes, some partici-
pants are almost incensed with the suggestion that the name
"Jesus" is not the "Name above every name." They point to their
English translation

> *. . . therefore God exalted him to the highest place*
> *and gave him the name that is above every name,*
> *that at the name of Jesus every knee should bow,*
> *. . . ,*
> *and every tongue confess that Jesus Christ is Lord,*
> *to the glory of God the Father. (Phil 2:9-11 NIV)*

And so they say, "It's pretty clear from the Bible that God
lifted the name 'Jesus' above all other names." They then might
turn to Acts 4:12 and say, "See, here it says,

> *Salvation is found in no one else, for there is no other*
> *name under heaven given to men, by which we must be*
> *saved. (NIV)*

It doesn't matter which English translation you pick, they all
do pretty much the same thing: render the text somewhat
straightforwardly. Of course, it is no sin to do so; however, doing so in this case may leave the biblical text at the mercy of
readers who tend not to know much about ancient words or con-

texts. As Jesus says, "Seeing they do not see, and hearing they do not hear." (And God forbid that anyone should have an NASV [New American Standard Version], since for many that is far better than a Greek text, it being the translation sitting at the left hand of God—at the right hand being the KJV.)

For me, it is annoying, although extremely sad, that Christians don't know something as basic and as fundamentally Christological as this—and even more annoying that many Christian teachers do not seem to know it either. Both Philippians 2:9-11 and Acts 4:11-12 speak of the significance of the name of Jesus: a *human* name (i.e., a name "given to men") that in Hebrew is Joshua (*Y.hoshua*) and in Greek *Iēsous*. The name means "Yahweh Saves" and was a very common name (as it still is). Of course, there is nothing special about the name itself—*as a name*—as to why it receives accolades.

What is special in early Christian terms is rather the claim that the one with the human name Jesus of Nazareth is actually *Lord and Messiah*.

What is the basis of this claim? Both texts are pulling from concepts rooted in ancient sacred texts identifying Jesus with "Lord." Acts 4:11 directly quotes Psalm 118:22, about the rejected stone: clearly a text about the Lord (go read the whole of Psalm 118 and cf. Isa 8:14). This is the same text used in all four Gospels of Jesus riding into Jerusalem on a donkey, in which the crowd cries "Hosanna ('save us'), O Lord." (v. 25. This is the only place where the Hebrew *hoshiya na* occurs in the OT.) Psalm 118 is quoted or alluded to numerous times in the NT and was clearly regarded as a Messianic Psalm. Acts 4 is fairly subtle in this association and assumes that its readers and hearers are familiar with Psalm 118.

This is not a safe assumption nowadays. It is safer to guess that contemporary Christians have their Christology shaped more by popular Christian songs than by ancient sacred text. So we sing about the special name of Jesus or about Jesus being the name above all names or several other songs of similar misdirection. And of course, we don't just sing these songs, we repeat the phrases a hundred times each occasion, as is the laborious habit of contemporary Christian singing—all the while maintaining an emotional state that approaches sanctimonious delirium.

You might or might not forgive my understated tirade (believe me, it is understated), but I do not intend to be offensive. I greatly appreciate the dedicated work of many Christian musicians and I personally enjoy all kinds of good Christian music. Nor am I denigrating the name of Jesus! Hardly. Rather, the basis of my demurrer is that I have grown weary of so often being offended by the sound of pretty songs that make us "move," but are also destitute of theological substance—songs that are misleading and that devalue the pursuit of well-founded Christology. Not all songs do this, but enough do.

B. An Illustration

Allow me, please, to illustrate this from someone who apparently never knew Jesus and was certainly not a believer. And yet, during the middle ages he reached the status among Christian authors as "Bishop," at least many thinking him to have become Christian. Let me quote for you a simply marvelous text that was in existence before Paul ever wrote even one word of his letters (Paul, of course, was the earliest Christian author of record). Look carefully at this text which was originally in Greek:

> But if there be any as yet unfit to be called a _Son of God_, let him press to take his place under God's _First-born, the Word_, who holds the _eldership_ among the angels, their _ruler_ as it were. And many names are his, for he is called, "the _Beginning_," and the _Name of God_, and _His Word_, and the _Man after His image_, and "he that sees," that is Israel. [I praise those who say] "We are all sons of one man" (Gen 42:11). For if we have not yet become fit to be thought _sons of God_ yet we may be sons of _His invisible image, the most holy Word_. For _the Word_ is the _eldest-born image of God_.

There is simply not enough time or space to write thoroughly about this quote. But as 21st century Christians looking back without contextual reference, we might be tempted to read this quote as referring to Jesus. We can think of numerous NT texts that use this very language. By listing some of the Greek words of this text here—*huios theou, prototokos, arkē, presbutatos, archaggelos, onoma theou, eikōn (son of God, first-born, beginning, eldest-born, archangel, name of God, image of God)*—this would make anyone with an ounce of familiarity with NT Christological terms to start hyperventilating! If you want to talk about emotional states of delirium, this can cause it!

Philo of Alexandria, who wrote this piece,[159] died at the very time Paul was beginning to write his letters. Philo is not talking about Jesus at all, but about the divine Logos or Word, which for him was the Reason of God. He is prolific about this, and it is far more than what I have just stated—but we simply can't go there now. We must note, however, that even though most Christians today never heard of him, Philo himself lived in, wrote for, and influenced the self-same thought-world as some of the NT writers, especially Paul, John, and Hebrews. Whether these NT authors were influenced directly by Philo or not, they sure spoke the same language—only now they focused on Jesus Christ as Lord.

Philo was a devout Jew, highly-educated in the Greek philosophy of the day and was fluent in the Greek OT. Even though it is doubtful that he knew Hebrew at all, in the text quoted above, he still refers to the name of God *(nomos theou)* without saying the name. Why? Because Jews did not pronounce the name of God. Yet for Philo, "the Word" is the same person as the "Name of God."

C. Phil 2:9-11

The bottom line is fairly simple: Paul does the very same thing in Phil 2:9-11. The text begins and ends with the concept that Jesus is God:

---

[159] *The Confusion of Tongues*, 146-147. See also the definitive work on Philo by David T. Runia, *Philo in Early Christian Literature: A Survey* (Fortress: 1993).

v. 6 "equality with God"

v. 11 *"KYRIOS* (emphatic) is Jesus Christ"

In this text, "The Name" of God is called upon as in the OT: "praise the Name," "bless the Name," "fear the Name," "call upon the Name." All of these refer unequivocally to "YAHWEH" (Greek, "LORD").

Unlike the Philo text we looked at, Paul (in Phil 2:11) actually states the name in Greek—and it is not Jesus. It is the Name above every name. "You shall not take the Name of YAHWEH (Greek, LORD) your God in vain." Paul says God lavished this Name on Jesus Christ so that when Jesus' name is spoken people will know that *"Jesus Christ—his name is KURIOS!"*

Now for those who are Greek minded, my point is not that "Lord" is the subject. I said earlier that the typical translation is technically correct: "Jesus Christ is Lord." The word "Lord" is a predicate nominative that has a qualitative/definite force.[160] This means that Jesus Christ is identified as the very KYRIOS of the Greek OT texts—texts that are clearly referring to Yahweh. The verb is not stated, but it doesn't need to be; and the predicate nominative has been moved to the front of the phrase for emphasis. And we can see parallels to this:

theos estin ho logos = **God** is the Word (Jn 1:1)

KYRIOS Iēsous Xristos = **LORD** is Jesus Christ

It would have been scandalous to equate Jesus with the very name *KYRIOS*—and that is why Paul is urging humility and service like Jesus, who did not use his equality with God to his own advantage, and yet had it lavished upon him.

---

[160] Daniel B. Wallace, *Greek Grammar Beyond the Basics* (Zondervan, 1996) pp. 270, 288 and 474 identifies this as definite: *"the* Lord" (namely, Yahweh). By Wallace's own categories (p.263), the force appears rather to be a qualitative/definite overlap inasmuch as Jesus takes on the quality, nature, and essence of KYRIOS, personifying in himself that very identification: it is more than a title.

D. Why So Technical?

There are those, of course, who wonder why this has to be so technical and difficult: "Why can't we just take the '*plain meaning* of the text'?" Perhaps this will help: Have you ever changed your mind about the meaning of a Bible text? Have you ever noticed how the "plain meaning of the text" changes the more you learn about the Bible? Consider that what is not so plain to us was plain to those who were there.

For your own edification do this: Go read Isaiah 45 and Psalm 117[161] from the following website (the Greek OT in a new English translation):

http://ccat.sas.upenn.edu/nets/edition/

Look for the word "Lord" in the text and how it functions. Imagine yourself an early follower of Jesus believing that Jesus is LORD in sacred texts. What might you see from these two chapters alone?

E. *KYRIOS* (LORD) as the Divine Name of God

It is helpful to remember that the NT documents have what can best be described as *relational or contextual Christology*—alive, compelling, and explained "as needed." Sometimes, such statements appear not to fit easily with other statements, but that is the price paid for a living, inductive approach. There is no 200-page, systematic handbook entitled "Jesus as LORD" or "Jesus as Christ" anywhere in the NT. Rather, we find "Christology on the move." Not haphazard; just at work in the many contexts and situations facing early believers. In the end, NT Christology is very practical, and it is always presented in a way that makes sense to life and living.

To understand about the Divine Name of God, it is important to understand some things about the sacred writings of the early church. Scholars don't agree on how to evaluate all the issues

---

[161] Psalm 118 in Hebrew and English is Psalm 117 in the Greek OT.

involved, but here is a general summary and some observations. Also keep in mind that we are not talking about a finalized "canon" here; we are talking about the documents from which early Christians read.

By and large, the Christians of the 1st century read from Greek holy writings—that is to say, Hebrew holy texts now in Greek. This is more important than most people realize. The Greek sacred writings had been translated from Hebrew manuscripts 200 years or so prior to Jesus' birth. These are the holy texts predominantly used by early Christians, including Paul (even though he also knew Hebrew).

In Hebrew manuscripts of the OT, God's holy name is יהוה (YHWH or JHVH). It is regarded as the highest of all names and is often called the "Divine Name" or the "Tetragrammaton" (meaning "four letters"). This Hebrew name was considered so holy that early Jewish scribes inserted the Hebrew name יהוה into Greek translations. All of the surviving Greek OT manuscripts that we have from 50 B.C. to A.D. 100 follow this practice.[162]

Remember also that early texts were always read aloud. So, when reading aloud from the manuscripts, early Jews developed the practice of not pronouncing the Divine Name of God so as not to take it in vain. (Hence, we now don't know how to pronounce it. The best we can do in English is "Yahweh" or "Jehovah.") A reader would see the name יהוה but would say another word: *adonai* (if speaking Hebrew); or *KYRIOS* (if speaking Greek).[163] Both of the substitute words meant "Lord." This

---

[162] For examples of this, go to the website by Robert Kraft: http://www.sas.upenn.edu/religious_studies/rak/earlylxx/EARLYPAP.HTM and click on any of the many links. You might also type in a Google image search for "tetragrammaton in Greek Manuscript."

[163] By the time of the NT, the majority of Jews lived outside of Palestine and many spoke Hebrew as a second language, if at all. Philo of Alexandria is a good example. A wealthy and highly educated Jewish resident in Egypt, this older contemporary of Paul was fluent in Greek philosophy and language, as well as the Greek OT; but it appears he did not know Hebrew well, if at all.

practice was intended as a show of respect and sanctity for the name of God.

Starting about the 2nd century A.D., Christian scribes who were copying OT texts in Greek (and who did not know Hebrew) began replacing all the occurrences of יהוה with the Greek translation *KYRIOS* or some form of it. Today, all copies of the Greek OT sold in bookstores have the Greek word *KYRIOS* in place of the Hebrew word יהוה .

Keep in mind this is a general summary. There is ongoing and lively debate among biblical scholars on the topic of God's Divine Name, and some would challenge the picture just painted. The primary question is this: *Did Jews in the early and mid-1st century A.D. refer to God using the Greek word KYRIOS?* There is ample external evidence that they did (e.g., from Philo of Alexandria) and internal evidence (e.g., why are NT authors so readily able to refer to God as *KYRIOS* if it was not an accepted practice?). Some have speculated that the original NT documents themselves may have included the Hebrew name of God in OT quotations instead of the Greek word *KYRIOS,* but this is both beyond current demonstration and still does not address the question just asked.

There is good reason to believe that early Greek speaking Jews spoke the word *KYRIOS* as the Divine Name in Greek (in place of יהוה). It is certainly used throughout the NT in this manner.

F. The Uses of the Word *Kyrios*

As to the meaning of the Greek word *kyrios,* it is used in five basic ways in the Greek NT: (1) to mean "sir"; (2) to designate a "master" of one or more slaves; (3) to denote a "deity" of some kind, including Roman emperors; (4) as a title for Jesus; and (5) as God's Divine Name where the OT Hebrew text has יהוה (YHWH).

When referring to God's Divine Name, most English translations use "LORD" (all caps) in the OT and "Lord" in the NT. This is a longstanding practice. However, it tends to obscure the issue for English readers, since (1) the word is not a name but a title; and (2) it gives the appearance of a clear distinction between the LORD of the OT and the Lord of the NT, even when they both refer to the same Hebrew personal name: יהוה .

Although many English readers never notice the capitalizations, the distinctions are beneficial for careful reading in English. However, more germane to our purpose is *the manner in which early Christians understood and applied the word KYRIOS in relation both to God and to Jesus Christ.* For, despite the effort of some to deny this usage (e.g., Jehovah's Witnesses), early Christians applied the Divine Name to Jesus in certain contexts, putting Jesus on a par with God. The best known example is Phil 2:6 and 11, where (as was mentioned) two phrases are juxtaposed:

> v. 6 "equality with God"
> v. 11 "*KYRIOS* (emphatic) is Jesus Christ"

See also John 5:18 where Jesus is accused of putting himself on par with God by calling him "Father." This is just a start.

It is not my purpose, here, to force Greek words on English readers or to advocate some kind of fad. The point is, rather, to make it possible for readers to reflect on the significance of the use of the term "LORD/Lord/ lord" in the OT and NT, but also to see and hear the term *KYRIOS* as it might have been seen and heard by early believers.

Although technically a title, in the NT it can be used as the Divine Name of God to show Jesus on a par with God.

"Jesus Christ—his name is KURIOS!"

G. Reading List for the Name

For those who want to do some detailed reading on the matter, here is a selected reading list.

Joseph Fitzmyer, "New Testament Kyrios and Maranatha and Their Aramaic Background," in *To Advance the Gospel* (New York: Crossroad, 1981).

George Howard, "The Tetragram in the NT," *JBL* 96 (1977): 63-83; also, *The Gospel of Matthew According to a Primitive Hebrew Text*, 1987.

Larry Hurtado, *LORD Jesus Christ: Devotion to Jesus in Earliest Christianity* (Eerdmans, June 1, 2003); also, *One God, One Lord: Early Christian Devotion and Ancient Jewish Monotheism* (T. & T. Clark, November 1, 2003); also, *How On Earth Did Jesus Become A God?: Historical Questions About Earliest Devotion To Jesus* (Eerdmans, November 15, 2005).

C. F. D. Moule, *The Origin of Christology* (Cambridge University Press, 1977).

A. Pietersma, "Kyrios or Tetragram: A Renewed Quest for the Original Septuagint" in *De Septuaginta,* Studies in Honor of John William Wevers on his sixty-fifth birthday, ed. A. Pietersma and C. Cox (Mississauga, Ont., Canada: Benben Publications, 1984).

J. R. Royse, "Philo, Kyrios, and the Tetragrammaton," *The Studia Philonica Annual,* Vol. 3, ed. D. T. Runia (Atlanta: Scholars Press, 1991), 167-83.

Emmanuel Tov, *The Greek Minor Prophets Scroll from Nahal Hever* (Oxford: Clarendon Press; 1990); also, *The Text-Critical Use of the Septuagint in Biblical Research* in Jerusalem Biblical Studies 8, 2nd ed., rev. and enlarged (Jerusalem: Simor, 1997).

N. T. Wright, *The Resurrection of the Son of God: Christian Origins and the Question of God* (Augsburg Fortress Publishers, April 1, 2003).

PART 3:
Partners in
the Conversation

ΒΙΒΛΙΟΘΗΚΗ

(bibliothēkē)
book case, library

Tools to facilitate conversation.

1. Conversation Partners
2. Abbreviations
3. Index
4. About the Author

Conversation Partners

(A Highly Selective List)

The Bible is a faith-community effort. For that reason alone, it is no mere book to be owned. Its nature and use cannot be determined whimsically or ritually or forcefully or in isolation.

Determining the nature and use of the Bible is not about justifying previous or long-held conclusions. It is not about pleasing our parents or kowtowing to college teachers or blindly following religious leaders. It is not about keeping our jobs or protecting our own sense of order in the world. And it is not about showing up Bible critics in a fight—or even forming little camps and killing off one another.

This is about the heartbeat of an ancient understanding of God in the world. It is a moment of truth. And the most crucial of all questions is not, "Who is right and who is wrong?" It is rather **"How do we create a culture of open and engaged conversation in which we can *think* together without acrimony?"**

For this, we need each other in all our variety to become conversation partners. Partners who will both challenge and encourage each other on multiple levels.

For this we do not want to only read authors that support our previous beliefs. We should want to be challenged, made uncomfortable, and engaged on the deepest levels.

You can do this privately or in study groups. But study groups need to understand their function: to study and consider, even amid disagreement.

Following is a very selective list that represents a wide array of approaches and positions. Naturally, the more detailed the study, the more conversation partners we will need at the table.

This list should be seen as suggestive, and it is listed twice: by alphabet and by year.

Alphabetical Listing

Abraham, William J., Jason E. Vickers, Natalie B. Van Kirk (eds). *Canonical Theism: A Proposal for Theology and the Church.* Eerdmans, 2008.

Achtemeier, Paul J. *Inspiration and Authority: Nature and Function of Christian Scripture.* Hendrickson, 1999.

Allert, Craig D. A High View of Scripture? The Authority of the Bible and the Formation of the New Testament Canon. Baker Academic, 2007.

Barton, John. *Holy Writings, Sacred Text: The Canon of Early Christianity.* Westminster John Knox, 1998.

Beckwith, R. T. "The Formation of the Hebrew Bible." Pages 39-86 in *Mikra: Text, Translation, Reading, and Interpretation of the Hebrew Bible in Ancient Judaism and Early Christianity.* Edited by Martin Jan Mulder and Harry Sysling. Compendium rerum iudaicarum ad Novum Testamentum 2.1. Fortress, 1991.

Best, Ernest. "Scripture, Tradition, and the Canon of the NT." *Bulletin of the John Rylands University Library,* 61 (1978-79): 258-89.

Brown, William P. (ed). *Engaging Biblical Authority: Perspectives on the Bible as Scripture.* Westminster John Knox, 2007.

Bruce, F. F. *The New Testament Documents: Are They Reliable?* 5th rev. ed. Eerdmans, 1960.

Childs, Brevard. *The New Testament as Canon: An Introduction.* Fortress, 1985.

Christensen, Duane L. *Explosion of the Canon: The Greek New Testament in Early Church History.* BIBAL Press, 2004.

Comfort, Philip Wesley (ed). *The Origin of the Bible.* Tyndale House, 1992.

Dogmatic Constitution On Divine Revelation: Dei Verbum solemnly promulgated by His Holiness Pope Paul VI on November 18, 1965. Boston: Pauline Books & Media,1966. [http://www.vatican.va/archive/hist_councils/ii_vatica n_council/documents/vat-ii_const_ 19651118_dei-verbum_en.html].

Ehrman, Bart D. *Forged: Writing in the Name of God—Why the Bible's Authors Are Not Who We Think They Are.* HarperOne, 2011.

_____. The Orthodox Corruption of Scripture: The Effect of Early Christological Controversies on the Text of the New Testament. Oxford University Press, 1993.

Evans, Craig A. and Emmanuel Tov (eds). *Exploring the Origins of the Bible: Canon Formation in Historical, Literary, and Theological Perspective.* Baker Academic, 2008.

Finkelberg, Margalit and Gedaliahu A. G. Stroumsa. *Homer, the Bible, and Beyond: Literary and Religious Canons in the Ancient World.* Jerusalem Studies in Religion and Culture, 2. Brill Academic Pub, 2003.

Gamble, Harry Y. *Books and Readers in the Early Church: A History of Early Christian Texts.* Yale University Press, 1995.

_____. *The New Testament Canon: Its Making and Meaning.* Guides to Biblical Scholarship. Fortress, 1985.

Geisler, Norman L., and William C. Roach. *Defending Inerrancy: Affirming the Accuracy of Scripture for a New Generation.* Baker Books, 2012.

Gnuse, Robert Karl. *Authority of the Bible: Theories of Inspiration, Revelation, and the Canon of Scripture.* Paulist Press, 1985.

Harris, Robert Laird. *Inspiration and Canonicity of the Bible: An Historical and Exegetical Study.* Zondervan, 1971.

Kasser, Rodolphe, Marvin Meyer, and Gregor Wurst (eds). *The Gospel of Judas.* National Geographic, 2006.

Köstenberger Andreas J. and Michael J. Kruger. *The Heresy of Orthodoxy: How Contemporary Culture's Fascination with Diversity has Reshaped Our Understanding of Christianity.* Crossway, 2010.

McDonald, Lee Martin, and James A. Sanders (eds). *The Canon Debate.* Baker Academic, 2011.

McDonald, Lee Martin. *Forgotten Scriptures.* Westminster John Knox, 2009.

_____. The Biblical Canon: Its Origin, Transmission, and Authority. 3rd corrected ed. Baker Academic, 2011.

_____. The Origin of the Bible: A Guide for the Perplexed. T & T Clark, 2011.

Metzger, Bruce M. *The Canon of the New Testament: Its Origin, Development, and Significance.* Oxford University Press, 1987.

Metzger, Bruce M., and Bart D. Ehrman. *The Text of the New Testament: Its Transmission, Corruption, and Restoration.* 4th ed. Oxford University Press, 2005.

Meyer, Marvin W., and Harold Bloom. *The Gospel of Thomas: The Hidden Sayings of Jesus.* 2d ed. HarperSanFrancisco, 2004.

Sanders, James A. *From Sacred Story to Sacred Text: Canon as Paradigm.* Fortress, 1987.

Schneiders, Sandra Marie. *The Revelatory Text: Interpreting the New Testament as Sacred Scripture.* HarperSanFrancisco, 1991.

Sundberg, Albert C. "The Bible Canon and the Christian Doctrine of Inspiration." *Interpretation* 29 no. 4 (October 1975): 352-71.

The Chicago Statement on Biblical Inerrancy. International Council on Biblical Inerrancy 1978.

Ulrich, Eugene Charles. *The Dead Sea Scrolls and the Origins of the Bible.* Studies in the Dead Sea Scrolls and Related Literature. Eerdmans, 1999.

Warfield, Benjamin Breckinridge, Samuel G. Craig, and Cornelius Van Til. *Inspiration and Authority of the Bible.* Presbyterian and Reformed Publishing, 1948.

Zia, Mark J. *What Are They Saying About Biblical Inspiration?* Paulist Press, 2011.

Listing By Year

2012—Geisler, Norman L., and William C. Roach. *Defending Inerrancy: Affirming the Accuracy of Scripture for a New Generation.* Baker Books, 2012.

2011—Ehrman, Bart D. *Forged: Writing in the Name of God—Why the Bible's Authors Are Not Who We Think They Are.* HarperOne, 2011.

2011—McDonald, Lee Martin, and James A. Sanders (eds). *The Canon Debate.* Baker Academic, 2011.

2011—McDonald, Lee Martin. The Biblical Canon: Its Origin, Transmission, and Authority. 3rd corrected ed. Baker Academic, 2011.

2011—McDonald, Lee Martin. The Origin of the Bible: A Guide for the Perplexed. T & T Clark, 2011.

2011—Zia, Mark J. *What Are They Saying About Biblical Inspiration?* Paulist Press, 2011.

2010—Köstenberger Andreas J. and Michael J. Kruger. *The Heresy of Orthodoxy: How Contemporary Culture's Fascination with Diversity has Reshaped Our Understanding of Christianity.* Crossway, 2010.

2009—McDonald, Lee Martin. *Forgotten Scriptures.* Westminster John Knox, 2009.

2008—Abraham, William J., Jason E. Vickers, Natalie B. Van Kirk (eds). *Canonical Theism: A Proposal for Theology and the Church.* Eerdmans, 2008.

2008—Evans, Craig A. and Emmanuel Tov (eds). *Exploring the Origins of the Bible: Canon Formation in Historical, Literary, and Theological Perspective.* Baker Academic, 2008.

2007—Allert, Craig D. A High View of Scripture? The Authority of the Bible and the Formation of the New Testament Canon. Baker Academic, 2007.

2007—Brown, William P. (ed). *Engaging Biblical Authority: Perspectives on the Bible as Scripture.* Westminster John Knox, 2007.

2006—Kasser, Rodolphe, Marvin Meyer, and Gregor Wurst (eds). *The Gospel of Judas.* National Geographic, 2006.

2005—Metzger, Bruce M., and Bart D. Ehrman. *The Text of the New Testament: Its Transmission, Corruption, and Restoration.* 4th ed. Oxford University Press, 2005.

2004—Christensen, Duane L. *Explosion of the Canon: The Greek New Testament in Early Church History.* BIBAL Press, 2004.

2004—Meyer, Marvin W., and Harold Bloom. *The Gospel of Thomas: The Hidden Sayings of Jesus.* 2d ed. HarperSanFrancisco, 2004.

2003—Finkelberg, Margalit and Gedaliahu A. G. Stroumsa. *Homer, the Bible, and Beyond: Literary and Religious Canons in the Ancient World.* Jerusalem Studies in Religion and Culture, 2. Brill Academic Pub, 2003.

1999—Achtemeier, Paul J. *Inspiration and Authority: Nature and Function of Christian Scripture.* Hendrickson, 1999.

1999—Ulrich, Eugene Charles. *The Dead Sea Scrolls and the Origins of the Bible.* Studies in the Dead Sea Scrolls and Related Literature. Eerdmans, 1999.

1998—Barton, John. *Holy Writings, Sacred Text: The Canon of Early Christianity.* Westminster John Knox, 1998.

1995—Gamble, Harry Y. *Books and Readers in the Early Church: A History of Early Christian Texts.* Yale University Press, 1995.

1993—Ehrman, Bart D. The Orthodox Corruption of Scripture: The Effect of Early Christological Controversies on the Text of the New Testament. Oxford University Press, 1993.

1992—Comfort, Philip Wesley (ed). *The Origin of the Bible.* Tyndale House, 1992.

1991—Beckwith, R. T. "The Formation of the Hebrew Bible." Pages 39-86 in *Mikra: Text, Translation, Reading, and Interpretation of the Hebrew Bible in Ancient Judaism and Early Christianity.* Edited by Martin Jan Mulder and Harry Sysling. Compendium rerum iudaicarum ad Novum Testamentum 2.1. Fortress, 1991.

1991—Schneiders, Sandra Marie. *The Revelatory Text: Interpreting the New Testament as Sacred Scripture.* HarperSanFrancisco, 1991.

1987—Metzger, Bruce M. *The Canon of the New Testament: Its Origin, Development, and Significance.* Oxford University Press, 1987.

1987—Sanders, James A. *From Sacred Story to Sacred Text: Canon as Paradigm.* Fortress, 1987.

1985—Childs, Brevard. *The New Testament as Canon: An Introduction.* Fortress, 1985.

1985—Gamble, Harry Y. *The New Testament Canon: Its Making and Meaning.* Guides to Biblical Scholarship. Fortress, 1985.

1985—Gnuse, Robert Karl. *Authority of the Bible: Theories of Inspiration, Revelation, and the Canon of Scripture.* Paulist Press, 1985.

1979—Best, Ernest. "Scripture, Tradition, and the Canon of the NT." *Bulletin of the John Rylands University Library,* 61 (1978-79): 258-89.

1978— *The Chicago Statement on Biblical Inerrancy.* International Council on Biblical Inerrancy 1978.

1975—Sundberg, Albert C. "The Bible Canon and the Christian Doctrine of Inspiration." *Interpretation* 29 no. 4 (October 1975): 352-71.

1971—Harris, Robert Laird. *Inspiration and Canonicity of the Bible: An Historical and Exegetical Study.* Zondervan, 1971.

1965—Dogmatic Constitution On Divine Revelation: Dei Verbum solemnly promulgated by His Holiness Pope Paul VI on November 18, 1965. Pauline Books & Media,1966. [http://www.vatican.va/archive/hist_councils/ii_vatica n_council/documents/vat-ii_const_19651118_dei-verbum_en.html].

1960—Bruce, F. F. *The New Testament Documents: Are They Reliable?* 5th rev. ed. Eerdmans, 1960.

1948—Warfield, Benjamin Breckinridge, Samuel G. Craig, and Cornelius Van Til. *Inspiration and Authority of the Bible.* Presbyterian and Reformed Publishing, 1948.

Abbreviations

English Translations of the Bible

Amplified	The Amplified Bible
BBE	Bible in Basic English
CEV	Contemporary English Version
CWPT	Coffee With Paul Translation
KJV	King James Version
LB	Living Bible Paraphrase
Moffat	Moffat, James. *The Translation of the Bible Containing the Old and New Testaments.* Harper, 1935.
MSG	The Message
NAB	New American Bible (Original version, 1970)
NASV	New American Standard Version
NEB	New English Bible
NETB	NET Bible
NIV	New International Version
NJB	New Jerusalem Bible
NLT	New Living Translation
NRSV	New Revised Standard Version
REB	Revised English Bible
RSV	Revised Standard Version
SEB	Simple English Bible
TEV	Today's English Version
WWE	World Wide English translation
YLT	Young's Literal Translation

Abbreviations for Greek and English

Within the body of the book, words from the Greek NT are "transliterated" (i.e., brought into English, letter by letter). For example, λόγος = *logos*. This way, if you are interested, but do not know the Greek alphabet, you will still be able to pronounce the Greek word.

Transliteration Chart, Greek to English

Name	Greek Letter	Translit- eration	Special Notes
alpha	α	a	
beta	β	b	
gamma	γ	g	gg, kg, and xg = ng— ἄγγελος = angelos ("angel")
delta	δ	d	
epsilon	ε	e	
zeta	ζ	z	
eta	η	ē	
theta	θ	th	
iota	ι	i	
kappa	κ	k	
lambda	λ	l	
mu	μ	m	
nu	ν	n	
xi	ξ	x	
omicron	o	o	
pi	π	p	
rho	ρ	r	
sigma	σ or ς	s	So, πίστις = pistis ("faith")
tau	τ	t	
upsilon	υ	u	For simplicity, u is always u, instead of y.
phi	φ	ph	
chi	χ	ch	As in Christ, never as in church.
psi	ψ	ps	
omega	ω	ō	

Abbreviations for Biblical Documents

Gen	1, 2Chr	Jer	Nah	Ac	Phlm
Ex	Ezra	Lam	Hab	Rom	Heb
Lev	Neh	Ezek	Zeph	1,2Cor	Jas
Num	Esth	Dan	Hag	Gal	1, 2Pt
Deut	Job	Hos	Zech	Eph	1, 2, 3Jn
Josh	Ps (Pss)	Joel	Mal	Phil	Jude
Judg	Prov	Amos	Mt	Col	Rev
Ruth	Eccl	Obad	Mk	1, 2Th	
1, 2Sam	Song	Jonah	Lk	1, 2Tim	
1, 2Kgs	Isa	Mic	Jn	Titus	

Abbreviations for Apocrypha & Pseudepigrapha

Wis	*Wisdom of Solomon*
1, 2Esd	1, 2 Esdras
1En	1 Enoch
1, 2, 4Macc	1, 2, and 4 Maccabees

Abbreviations for Philo

Abr	*De Abrahamo*
Agr	*De agricultura*
Cher	*De Cherubim*
Conf	*De confusion linguarum*
Congr	*De congress eruditionis gratia*
Decal	*De Decalogo*
Ebr	*De ebrietate*
Flacc	*In Flaccum*
Fug	*De fuga et inventione*
Her	*Quis rerum divinarum heres sit*
Legat	*Legatio ad Gaium*
Migr	*De migration Abrahami*
Mos	*De vita Moysis*
Opif	*De opificio mundi*
Post	*De posteritate Caini*
Praem	*De praemiis et poenis, De exsecrationibus*
Prob	*Quod omnis probus liber sit*
Prov	*De Providentia*
QG	*Quaestiones et solutiones in Genesim*
Sacr	*De sacrificiis Abelis et Caini*
Somn	*De somniis*
Spec	*De specialibus legibus*
Virt	*De virtutibus*

Abbreviations for Josephus

Ap	*Contra Apionem*
Ant	*Antiquitates Judaicae*

Abbreviations for Resources

AB	Anchor Bible Reference Library
ABD	*Anchor Bible Dictionary.* 6 volumes. Doubleday, 1992.
Apoc	Apocrypha

BDAG	Bauer, Danker, Arndt, and Gingrich, *A Greek-English Lexicon of the New Testament and Other Early Christian Literature*. 3rd edition. Chicago, 2000.
BDF	Blass, DeBrunner, Funk, *A Greek Gammar of the New Testament and Other Early Christian Literature*. Chicago, 1961.
BG	Zerwick, Maximilian. *Biblical Greek*. Scripta Pontificii Instituti Biblici. Rome 1963.
CBQ	*Catholic Biblical Quarterly*.
CRINT	Compendia Rerum Iudaicarum ad Novum Testamentum.
DNTB	Hawthorne, Martin, Reid. *Dictionary of New Testament Background*. IVP, 2000.
DPL	*Dictionary of Paul and His Letters*. IVP, 1993.
DSST	Martinez, Florentino Garcia. *The Dead Sea Scrolls Translated: The Qumran Texts in English*. 2nd edition. Grand Rapids: Eerdmans, 1992.
HCNT	Boring, Berger, Colpe. *Hellenistic Commentary to the New Testament*. Abingdon, 1995.
ISBERev	*International Standard Bible Encyclopedia*. 4 volumes. Eerdmans, 1979-1988.
IVP	Inter-Varsity Press
JBL	*The Journal of Biblical Literature*
JSNT	*The Journal for the Study of the New Testament*
JWSTP	*Jewish Writings of the Second Temple Period: Apocrypha, Pseudepigrapha, Qumran Sectarian Writings, Philo, Josephus.* The Literature of the Jewish People in the Period of the Second Temple and the Talmud. Section 2. CRINT. Fortress, 1984.
LS	Liddell, Scott, and Jones. *A Greek English Lexicon*. Oxford, 1968.
LXX	Septuagint (the Greek OT)
NA27	Nestle-Aland. *Novum Testamentum Graece*. 27th edition. Stuttgart, 1993.
NETS	*A New English Translation of the Septuagint*, by the International Organization of Septuagint and Cognate Studies, Inc., 2007.
NIDB	*The New Interpreters Dictionary of the Bible*. 5 volumes. Abingdon Press, 2009.
NIGTC	New International Greek Testament Commentary
NT	New Testament
NTMI	*The New Testament and It's Modern Interpreters*. Ed. by Eldon Epp and George McRae. Scholars Press, 1988.
NTS	*New Testament Studies*
OT	Old Testament
PACE	Project on Ancient Cultural Engagement

PG	*Patrologia graeca.* Edited by J. P. Migne. 162 volumes. Paris, 1857-1886.
pl	plural
Pseud	Pseudepigrapha
sg	singular
TDNT	*Theological Dictionary of the New Testament.* 10 volumes. 1964-1976. Ed. by G. Kittel, G. W. Bromiley & G. Friedrich.
TR	Textus Receptus, or "Received Text," the form of the Greek text commonly accepted and in use at the time the KJV was translated in the early 17th century.
UBS4	United Bible Society Greek NT, 4th ed.

Index

Apologies to all in advance for this kind of "group" indexing of Ancient References.
I do not have the tools to produce a proper one at this time.

1

1 OT TEXTS
1 General . 80, 90, 96, 100, 101, 102, 125, 141, 156, 163, 164, 190, 193, 196, 201, 202, 215, 216, 217, 218, 220, 221, 223, 230, 246, 248, 257, 262, 264, 266, 267, 268, 270, 271, 274, 275, 276, 280, 283, 284, 285, 286, 287
1Chronicles 198, 200, 214
1Kings 221
2Chronicles 198, 200, 201, 214, 274
2Esdras 198
2Kings 221, 254
Daniel 149, 201, 214, 254, 255, 275, 283
Deuteronomy 89, 141, 149, 156, 184, 197, 198, 202, 203, 220, 239, 255, 263
Ecclesiastes 274
Exodus . 70, 114, 196, 202, 203, 253, 263
Ezekiel 214, 251, 252, 254, 255, 274
Ezra 196, 198
Genesis .. 68, 69, 149, 150, 156, 220, 255, 281
Habakkuk 220
Isaiah ... 70, 114, 119, 148, 163, 165, 167, 201, 202, 214, 220, 221, 223, 238, 239, 244, 251, 252, 253, 254, 255, 259, 266, 268, 280, 284
Jeremiah 126, 151, 163, 201, 251, 252, 254, 263, 269, 274
Joshua 239, 251, 280
Judges 251, 263
Kings 69, 251, 274
Lamentations 254
Leviticus 148, 199, 220
Malachi 163, 263
Minor Prophets 251, 252
Nehemiah 70, 198, 218, 254
Numbers 70, 202, 235, 237, 238, 239, 253, 255, 263
Proverbs 89, 184, 252, 255
Psalms .. 70, 163, 214, 221, 223, 224, 230, 231, 232, 233, 240, 252, 253, 255, 257, 258, 259, 260, 264, 268, 280, 284
Ruth 148
Samuel 251, 275, 295, 299
Zechariah 163, 224, 254
Zephaniah 254

2

2 NT TEXTS
1 General 30, 33, 34, 35, 60, 80, 84, 90, 96, 97, 100, 101, 102, 122, 125, 127, 129, 136, 150, 151, 152, 156, 158, 163, 164, 185, 186, 190, 192, 193, 199, 200, 201, 202, 213, 214, 215,

216, 217, 219, 220, 221,
222, 223, 229, 230, 237,
238, 246, 247, 248, 249,
254, 256, 260, 262, 264,
265, 266, 267, 268, 271,
272, 273, 274, 275, 276,
280, 282, 284, 285, 286,
287, 288, 292, 297, 298
1Corinthians 63, 64, 70, 83, 89,
114, 162, 167, 185, 199,
222, 227, 230, 238, 241,
243, 246, 267, 268, 269, 270
1John................................. 230
1Peter 163, 167, 214, 215, 221,
265, 267
1Thessalonians.. 152, 262, 267,
268, 269, 270, 271, 273, 274
1Timothy..... 71, 221, 222, 223,
266, 267, 269
2Corinthians.. 89, 91, 124, 125,
163, 167, 183, 222, 230,
267, 271
2Peter 83, 89, 183, 214, 215,
221, 258, 259
2Thessalonians................... 270
2Timothy28, 41, 71, 80, 83, 84,
112, 122, 191, 195, 214,
220, 221, 259, 265, 267, 269
Acts71, 97, 152, 155, 156, 163,
177, 191, 220, 221, 237,
243, 244, 257, 260, 280
Colossians 266, 267, 271
Ephesians 81, 222, 223, 230,
266, 267
Galatians 89, 183, 215, 220,
269, 273
Gospels.. 69, 70, 148, 152, 153,
154, 155, 163, 264, 280
Hebrews .. 34, 81, 91, 101, 155,
163, 227, 230, 238, 266,
267, 271, 282
James. 101, 155, 199, 212, 215,
222, 223, 238, 270
John. 29, 34, 83, 149, 150, 152,
154, 155, 163, 191, 212,
214, 221, 222, 223, 224,

225, 228, 229, 230, 232,
233, 234, 235, 236, 237,
238, 239, 240, 244, 245,
246, 247, 248, 253, 258,
266, 267, 283, 287, 288,
292, 298
Jude70, 81, 101, 102, 238, 253,
254, 259, 264
Luke....... 34, 89, 150, 155, 183,
184, 185, 191, 208, 228,
230, 240, 242, 243, 244,
256, 257, 260
Luke-Acts 34, 83, 114, 148,
150, 152, 153, 154, 155,
156, 163, 167, 267, 270,
271, 279, 280
Mark .. 149, 150, 153, 154, 163,
186, 187, 191, 228, 230,
238, 240, 241, 242, 243,
244, 256, 266, 267, 271,
295, 296
Matthew..... 8, 89, 91, 119, 150,
152, 153, 154, 155, 162,
163, 185, 228, 230, 240,
241, 242, 256, 260, 267,
271, 288
Philippians.149, 164, 280, 282,
287
Revelation64, 83, 89, 101, 148,
152, 184, 262, 266, 267,
271, 275
Romans...... 127, 129, 130, 150,
152, 214, 220, 221, 230,
258, 267, 268, 269
Titus...........................266, 267

3

3 OTHER ANCIENT TEXTS

1Enoch............70, 81, 253, 259
1Esdras 198, 201
1Maccabees 201, 214
2Esdras 200
2Maccabees 201, 217, 254
4Maccabees 201, 203, 255
Acts of Paul and Thecla........71
Apocalypse of Baruch 264

Apocalyptic ... 23, 64, 102, 148, 149
Apocrypha ... 90, 101, 115, 196, 198, 201, 210, 218, 230, 262, 275
Aristeas, Letter of 184, 203, 205, 211
Assumption of Moses 253
Church Fathers
   Didache 116
   Shepherd 116
Dead Sea Scrolls 116, 126, 239, 264
   Qumran 218, 238, 239
Josephus 116, 185, 208, 209, 210, 211, 212, 213, 220, 222, 227
Nag Hammadi 116
Philo .. 116, 203, 204, 205, 206, 207, 208, 211, 220, 273, 282, 283, 285, 286, 288
Psalms of Solomon 264
Pseudepigrapha ... 70, 116, 210, 218, 264
   1Enoch 70, 102, 264
Rabbinic
   Mishnah 69, 116
   Talmud 69, 116
Sirach 214, 255, 274
Temple Scroll 264
Tobit 264, 265

4

4 ANCIENT AUTHORS

Aquinas 117
Athanasius 96, 101, 119
Augustine 117
Herodotus 117
Homer 117
Luther, Martin 101, 113
Marcion 117
Thucidides 117

5

5 MODERN AUTHORS

Abraham, William J.. 172, 292, 296
Achtemeier, Paul J. 292, 297
Allert, Craig D. 292, 297
Barna, George ... 23, 54, 55, 56, 57
Barton, John 31, 292, 297
Bauer, Walter 98, 100
Beckwith, R. T. 31, 292, 298
Best, Ernest 292, 298
Bloom, Harold 294, 297
Borgen, Peder 204
Brown, Dan 30, 58, 59, 181
Brown, William P. 292, 297
Bruce, F. F. 31, 292, 299
Bruffee, Kenneth 47, 48
Bultmann, R. 230
Charlesworth, James H. 264
Childs, Brevard 31, 292, 298
Christensen, Duane L. 292, 297
Collier, Craig A. 47
Collier, Gary D. 8, 15, 238, 326
Comfort, Philip Wesley 293, 298
Craig, Samuel G. 295, 299
Ehrman, Bart D. 30, 31, 98, 100, 136, 293, 294, 296, 297
Evans, Craig A. 293, 296
Finkelberg, Margalit .. 293, 297
Fitzmyer 288
Gamble, Harry Y. 31, 293, 297
Geisler, Norman L. 293, 296
Gnuse, Robert Karl 293, 298
Harris, Robert Laird ... 294, 299
Howard, George 288
Hurtado, Larry 288
Kasser, Rodolphe 294, 297
Köstenberger, Andreas J. 89, 96, 98, 100, 101, 187, 294, 296
Kraft, Robert 285
Kruger, Michael J. 89, 96, 100, 101, 187, 294, 296
McDonald, Lee Martin . 31, 98, 294, 296
Metzger, Bruce M. 31

Metzger, Bruce Manning .. 294, 297, 298
Meyer, Marvin 294, 297
Moule, C. F. D. 288
Oakshott, Joseph 47
Pahl, Michael W................. 272
Rivkin, Ellis 212
Roach, William C....... 293, 296
Robertson, A. T................. 225
Royse, J. R. 288
Runia, Runia, David T. 282
Sanders, James A. 31, 119, 294, 296, 298
Savage, James C......... 212, 227
Schneiders, Sandra Marie . 294, 298
Silberman, Lou H. 119
Skarsten, Ronald 204
Smith, W. C. 48
Stroumsa, Gedaliahu A. G. 293, 297
Sundberg, Albert C. 31, 295, 299
Thompson, M. B. 228
Tov, Emmanuel... 31, 288, 293, 296
Ulrich, Eugene 31
Ulrich, Eugene Charles 295, 297
Van Kirk, Natalie B. . 172, 292, 296
Van Til, Cornelius...... 295, 299
Vermes, Geza............. 239, 264
Vickers, Jason E. 172, 292, 296
Wallace, Daniel B. 283
Warfield, Benjamin Breckinridge.......... 295, 299
Whiston, William 209, 212
Whitaker, Richard E........... 204
Wright, N. T..................... 288
Wurst, Gregor 294, 297
Yonge, C. D. 204, 207, 208
Zerwick, Maximilian.......... 271
Zia, Mark J................. 295, 296

A

Abortion 26, 52, 122
    Pro-Choice.........................139
    Pro-Life 139
Academic ...51, 75, 116, 117, 129, 136
Act of Faith See Bible:Act of Faith
Adaptability 32, 70, 114, 143, 144, 163, 175, 252
Agnosticism 136
Agreement..27, 28, 31, 35, 38, 40, 61, 64, 65, 72, 182, 284
    Agreeing to Disagree............24
    Disagreement 24, 26, 39, 60, 65
    Supportive Engagement........24
Ahab...............................274
Alexandrinus 214
All About Me 146, 276
American...........................60, 102
American Christians See Christian
Apocalyptic ....See 3 OTHER ANCIENT TEXTS
Apocrypha..............See 3 OTHER ANCIENT TEXTS
Apollos...................................118
Apostle 96, 97, 124, 155
Archaeology............................117
Argument64, 65, 68, 86, 105, 140, 155, 261, 262, 275
Atheism 53, 136, 139
Attitude...............................27, 34
Audience 147, 155
Author .63, 64, 123, 147, 162, 270
Authority .20, 37, 90, 93, 262, 271

B

Baal...69
Babies....................139, 141, 143
Balaam 263
Baptism 162
BDAG 200, 203, 205, 206, 208, 215, 216, 217, 226
Bel...69
Bible15, 19, 20, 21, 22, 23, 24, 25, 27, 28, 29, 30, 31, 33, 34, 35, 36, 37, 38, 40, 43, 44, 45, 46,

47, 48, 49, 50, 51, 52, 53, 54,
55, 56, 57, 58, 61, 62, 63, 64,
65, 66, 67, 68, 70, 71, 73, 74,
75, 77, 78, 79, 80, 81, 83, 84,
86, 87, 88, 89, 90, 91, 92,
93,94, 95, 96, 100, 101, 102,
103, 104, 105, 106, 107, 109,
110, 111, 112, 113, 115, 120,
121, 122, 123, 124, 125, 126,
131, 132, 133, 135, 136, 138,
139, 140, 141, 142, 143, 144,
145, 146, 148, 149, 156, 157,
158, 159, 160, 162, 168, 171,
172, 174, 175, 181,182, 183,
186, 187, 189, 190, 217, 219,
247, 251, 261, 262, 269, 275,
276, 279, 284, 285, 291, 292,
293, 294, 295, 296, 297, 298,
299, 326

Act of Faith .38, 46, 49, 50, 71,
  73, 94, 104, 110, 111, 119,
  120, 121, 131, 135, 136,
  140, 172, 174, 180

Battles... 88, 103, 105, 125, 150

Bible Translations
  The Message.................. 246

Biblical 8, 14, 21, 22, 23, 24,
  26, 28, 31, 32, 33, 34, 45,
  55, 56, 58, 64, 66, 75, 77,
  82, 83, 86, 88, 89, 90, 91,
  95, 96, 98, 102, 114, 115,
  116, 117, 119, 123, 124,
  135, 142, 187, 219, 246,
  251, 252, 261, 262, 274,
  276, 279, 286, 326

Biblical Documents 90, 123,
  188

Blueprint...............................52

Critics (negative) 74, 87, 93,
  136, 138, 139, 143, 144, 291

Evolved 30, 59, 87, 181

Idea, Dream 49, 50, 111

Parts is Parts 146

'The Bible' as exclusive 105

'The Bible' as inclusive 105

'The Bible' as Jargon........... 105

Bible Class......................... 25, 28

Bible Study 22, 35, 193, 326

Bible Translations
  KJV 101, 192, 199, 214, 222,
    246, 280
  NASB 199, 246
  NASV 280
  NEB 199, 246
  NIV 199, 222, 246, 271, 279
  NJB 199, 246
  NKJV 199, 246
  NRSV 199, 222, 246
  The Message 246

Book of Glory......................... 233

Book of Signs 232, 235

Bridwell Library 127

c

Cannibalism........................... 141

Canon ...15, 22, 29, 31, 32, 34, 48,
  50, 60, 61, 73, 75, 76, 77, 78,
  79, 80, 81, 82, 83, 87, 88, 89,
  90, 92, 93, 95, 96, 97, 98, 99,
  100, 101, 102, 103, 104, 105,
  106, 107, 109, 110, 111, 112,
  113, 114, 115, 116, 117, 119,
  120, 121, 122, 131, 132, 133,
  135, 139, 140, 149, 150, 157,
  158, 159, 160, 168, 169, 171,
  172, 174, 175, 179, 180, 183,
  184, 185, 186, 187, 188, 189,
  190, 195, 201, 202, 209, 212,
  213, 216, 217, 218, 220, 221,
  223, 224, 246, 248, 252, 253,
  256, 257, 258, 259, 260, 262,
  264, 265, 266, 276, 285, 292,
  293, 294, 295, 296, 297, 298,
  299

7-Tier Universe.................. 107

Act of Faith .... See Bible:Act of
  Faith

Arrangement 152, 156
  TNK 149, 150, 251, 257
  Torah........................... 264

Canon Consciousness ... 89, 90,
  168, 187, 218, 246

Canonical 30, 79, 94, 100, 104,
105, 106, 107, 124, 126,
131, 132, 133, 161, 253,
260, 264
Canonical Conversation 94,
106, 107
Canonical filters 132
Canonical Process 31, 114, 143,
187
Canonical Variety 104, 105,
106
Canonization 136
Closed Canon.... 78, 79, 80, 81,
89, 90, 92, 99, 105, 109,
113, 118, 120, 174, 187,
189, 218, 249, 257, 262, 276
Collection.... 31, 44, 51, 67, 69,
106, 109, 110, 111, 115,
155, 157, 168, 182, 276
Implications 32, 90, 99, 102,
109, 132, 188, 189
Jars of Clay 107, 121, 124, 126,
131, 133, 171, 174
Muratorian Canon 100
Only One.................... 103, 113
Open Canon 110, 112, 249
Origins 19, 103, 171
Ownership 106
Should-a-Coating 113
Specific
Greek Orthodox.... 102, 109,
172
Orthodox Tewahedo 102,
253
Protestant...... 102, 105, 109,
113, 115, 116, 123, 156,
172, 184, 190, 217, 219,
248
Roman Catholic.... 100, 102,
105, 109, 116, 172, 190,
248
Western Canon.................... 77
Century 280, 285
01st Century 89, 186, 187, 189,
195, 198, 213, 246, 247,
251, 252, 254, 264, 285, 286

02nd Century 65, 66, 71, 89,
100, 101, 113, 187, 198,
251, 254, 260, 286, 288
03rd Century...... 77, 84, 89, 99,
100, 150, 187, 214, 251
04th Century 78, 84, 89, 99,
100, 101, 106, 113, 123,
187, 214, 252, 294, 297
05th Century 110, 120, 214,
292, 299
06th Century 113
07th Century 100, 133
15th Century 113
19th Century 123
20th Century 123
21st Century 19, 21, 22, 24, 32,
141, 142, 147, 281
Challenge .36, 40, 60, 67, 71, 286,
291
Children.................. 111, 141, 164
Christian 12, 21, 23, 24, 25, 27, 28,
29, 30, 31, 32, 33, 34, 37, 38,
47, 52, 54, 57, 60, 61, 62, 70,
71, 74, 75, 77, 81, 82, 87, 88,
90, 91, 93, 100, 101, 103, 104,
105, 106, 109, 115, 116, 121,
123, 131, 132, 135, 136, 151,
159, 162, 164, 166, 168, 171,
194, 195,259, 266, 272, 273,
280, 281, 282, 286, 288, 292,
293, 295, 297, 299, 326
American Christians 54, 56, 57,
102
Christian History 60, 101, 102,
105, 136
Christianity .34, 58, 59, 60, 61, 62,
118, 136, 152, 155, 190, 267,
288, 292, 294, 296, 297, 298
Christians ... 19, 20, 23, 26, 27, 28,
29, 30, 31, 32, 39, 43, 44, 51,
52, 53, 55, 57, 58, 59, 60, 61,
62, 63, 67, 68, 70, 73, 75, 77,
86, 93, 94, 95, 97, 101, 102,
105, 113, 136, 140, 151, 154,
159, 161, 162, 165, 167, 168,
171, 172, 174, 179, 184, 186,

198, 203, 204, 208, 223, 227,
232, 246, 252, 254, 257, 259,
262, 264, 268, 273, 280, 281,
282, 285, 287
Christology.............. 162, 163, 280
Above Every Name ... 164, 165,
166, 279, 283
Ascension ... 231, 234, 237, 239
Christ ... 70, 72, 90, 91, 97, 112,
133, 140, 161, 162, 163,
166, 168, 175, 199, 257,
262, 265, 266, 267, 268,
269, 270, 271, 272, 273,
274, 276, 277, 283, 284,
287, 288
Glorification 230, 231, 234,
237, 238, 239, 244
I am 165, 224, 232, 236
Jesus 28, 29, 33, 59, 60, 61, 65,
66, 69, 70, 72, 112, 114,
133, 149, 150, 151, 153,
154, 155, 159, 161, 162,
163, 164, 166, 167, 168,
169, 175, 184, 186, 187,
201, 204, 218, 220, 224,
228, 229, 230, 231, 232,
233, 234, 235, 236, 237,
239, 240, 241, 242, 243,
244, 247, 253, 256, 257,
258, 264, 265, 266, 267,
270, 272, 274, 276, 279,
280, 281, 282, 283, 284,
285, 286, 287, 288, 294,
297, 326
Jesus Christ.. 33, 162, 166, 168,
258, 266, 279, 282, 283, 287
KYRIOS/LORD 148, 164, 165,
166, 167, 169, 263, 274,
283, 284, 285, 286, 287, 288
Lifted Up ... 235, 236, 237, 238,
239, 244
Logos/Word....... 124, 267, 274,
281, 282, 283
Lord 20, 124, 125, 133, 161,
162, 163, 164, 165, 166,
167, 168, 262, 263, 264,
265, 266, 267, 268, 270,
271, 272, 273, 274, 275,
280, 283, 284, 286, 287, 288
Lord Jesus 118, 165, 168
Messiah............... 163, 245, 280
Relational........................... 284
Resurrection 191, 225, 229,
230, 232, 233, 234, 239,
240, 241, 242, 243, 244,
245, 257
Son of God..224, 281, 282, 288
Son of Man 235, 236, 237, 239,
241, 242, 244
Chronology..................... 123, 152
Church .... *See* Community
Code 124, 125
Collection ..*See* Canon: Collection
Community.44, 45, 46, 51, 61, 74,
75, 83, 107, 109, 111, 112,
114, 115, 120, 121, 131, 133,
143, 155, 174, 182, 291
Christian Community24, 27, 38
Christian Culture....*See* Culture
Church ...21, 22, 23, 24, 25, 29,
31, 32, 34, 45, 52, 58, 63,
93, 102, 103, 112, 117, 135,
146, 151, 152, 155, 158,
168, 175, 284
Communities of Faith *See* Faith
Discourse Communities....... 48
Comparison 87, 124, 150
Concordance, Bible 190, 192, 193,
196, 213, 246
Confession 161, 166
Conscience.................... 24, 26, 27
Conservative 25, 102, 123, 133
Container 124, 125, 126, 130, 133,
174
Contemporary 276
Context .22, 24, 35, 45, 46, 55, 64,
68, 75, 88, 138, 142, 143, 144,
147, 156, 159, 175, 268, 274,
280, 282, 284, 287
Conversation.....20, 22, 23, 24, *25*,
27, 28, 29, *31*, 32, *33*, 35, 38,
40, 46, 47, 62, 63, 66, 67, 68,

69, 70, *71*, 72, *73*, 74, 75, 88, 92, 94, *104*, 105, 107, *109*, *110*, *111*, 112, *118*, 119, 120, *121*, *131*, *135*, 140, 147, *167*, *169*, 172, 174, 268, *291*
Canonical Conversation ......*See* Canon
Conversation with God . 38, 46, 71, 73, 94, 104, 105, 109, 110, 111, 112, 121, 131, 135, 144
Debate ... 25, 52, 60, 66, 68, 85, 94, 101, 112, 113, 124, 152, 272, 286
Discourse 25, 48
Discussion ... 31, 32, 37, 38, 40, 74, 85, 121, 152, 172
Engage 35, 67, 72, 85, 111, 112, 115
Engagement 28, 39, 49
Human Conversation 48
Council Of Nicaea 100
Countries................................ 141
Borneo................................ 141
China................................ 141
Europe............................ 142
India 141
Japan 141
Melanesia 141
Nigeria 141
Russia.............................. 137
Taiwan 141
Creed..................................... 122
Critics.....*See* Text:Textual Critics, *See* Bible:Critics
Culture
Christian Culture 25, 35, 291
Human Culture............. 56, 160

D

Da Vinci Code ... *See* Movies: The Da Vinci Code
Dangerous 74
Dates

A.D. 78, 100, 101, 113, 119, 127, 150, 153, 187, 251, 252, 264, 285, 286
B.C. 198, 251, 254, 285
David...... 198, 200, 201, 218, 221, 225, 245, 252, 255, 263
Dead Sea Scrolls 252, 295, 297
Dead-End Road 105
Death 124, 125, 137
Debate .... *See* Conversation
Dei Verbum... *See* Inspiration, *See* Inspiration
Dictionary, Bible .*See* Study Tools
Disciples..229, 230, 231, 234, 240
Discipleship............................ 154
Discipline 116, 137
Dispute 49, 71
Diversity..... 31, 32, 44, 45, 55, 57, 67, 86, 90, 109, 156, 157, 161, 162, 175, 182, 291, 294, 296
Divine..... 37, 69, 90, 93, 165, 167, 171, 261
Doctrine 66, 82, 83, 86, 88, 91, 93, 94, 96, 103, 106, 123, 132, 136

E

Ecclesiastical 94
Edification 284
Editing....................................156
Education 121
Elijah 221, 254
Elisha....................................221
Endurance...............................143
Engagement .... *See* Conversation
English 85, 164, 165, 264, 267, 268, 279, 284, 285, 286, 287
Ephraemi Rescriptus 214
Ethics...............................52, 139
Evangelical..53, 82, 102, 132, 133
Evidence..... 88, 94, 103, 106, 110, 132, 143, 174, 286
Evil...66
Exclusive...........99, 105, 107, 160
Experience................36, 116, 117

F

Facts 24, 69, 87, 138, 141
Faith 19, 20, 29, 37, 45, 46, 49, 51,
    54, 61, 62, 74, 75, 82, 88, 90,
    94, 105, 107, 109, 111, 112,
    114, 115, 118, 121, 129, 130,
    131, 133, 135, 136, 140, 143,
    174, 182, 268, 291
    Act of Faith ... See Bible:Act of
      Faith
    Belief 54, 55, 274
    Believe .. 37, 39, 40, 52, 55, 58,
      114, 140, 146, 159, 264,
      276, 286
    Believers 88, 94, 103, 109, 111,
      143, 155, 270, 273, 284, 287
    Communities of Faith 119
    Disbelief 135
    Faith by inertia 34
    Faith Communities .. 44, 45, 46,
      105, 106, 109, 111, 114,
      115, 121, 129, 135, 138,
      140, 172
    Faith Community 119
    Non-Believers 19
Family 44, 45, 56, 60, 121, 265
Father 166, 167, 287
Fear 38, 49, 51, 168, 283
    Fearless 38
Flat Earth 92, 148
Flexibility 252, 253, 254
Focus 35, 58, 86, 93, 103, 106,
    107, 114, 160, 263, 271, 276
Forgiveness 143
Function 94, 143, 171, 172
Fundamental 55, 94, 147

G

Gauntlet 20, 40
Genetic Engineering 169
Genie 145
Goal 35, 36, 54, 147, 161, 171
God. 15, 19, 29, 30, 33, 34, 38, 41,
    44, 46, 48, 50, 52, 53, 58, 62,
    63, 64, 65, 67, 69, 71, 73, 74,
    76, 77, 80, 81, 83, 85, 87, 88,

89, 90, 93, 94, 95, 96, 97, 99,
    102, 103, 104, 105, 106, 107,
    109, 110, 111, 112, 114, 119,
    120, 121, 124, 125, 126, 129,
    130, 131, 133, 135, 139, 140,
    143, 144, 146, 147, 148, 149,
    154, 158, 161, 162, 164, 165,
    166, 167, 171, 172, 174, 177,
    179, 180, 181, 182, 184, 185,
    186, 197, 201, 202, 203, 209,
    210, 212, 218, 220, 221, 222,
    224, 228, 230, 231, 234, 236,
    237, 247, 248, 253, 254, 258,
    262, 263, 264, 265, 266, 267,
    268, 270, 271, 274, 275, 276,
    279, 280, 282, 283, 284, 285,
    286, 287, 288, 291
    Existence 52, 65, 129
    Godhead 123
    Name Of .. 30, 67, 68, 164, 281,
      282, 284, 285, 286, 287,
      293, 296
    YHWH/JHVH .. 126, 164, 280,
      283, 285, 286, 287
Gospel... 23, 60, 70, 116, 130, 148,
    149, 152, 153, 154, 265, 266,
    267, 268, 270, 272, 273, 276,
    288
Greek Orthodox .... *See*
    Canon:Specific
Greek OT .... *See* Septuagint

H

Heartbeat 130, 291
Heaven 50, 52, 156, 279
Hell 52
Heresy .. 26, 27, 31, 71, 74, 95, 122
Hermeneutic of Interchangeability
    .... 80, 81
Hermeneutics 121
Hezekiah 274, 275
History .. 23, 30, 34, 37, 52, 53, 58,
    63, 69, 70, 87, 93, 94, 105,
    116, 117, 118, 123, 135, 138,
    147, 149, 181, 182, 272

Holy 52, 66, 81, 83, 87, 94, 99, 107, 156, 161, 162, 163, 164, 171, 262, 264, 276, 285
Holy Texts .... *See* Scripture
Homosexuality 52, 122
Hosanna 280
Human . 65, 94, 95, 105, 106, 112, 122, 123, 125, 126, 135, 141, 154, 171, 261, 280
Humility 283
Hunger 137, 138
Hypocrisy 139
Hyrcanus, John 212

I

Ignorance 23, 27, 34, 53, 60, 61
Illiterate 23, 54, 61, 73, 93, 174
Imperfect 65
Implications 57, 172, 189, 262
Indoctrination 24, 25, 27, 29
Inerrancy .... *See* Inspiration
Inertia 33
Infallibility .... See Inspiration
Inspiration 22, 29, 96, 104, 121, 122, 123, 132, 169, 171, 254
   Chicago Statement on Biblical Inerrancy 82, 132
   Definition 131
   Dei Verbum.. 83, 132, 293, 299
   Inerrancy 26, 37, 81, 82, 83, 87, 91, 103, 122, 123
   Inerrancy Code 36, 83, 87
   Infallibility .. 37, 79, 81, 83, 87, 122, 123
   Original Autographs 37, 81, 83, 87, 91, 122, 123, 130, 133, 143, 276, 286
   Phenomena of Scripture 123, 132, 172
Integrity 152
Interdisciplinary 121
Interpretation . 64, 85, 86, 87, 106, 115, 264, 268, 272
   Allusion 118
   Comparative Midrash 118
   Conflation 106

Context .... *See* Context
Echo 118, 166
Echoes Of Scripture 268
Interpreters 85, 122
Intertextuality .67, 70, 118, 202
Motif ... 229, 230, 231, 235, 238
Personification 50, 111
Plain Meaning 284
Pre-Critical 147, 157
Process. 31, 32, 66, 83, 90, 106, 113, 114, 136, 187
Reapplication 119
Says vs Means ... 37, 83, 84, 85, 96, 183, 246
Understanding ... 43, 55, 56, 60, 65, 152, 171, 268
Wrestling 119
Israel 116, 126, 162, 263, 264, 265, 275

J

James 97
Jars of Clay .... See Canon
Jeroboam 274
Jerusalem 252, 256, 264, 280, 288, 293, 297
Jesus .... *See* Christology
Jesus ben Sirach 255
Jews ..*See* Nationalities/Languages
John 118
Judas 60, 65
Justice 52, 143
Justified 166

K

Kirk, James T. 46
Klatu 20, 33, 40
Koine *See* Nationalities/Languages

L

Languages .... *See* Nationalities/Languages
Law ... 23, 125, 141, 146, 147, 149
Law and Prophets ... 150, 251, 254, 255, 256, 257, 258, 260
Leadership

Church Leaders .22, 23, 24, 26, 29, 31, 34, 135, 169
Elders 25, 26, 45
Musicians 281
Pastors 22
Preachers 40, 55, 57, 85, 135
Teachers 22, 23, 24, 29, 30, 31, 36, 55, 57, 72, 81, 121, 155, 291
Letter 23, 71, 90, 106, 128, 152, 264, 268, 269, 273, 274
Lexicon, Greek .... *See* Study Tools
Life. 37, 44, 45, 52, 55, 66, 70, 81, 83, 87, 90, 94, 106, 114, 117, 125, 147, 148, 149, 153, 155, 162, 265, 268, 270, 284
Life and Death 49, 152
Literal 148, 149, 271, 275
Literary 147, 149, 157
Literature.. 23, 117, 147, 149, 157, 161, 187, 263, 265, 274
Logic 88
Lord .... *See* Christology
Love 29, 36, 44, 49, 129, 133, 268
Act of Love 49
Love Affair 62
Luther, Martin .... *See* 4 ANCIENT AUTHORS
LXX .... *See* Septuagint
Lydia 118

M

Majority Text .... *See* Text
Man of God 221
Manuscripts .... *See* Text
P26 .... 126, 127
P72 214
Marcus Aurelius 49
Marduk 69
Mariam 234
Marriage 49, 69
Remarriage 52
Mary Magdalene 29, 59
Masoretic Text .... *See* Text
McCoy, Leonard H. 46
Memory 123

Men.30, 58, 59, 87, 112, 137, 141, 181, 262, 271, 279, 280
Methods 23, 27
Morals, Morality.47, 52, 117, 139, 212
Moses .97, 99, 125, 159, 161, 162, 163, 184, 196, 198, 199, 221, 224, 252, 254, 256, 257, 258, 263
Motif .... *See* Interpretation
Movies 20, 44, 58, 59, 60, 103, 145, 153
50 First Dates 43, 44, 46
Gladiator 49
Star Trek (V) 46
The Da Vinci Code .. 29, 30, 58, 60, 74, 87, 88, 98, 136, 181
The Day The Earth Stood Still 20
The Highlander 103
The Last Temptation Of Christ 60
The Secret 145
Muratorian Canon .... *See* Canon
Musicians .... *See* Leadership
Mystery 265, 267, 268, 272, 277

N

NA27 .... 84, 222
Napoleon 137
Nationalities/Languages
Aztechs 141
Canaanites 141
Greek 84, 91, 116, 117, 122, 124, 136, 150, 151, 155, 161, 162, 164, 165, 268, 271, 274, 275, 280, 282, 283, 284, 285, 286, 287, 288
Greek--Holy Spirit Language 33, 34
Greek--Koine 33
Hebrew ..84, 91, 100, 101, 116, 124, 149, 150, 161, 162, 164, 268, 275, 280, 284, 285, 286, 287, 288

Jews... 32, 66, 69, 86, 101, 115, 116, 125, 141, 142, 148, 150, 155, 161, 163, 164, 282, 285, 286, 288

Latin 84, 117

Scythians 142

Nazareth 280

NETS .... *See* Septuagint

Newsweek 53

Novel 60

O

Obedience 147

Original Autographs .... *See* Inspiration

Origins 34, 69, 93, 94, 99

Orthodox 30

Orthodox Tewahedo .... *See* Canon:Specific

P

Papyrus 126, 127

Paradosis . *See* Tradition:Paradosis

Parents 54, 56, 111, 141, 291

Passover 60

Pastors .... *See* Leadership

Paul 40, 54, 65, 70, 89, 91, 99, 114, 116, 118, 119, 124, 125, 128, 129, 130, 131, 133, 152, 155, 156, 162, 163, 166, 167, 183, 191, 195, 201, 203, 204, 215, 218, 220, 221, 227, 228, 238, 239, 240, 241, 243, 244, 245, 247, 253, 255, 257, 258, 259, 268, 269, 270, 271, 272, 273, 274, 275, 276, 281, 282, 283, 285, 292, 293, 297, 299, 326

Peace 27, 72

Pentateuch 149, 150, 161, 196, 197, 204, 207, 210, 251, 260

Samaritan Pentateuch 150

Perkins School of Theolgy 127

Pervasive Witness 191, 233

Peter .. 65, 155, 220, 229, 230, 231

Pharisees . 159, 186, 212, 227, 256

Phenomena of Scripture .... See Inspiration

Philo .... *See* 3 OTHER ANCIENT TEXTS

Philosophy. 86, 112, 117, 139, 285

Phoebe 118

Point

Starting Point 74, 75, 115

Tipping Point 74

Politics 28, 65, 69, 121, 142

Polygamy 92, 142

Popular . 30, 35, 87, 136, 145, 146, 159, 171, 280

Prayer 22, 53, 122

Priscilla 118

Process .... *See* Interpretation

Promise 126, 171

Prophecy 70, 81, 99, 149, 161, 163, 253, 254, 258, 263, 265, 269, 272, 273, 274, 275

Prophets .. 150, 151, 217, 251, 252, 254, 255, 257, 258, 260, 288

Protestant .. 19, 29, 35, 78, 86, 101, 105, 106, 110, 171, *See* Canon:Specific

Pseudepigrapha ...... *See* 3 OTHER ANCIENT TEXTS

Ptolemy Philadelphus 211

Pursuit of God .. 29, 35, 38, 46, 71, 73, 94, 104, 106, 110, 111, 121, 131, 135, 168

R

Rabbouni 234

Relic 51, 62, 63, 73, 93, 120

Religion 53

Resurrection ... 231, 232, 233, 234, 235, 237, 239, 241, 243, 244, 266

Revelation (Divine) 33, 37, 45, 64, 118, 119, 120, 161, 174, 182, 293, 299

Where is God? 120

Revolutionary 39, 162

Right 52, 56, 57, 65, 66, 69, 71, 83, 85, 86, 87, 88, 93, 103,

110, 112, 125, 129, 136, 143, 145, 156, 157, 291
Righteous.............................165
Righteousness.......57, 112, 165
Rock.........................70, 162, 163
Stone.............66, 125, 163, 280
Roman Catholic .58, 83, 100, 105, 106, 113, 122, 132, 171, *See* Canon:Specific
Roman Roads.............................40
Rome.................................49, 130
Rorschach Test.........................43

S

Sacred Story............114, 294, 298
Sacred Writings, Sacred Text.. *See* Scripture
Sacrifice.................................141
Sadducees...............................212
Salt and Light...........................28
Salvation.................122, 130, 275
Santa Claus...............................88
Satan..52
Says vs Means..*See* Interpretation: Says vs Means
Scholars 23, 36, 60, 61, 65, 84, 89, 135, 152, 158, 187, 272, 286
Science...20, 23, 52, 68, 117, 118, 123, 140, 142, 150
Evolution................52, 68, 122
Scribe.....128, 130, 131, 162, 214, 217, 285, 286
Scribes for K/H.....................162
Scripture
1 Scripture...1, 7, 8, 29, 30, 41, 48, 73, 75, 76, 79, 80, 81, 83, 85, 87, 89, 90, 92, 95, 98, 101, 102, 104, 122, 171, 174, 177, 189, 190, 199, 200, 203, 204, 205, 209, 212, 213, 215, 216, 217, 219, 220, 222, 224, 226, 246, 248, 253, 258, 262, 268, 269, 292, 293, 294,296, 297, 298

2 scripture 22, 29, 32, 35, 37, 45, 48, 58, 61, 62, 67, 70, 72, 73, 74, 76, 77, 78, 79, 80, 81, 82, 83, 86, 87, 88, 89, 90, 92, 96, 99, 102, 104, 109, 110, 114, 116, 117, 119, 124, 126, 131, 132, 133, 156, 159, 171, 174, 180, 181, 182, 183, 189, 190, 191, 193, 194, 195, 196, 199, 200, 201, 202, 203, 204, 205, 206, 207, 208, 209, 210, 211, 212, 213, 215, 216, 217, 218, 219, 220, 221, 224, 225, 226, 244, 248, 258, 261, 268, 270
3 scriptures...15, 24, 32, 33, 48, 51, 55, 71, 75, 76, 79, 82, 83, 91, 92, 95, 99, 100, 104, 107, 112, 118, 120, 124, 125, 126, 132, 138, 140, 143, 149, 150, 151, 156, 157, 171, 183, 185, 186, 187, 188, 191, 196, 202, 205, 206, 207, 210, 227, 244, 246, 256, 261, 266, 267
graphē......76, 84, 90, 122, 189, 194, 195, 196, 197, 198, 200, 201, 202, 203, 204, 205, 206, 207, 208, 209, 210, 211, 212, 213, 214, 215, 216, 219, 220, 221, 222, 223, 224, 225, 226, 227, 228, 229, 240, 244, 245, 246, 247, 248, 258, 260, 262, 264, 269
Holy Scrolls.......................165
Holy Texts ..202, 217, 266, 285
Holy Writings ... 106, 107, 110, 116, 122, 132, 161, 162, 168, 195, 254, 255, 257, 260, 268, 269, 292, 297
Sacred Texts 62, 70, 76, 91, 94, 110, 112, 161, 163, 164, 168, 169, 191, 198, 200,

203, 206, 207, 208, 210,
212, 214, 217, 219, 220,
221, 222, 225, 229, 231,
232, 239, 241, 244, 245,
248, 256, 257, 258, 259,
260, 268, 269, 270, 271,
273, 280, 284, 292, 294,
297, 298
Sacred Writing .. 109, 219, 221,
224, 254
Sacred Writings. 62, 90, 91, 92,
94, 109, 160, 161, 192, 214,
221, 249, 255, 256, 257,
258, 259, 260, 267, 284, 285
scriptura 76, 202
Tradition and Scripture 83
Undefined References . 76, 102,
189, 191, 206, 208, 211,
213, 215, 217, 220, 221,
223, 226, 241, 246, 247,
255, 256
Scroll of King David 202
Scroll of the Kings 202
Scroll of Truth 202, 214
Scrolls 126, 149, 150, 151, 161,
198, 217, 218, 251
Septuagint .. 33, 91, 184, 193, 196,
198, 199, 203, 211, 214, 247,
252, 254, 288
Greek OT ... 282, 283, 285, 286
Greek Translations 33, 184, 251
LXX .. 194, 214, 221, 224, 252,
253
NETS 166, 199, 284
Sermon 25, 63, 64, 149
Serving Together 283
Sinaiticus 214, 265
Situation 114, 168
Slavery 52, 66, 92, 141, 142
Social Justice 169
Society 52, 57, 138, 143
Solomon 70, 198, 252, 255
Son of God *See* Christology: Son of
God
Songs
Row Your Boat 46

Sosthenes 91
Soul 61, 67
Soul-Battering 67
Speakers 136
Spirit 21, 29
Holy Spirit . 33, 34, 89, 90, 107,
133, 135, 154, 155
Spirit of God 112, 172
Spiritual 115, 116, 117, 129,
136, 139, 162
Spiritual Gifts 26, 169
Spock, Mr. 46
Status Quo 28, 30
Stone .... *See* Rock
Story 29, 68, 88, 114, 148, 152,
153, 154, 156, 161, 163, 262
Straight Jacket 132
Studies 30, 53, 117
Study 38, 55, 56, 57, 116, 136,
276, 291
Study Tools
Bible Software 23, 193, 204,
213
Dictionary, Bible 100, 190, 192,
193, 215, 216
Lexicon, Greek .. 192, 193, 200,
215
Study Bible 190, 276
Style 27, 28, 35, 147, 155
Supportive Engagement .... *See*
Agreement
Synoptic Gospels 223, 228, 239,
240, 242, 244

T

Table 20, 75, 128, 291
TDNT 205, 215, 216, 226, 230,
266, 268
Teachers .... *See* Leadership
Teaching 54, 56, 69, 112, 140,
266, 269, 273
Teach 22, 116
Tetragrammaton ...... 285, 288, *See*
God: YHWH/JHVH
Text 27, 58, 84, 85, 86, 89, 91,
118, 121, 123, 124, 128, 130,

132, 139, 164, 166, 187, 262, 263, 265, 266, 267, 270, 271, 272, 273, 275, 276, 277, 280, 284, 286

Document 22, 44, 67, 89, 91, 104, 116, 117, 123, 143, 144, 149, 152, 154, 155, 156, 157, 158, 161, 162, 163, 175, 262, 268, 273, 274, 276, 284, 286

Majority Text 214

Manuscripts . 34, 124, 126, 127, 128, 130, 136, 182, 285

Masoretic Text 252

Sacred Texts .... *See* Scripture

Scroll 150

Textual Critics 84

Textual Variants .. 84, 124, 128, 214

Transmission 93

Writings. 22, 62, 69, 70, 90, 94, 99, 104, 107, 114, 115, 116, 123, 124, 125, 126, 142, 150, 151, 152, 155, 161, 162, 163, 262, 263, 264, 266, 267, 268, 273, 274, 276

Textual Critics .... *See* Text/Textual Critics

Theology .. 21, 23, 37, 57, 82, 112, 117, 121, 123, 156, 276

Theory 52, 61, 63, 87, 276

Thinking ... 24, 25, 28, 39, 40, 103, 107, 111, 115, 121, 148, 168, 169, 291

Timothy 221

Titus (Roman General) 252

Tongue-Speaking 52

Topical 156, 157, 175

Tradition 37, 87, 89, 101, 104, 113, 114, 131, 152, 163, 168, 179, 182, 184, 202, 205, 211, 214, 222, 228, 238, 239, 240, 241, 242, 243, 244, 252, 256, 269, 270, 272

Paradosis ... 212, 227, 228, 245, 247, 270, 272

Quotes of Known Conclusion 224, 226, 244, 245, 246, 247

Shared Tradition 226, 228, 229, 244, 245, 248

Traditions . 69, 102, 161, 179, 182, 212, 220, 227, 245, 247, 270

Tranquility 27

Translation 85, 165, 267, 271, 273, 275, 279, 284, 286

Translators 85, 199, 200, 202, 203, 204, 207, 210, 214

Treasure 124

Truth ... 28, 54, 57, 59, 65, 67, 121, 154, 162, 165, 168, 175, 265, 267, 268, 291

U

U.S. 52, 54, 69

Unity 20, 67

Illusion of Unity 25, 27, 29

Universe 114, 117, 145

V

Vaticanus 214

Version 30, 59, 69, 87, 88, 101, 181, 182

W

Western Canon .... *See* Canon

Women 25, 26, 44, 52, 58, 59, 122, 142, 149, 169

Word of God 19, 36, 37, 52, 61, 64, 79, 81, 82, 83, 87, 89, 90, 122, 124, 198, 224, 261, 262, 263, 264, 265, 266, 267, 268, 269, 270, 271, 273, 276, 277

Word Studies, Doing 193, 213, 267

World 23, 36, 51, 52, 53, 57, 58, 61, 63, 65, 67, 68, 69, 70, 72, 73, 115, 117, 137, 138, 139, 171, 266, 291

Earth 20, 86, 103, 138, 142, 148, 165

Worship 53, 133, 264

Notes

Notes

Notes

Notes

Meet the Author

Gary D. Collier *is founder and director of The Coffee With Paul Classroom. He is author of <u>Reading the Bible Like Jesus</u> and of two innovative forthcoming Bible study series: <u>40 Things Everybody Should Know about the Bible</u> and <u>Unrelenting Faith</u>.*

In contact with people from numerous countries around the world, he is uniquely qualified as the Bible translator, developer, and teacher of an innovative new approach to adventurous Bible study. As the founder and co-chairman of the one-time Seminar for Biblical Hermeneutics at Christian Scholar's Conferences held at college campuses throughout the United States, as a former teacher of biblical languages at Fuller Theological Seminary and the Iliff School of Theology, and biblical languages and literature at Martin University, and as a minister in California, Tennessee, and Indiana, Gary has devoted his life to the innovative, responsible, and contextual application of the Bible.

Gary and his wife Lanette live happily in rural Indiana, together patiently working to build The Coffee With Paul Classroom:

www.CoffeeWithPaul.com

Made in the USA
Lexington, KY
28 September 2017